NATIONAL
FAMILY MEDIATION
GUIDE TO
SEPARATION
AND
DIVORCE

NATIONAL FAMILY MEDIATION GUIDE TO SEPARATION AND DIVORCE

The complete handbook for managing
a fair and amicable divorce

THELMA FISHER OBE

VERMILION
LONDON

1 3 5 7 9 10 8 6 4 2

First published in the United Kingdom in 1997 by
Vermilion
an imprint of Ebury Press

Random House UK Ltd
20 Vauxhall Bridge Road, London SW1V 2SA

Random House, Australia (Pty) Limited
20 Alfred Street, Milsons Point,
Sydney, New South Wales 2061, Australia

Random House New Zealand Limited
18 Poland Road, Glenfield, Auckland 10, New Zealand

Random House, South Africa (Pty) Limited
Endulini, 5a Jubilee Road, Parktown 2193, South Africa

Random House UK Limited Reg. No. 954009

A CIP catalogue record for this book is available
from the British Library.

ISBN 0 09 181465 0

Typeset in Century Old Style

Design & page make-up by Roger Walker

Printed and bound in the United Kingdom by
Mackays of Chatham, Ltd.

Papers used by Vermilion are natural, recyclable products made
from wood grown in sustainable forests.

CONTENTS

Foreword by Dame Brenda Hale DBE   vii

Introduction   1

PART 1:
THE EXPERIENCE OF SEPARATION AND DIVORCE

1	The Decision	11
2	If your Marriage Is Over	20
3	Separating	28
4	New Relationships	37
5	Your Needs	43
6	The Needs of your Children	50
7	Telling the Children	65
8	Your Culture: Kith and Kin	70

PART 2:
HOW TO WORK IT OUT

9	What is Family Mediation?	81
10	Preparing for Mediation	88
11	The Mediation Process	96
12	Making Arrangements for your Children	104
13	All Issues Mediation	116
14	Negotiation by Solicitors	145
15	The Court	151
16	Domestic Violence	154
17	Living in the Future	159

PART 3:
REFERENCE SECTION

18	Financial Considerations	175
19	Legal Aid	194
20	Current Law	198
21	The Family Law Act 1996	205
	Useful Addresses	209
	Recommended Reading	225
	Bibliography	227
	Index	228
	Acknowledgements	232

FOREWORD

by Dame Brenda Hale DBE
President of National Family Mediation

But who wants a fair and amicable divorce? We have all heard someone say: 'I am going to take that man for all he is worth' or 'No way am I going to let that woman see the children she walked out on.' On the other hand, 'She must see that I need somewhere to live – that house is much too big for her now' or 'He drove me to it – he was treating me so badly I felt like dirt.'

Conflicts like these can be addictive. It is easy to see why. When a marriage or relationship breaks down, there is usually a 'leaver' and a 'left'. As Thelma Fisher says, the path to separation or divorce is not a well planned journey. People do not start together with a common purpose.

This book is about trying to plan your own particular journey better and to stay in control of your own lives. You do not have to lose your capacity for careful thought and sensible action. But you do need to understand what you, your partner, your children, and your family and friends are feeling. You do need to explore the options which are available, whether the break with your partner is final, whether you should divorce, where the children are going to live, how much they will see of each parent, what you are all going to live on and where. You also need to know the different ways of getting to the end of your journey.

Most couples choose to get there by each consulting their own lawyers. Most lawyers then try very hard to negotiate a solution which comes as close as possible to what their client wants and they think that their client would get in court. If this cannot be done, they will ask the court to decide. Most people know that this ought to be the last resort. Taking a case to court costs money and energy which would be better spent on other things. Sometimes the situation is so bad, or one party is so devious, deceitful or abusive, that there is no alternative. Sometimes it is difficult to develop the options and the parties' different bargaining positions, especially at arms' length, without one or other of them feeling let down or unjustly treated unless they have their 'day in court'.

Some people do choose to get there by themselves, without any professional help. But this is difficult for most people to do. The information they need is quite hard to come by. There is always the fear that they will have

missed something important. More seriously, perhaps, it is hard to negotiate with your partner when feelings are bound to be running high, and one
of you is likely to be much more in charge of events than the other.

Family Mediation offers separating and divorcing couples a different
way of getting there. This is a neutral but skilled outsider who helps you to
communicate with one another so that you can conduct your own negotiation towards a solution to which you both agree because it suits your particular needs. 'The exchange of information between two people who have
become newly receptive to what they hear is the simple ingredient that settles most disputes.... Negotiation does not mean giving in.... It means talking and listening, and, in the process, seeing a way of reaching a solution.'

When the Family Law Act 1996 comes into force, it will be easier for
everyone to choose which of these routes will suit them best. But long
before that, this book should help to explain what is going on, why trying to
achieve a fair and amicable divorce is so important, and how you might go
about doing it.

Dame Brenda Hale
25 February 1997

INTRODUCTION

DIVORCE: A JOURNEY, NOT AN EVENT

Although the granting of a divorce is an event, the experience of a divorce is more like a journey. Divorce essentially brings about a change of legal status from a married person to a no-longer-married person. When it actually occurs, however, it may seem an anti-climax, whereas the journey leading to it is usually action-packed. People set off, or feel pushed, into a new land, where everything alters as they pass. Unlike the Shakespeare sonnet which says that 'love is not love, which alters when it alteration finds', divorce alters everything, as alterations tumble one upon the other.

There is no well-tried map to help you follow a clearly marked route. Most people think there is and ask 'What am I supposed to do?' It is however a journey with choices always to be made between several options. Your journey will not be the same as anyone else's. Your divorce will be as distinctively unique for you as has been your marriage.

Separation and the breakdown of a marriage jolt adults and children alike from the security of an established way of life. Even the one who chooses to end that security may feel out of control. The spouse who does not choose to have their way of life overturned and the children, who are caught in the middle, may feel even more out of control. The first stage of any crisis passes, however, and then the critical factor in recovery is how to handle the aftermath. To have a plan of action is more energising than being swept along by events.

A future focus

Taking charge of events requires sorting out the different issues that demand decisions and actions, planning to meet the needs of everyone involved, especially children, setting some broad goals for the future and deciding which route to follow. Many people nowadays have come to expect change in their working lives but are thrown totally off balance when they have to manage unexpected change in their private lives. At home, we depend on trust, support and routines. After the collapse of a marriage or long-term relationship, we miss these and find it painful and difficult to cope with conflict and loss, rebuild trust, find new sources of support and construct new routines. Expending energy on family change is emotionally and physically exhausting; divorce is acknowledged as one of the major stresses in adult life.

Although at times you may be overwhelmed by complex, angry, sad and turbulent feelings, you do not have to lose your capacity for careful thought and sensible action. You do not have to see your partner as an enemy. Trying to think out what outcomes you want for yourselves and your children involves a focus on the future which can pull you away from the griefs and angers of the present and the past. If you have no children, you will want to emerge from this experience positively and ready for a new life. Mediation is a route that focuses on the future.

THE PURPOSE OF THE GUIDE

This book aims to help you to decide whether to embark on your journey and, if you do, which route to take and how to conduct your divorce in such a way that you achieve a fair and amicable outcome.

The word 'amicable' is probably used only when people feel that things might very well *not* be amicable; they may be in the grip of strong emotions which they are trying to control or overcome. The mediators who have contributed to this book have years of experience of sitting as third parties while separating and divorcing couples negotiate fair and amicable outcomes despite being caught up in conflict and emotion.

Mediators invite you to come *together* in order to negotiate face to face and take charge of what is happening; to plan, to be aware of what issues are at stake for you, your partner and your family and to avoid the common pitfalls which can otherwise result in bitterness, blame and unfairness. Trying to co-operate, even in trying circumstances, can prevent each of you from acting in the dark to your own disadvantage, to the disadvantage of your partner and to the detriment of your children.

You may be able to read this book and use it to proceed co-operatively without the help of a mediator.

You may decide that you simply cannot sit down together and talk, even with a mediator, and that you prefer to have a solicitor negotiate on your behalf. The book might still be helpful in identifying what needs to be done.

If you should not be negotiating face to face at all for reasons of safety, the Guide provides information to assist you.

Much that is written here applies equally to cohabiting couples whose relationships come to an end. There are, however, important differences in financial rights and parental responsibilities. These are commented upon where they arise.

THE STRUCTURE OF THE GUIDE

This book is in three parts:

1 The Experience of Separation and Divorce
The journey of separation and divorce for children, adults and the wider family, starting by questioning whether the journey has to be made at all.

2 How to Work It Out
Working things out together, using mediation as a means of understanding and doing what needs to be done, referring also to the contribution of solicitors, courts and other sources of help, particularly for domestic violence. Also included is an important section about life after divorce. See chapter 17: Living in the Future.

3 Reference Section
This pulls together information about the law, legal aid, financial issues, the Child Support Agency, welfare benefits and sources of professional and community help.

It should not be thought that mediators are there to escort you up all the hills and through all the valleys of your divorce experience. Mediation has modest goals. It is not a form of therapy or counselling. It is a joint process in which you are helped to do the work of decision-making together. You do not have to do it without legal assistance; solicitors are a valuable and at times necessary resource of advice and support.

By the end of the book, after reading Parts 1 and 2 and dipping into Part 3, you should glimpse the land at the end of your journey, with its new hills and new valleys. You may even feel that you are ready to live in it!

FAMILY MEDIATION: A PRACTICAL FOCUS ON THE FUTURE

Family mediation helps you to work out your future plans. It will help you to decide whether your marriage is over, clarify your goals for the future, set targets and make plans that take account of everyone's needs.

Mediators understand that conflict and distress can make it hard for you to work things out without outside help but mediation does not remove your responsibility for doing so. In mediation you make your own decisions.

Family mediation plays its part best early on, at or around the point of decision or separation, although you can use it at any time. If you think that it is suitable for your situation, it gets you off to a good start and prevents both the anxiety and expense of conducting divorce proceedings separately.

What is family mediation?

Mediation is about directly negotiating your own decisions with the help of a third party. It is different from marriage or relationship counselling, which attend primarily to relationships and feelings. It is an alternative to solicitors negotiating for you, and to having decisions made for you by courts. It aims at a fair and amicable result by conducting a fair and thorough process in which differences are fully explored and common ground found. A definition is set out below.

> **Family Mediation** is a process in which trained and impartial mediators assist those involved in family or relationship breakdown, and in particular separating or divorcing couples, to communicate better with one another and to reach their own informed decisions about some or all of the related issues. The issues may concern their relationship, the present and future arrangements for any children, finance and property and any other practical matters.

Mediators can help you to resolve together:

- whether your marriage is over
- arrangements for the children
- financial arrangements for the future
- what to do about the family home and where everyone should live
- any other matters particular to your family or your situation

Research in the UK has established the benefits of mediation:

The Benefits of Family Mediation

- reducing conflict and bitterness
- improving communication
- helping parents to focus on the needs of children

Mediation and legal advice

Mediation does not mean you do not have solicitors. Mediation is not an alternative to legal advice but it is an alternative to lawyer representation, i.e. negotiation on your behalf by your solicitors. In mediation you negotiate with each other directly, face to face.

Mediation is for many but not for everyone

Mediation is good for many, perhaps most, families, but does not claim to be right for everyone. It may not be right, for example, if you or your partner have reason to be afraid of being together in the same room. It may prove to be unworkable if either of you does not intend to play fair in it or seeks only to have your own way rather than be prepared to listen and negotiate.

CHANGES IN DIVORCE LAW

Divorce law in the UK has been moving since the 1970s towards focusing on the future rather than concentrating on what has gone wrong in the past. There is a new divorce law for England and Wales which will come into effect probably just before the year 2000. Its aim is to make people thoroughly think through what they are doing before their divorce is granted. Can the marriage be saved? Have the consequences of divorce been faced and worked out? Instead of looking at what has gone wrong as one way of deciding *whether* people can be allowed to divorce, courts will look at people's practical plans for the future *before* they are allowed to have a divorce. The laws in Scotland and Northern Ireland are similar in principle and are moving in the same direction. The UK laws are explained in Part 4. The intentions of the Act are already pervading the way divorce is approached by the courts and the legal and helping professions.

Family Mediation and changes in the law

Family mediators have existed in the UK since 1978, but will be of particular assistance in making the best use of the new law, which essentially encourages divorcing couples to work out their future arrangements *before* they divorce. If they are parents, this will be beneficial for their children and will build upon the intentions of the Children Act 1989.

The principles of the new Family Law Act in England and Wales (not yet in operation) are set out overleaf.

The Principles of the Family Law Act 1996

a) that the institution of marriage is to be supported

b) that the parties to a marriage which may have broken down are to be encouraged to take all practicable steps to save it

c) that a marriage which has irretrievably broken down and is being brought to an end should be brought to an end:

(i) with minimum distress to the parties and to the children affected

(ii) with questions dealt with in a manner designed to promote as good a continuing relationship between the parties and any children affected as is possible in the circumstances; and

(iv) without costs being unreasonably incurred in connection with the procedures to be followed in bringing the marriage to an end

d) that any risk to one of the parties to a marriage, and to any children, of violence from the other party should, so far as reasonably practical, be removed or diminished

This gradual shift in the focus of the law, linked to the sheer numbers of people divorcing in the Western world and growing concern about the effects of divorce upon children, has contributed to the emergence of family mediation in the UK. It is legally aided in Scotland and will be fully aided in England and Wales when the new law takes over. Mediation is also developing in other European countries.

Changes in the law on children

The Children Act in force since 1991 creates a good base for mediation because of its emphasis on the continuing responsibility of each parent towards their children after divorce. Mediation had its roots in this country in the 1970s in helping parents to continue their parenting after divorce. By helping parents to maintain their attachments to their children when they are no longer partners, mediation can give practical reality, particularly for children, to their inner experience of their original family. Mediation can also help to keep children in touch with both sides of their wider families, especially grandparents. Some principles of the Children Act in England and Wales are set out opposite.

The Principles of the Children Act 1989

1 The Welfare of the Child (Section 1)

i When a court determines any question with respect to

a) the upbringing of a child...

the child's welfare shall be the court's paramount consideration.

2 Parental Responsibility (Section 3)

This means all the rights, duties, powers, responsibilities and authority which by law a parent has in relation to a child and his property.

3 Non-Intervention of the Court (Section 1(5))

'Where a court is considering whether or not to make one or more orders under this Act with respect to a child, it shall not make the order or any of the orders unless it considers that doing so would be better for the child than making no order at all.'

4 Delay is bad for children (Section 1(2))

'...the court must have regard to the general principle that any delay in determining the question is likely to prejudice the welfare of the child'.

The new Family Law Act adds to the Children Act by actually stating that it is important for children to keep in touch with their parents and members of their family. The wording of this is set out below.

Contact between parents and children after divorce

The Family Law Act (Section 11) says:

'The welfare of the child will be best served by:

(i) his having regular contact with those who have parental responsibility for him and with other members of his family; and

(ii) the maintenance of as good a continuing relationship with his parents as is possible.'

CHOOSING YOUR ROUTE THROUGH DIVORCE

This Guide can help you to decide which route to take through your divorce. The usual routes are listed in the order in which they logically come although, of course, you would not use all of these routes one after another.

Before court

Mediation as a means of negotiating your own agreed decisions

> about children (with solicitors dealing with financial issues),
> about all issues.

Negotiation between your solicitors on your behalf, to see if they can find a settlement

> about financial matters (with mediation helping with children issues),
> about all issues.

At court

Judges making 'consent' orders on the basis of your agreed decisions reached by mediation and/or by solicitor negotiation.

Judges seeing if unresolved disputes can nevertheless be resolved

> about children, by discussion between you and a family court welfare officer,
> about finances, by a Financial Dispute Resolution appointment with the judge (available in a few courts only).

Judges making decisions on the basis of:

> your proposals presented by your solicitors,
> barristers representing you in court, briefed by you and your solicitors,
> family court welfare officers reporting to the court on the welfare of your children.

Information

Most people say that they do not know what to do and become confused about the law and the legal process. Under the Family Law Act much more attention is to be given to the information people need to assist them to make choices about which route they will take. Compulsory information meetings will become the first essential step in the divorce process.

This Guide will help to fill the gap until such meetings are available and could then become useful additional reading.

PART 1

The Experience of Separation and Divorce

1
THE DECISION

Taking stock

Two couples had flats in the same big house. When they went away on holiday, their habits were markedly different. One couple left the place tidy to return to, the other couple left their flat in chaos, intending to clear it up on their return. Some marriages end with a clearing up, a stocktaking, and some do not.

There is phrase in the Book of Common Prayer: 'There is no health in us.' If you feel this way about your marriage, you need to take stock. The first step may be to talk to your partner. If you think you cannot for any reason, you might talk to a person who has both your interests at heart. Or you might talk to a counsellor confidentially. Sometimes acknowledging the problem brings relief and makes matters clearer. Taking stock can create the energy to tackle your uneasiness. Taking control of your situation requires energy.

WHY DO MARRIAGES BREAK DOWN?

Although this is not a book about marriage or marriage counselling but about the ending of a marriage and how to end it fairly and amicably, it must begin nevertheless with deciding whether or not the marriage has to end. Marriages and close relationships break down for many complex reasons. Robert Weiss, an American sociologist, says that the experience of lone parenthood, for example, is characterised by:

- responsibility overload
- task overload
- emotional overload

Many would agree that the pressures on modern marriages and on modern partnership arrangements are similar. The problem of overload does not end with divorce. The load doubles at divorce and further redoubles in stepfamilies, whether they are full-time or part-time. Divorce or separation create as many problems as they solve.

_____ HOW MARRIAGES BREAK DOWN _____

The seven levels of divorce

Over the years, marriage will have changed you inwardly and outwardly. To a varying extent, it will have defined you. Divorce redefines us. It may seem to be changing you back to the single person you once were, but it is really changing the future. This is what you have to come to terms with at a number of different levels.

The end of a marriage touches and changes us at every level: the personal – what we feel, think, and what we look like in the mirror; the emotional – what we show, tell, hide from our partner; the parental – what our children hear and sense and what we try to show them or not show them; the wider family – what our parents know and what we think they know or don't know; the community – what other people make of us now, as we walk, talk, drive past, or sit looking out of the train or office window; the economic – what the bank knows about the state of our accounts, and, lastly, the legal – what we fill in or sign on our divorce papers.

Seven Levels of Divorce

Personal	inner self
Emotional	close relationships
Parental	our children
Family	family and friends
Community	our wider networks
Economic	money and life-style
Legal	our legal status

(Adapted from Peter Bohannon, *Divorce and After*, Doubleday, New York, 1970, which lists the different levels of living affected by separation and divorce.)

The seven stages of marital breakdown

In Kessler's *The American Way of Divorce*, there is another set of sevens: the seven stages in the breakdown of a marriage. They may be helpful in positioning your relationship in the journey.

Seven Stages in the Breakdown of a Marriage

Disillusionment
Disappointment; doubts; admitting disquiet or negative feelings.

Erosion
A deeper estrangement.

Detachment
May coincide with involvement with another close relationship.

Physical separation
Either a sudden crisis or a joint decision.

Mourning the marriage
Overwhelming loss or rejection of the partner; turning from love to hate; from grief to anger.

Second adolescence
Plunging into new relationships and activities.

Integrating the trauma
The hard work of re-establishing the ability to cope and be positive.

(Kessler, S., *The American Way of Divorce*, Chicago, Nelson Hall, 1975.)

Most marriages do not end with the couple agreeing that their marriage is over. The experience is different for the leaver and the left. The very words 'leaver' and 'left' describe the activity of one and the enforced passivity of the other. Talking and understanding, reckoning and taking stock, are all needed if the inequality of the ending is not to sour relationships for ever.

The first three stages – disappointment, erosion and detachment – make up the private part of the journey, the period before separation, when a marriage is beginning to go awry. The divorce or separation is not yet public; the struggle between the two partners is still mostly within the four walls of their home, though it breaks out now and then if triggered by the level of tension or by outside events.

The first three levels – the personal, the emotional and the parental – are likely to be the most involved.

The more public journey begins at separation. The final stages may then follow: the mourning of the marriage, a second adolescence and eventually, depending on circumstances, the integration of the whole traumatic ordeal into a new way of life. All seven levels are likely to be involved once the breakdown becomes 'public'. The divorce happens at the personal, the emotional and the parental levels within the family but is also taking place at the social, community, legal and economic levels. And the inner journey takes longer than the public, legal journey.

Managing time

The final *legal* divorce will occur at a particular stage of the journey. It is quite possible to decide jointly *when* it should happen. It does not have to 'just happen' to you. Many people seem to rush in order to get it over, thinking that this will settle things. But things do not settle like that. They take time. You can try to take charge of time. That is the approach of the new Family Law Act. The preparation for a divorce is to be given time. The way we, as a nation, enter divorce is set out below.

Who Divorces in the UK

It is predicted that 4 out of 10 new marriages are likely to end in divorce.
Most divorces occur between 5 and 9 years after marriage.
72 per cent are filed by women.
The average age at divorce for women is 36.
The average age for men is 38.

(Most of the above statistics and those following are taken from the *One plus One* Information Pack obtainable from 14 Theobald's Road, London WC1X 8PF.)

Is it too late to turn back?

Few marriage partners are agreed on this question. Knowing whether you have reached the start of divorce is the first and maybe the worst hurdle. Robert Weiss once commented that people leave when 'home has become somewhere else'. Such a realisation may be such a shock to both the leaver and the left that it may not even be discussed. Having an affair is the way that some people act out their feelings, instead of talking about them, even in the early (and preventable) stages of breakdown.

————— ASKING FOR HELP —————

Asking for help is a thorough way of being quite sure of your intentions and their likely consequences and of trying to get things sorted out before you drift too far apart or get into conflict and dispute. Asking for help with a difficult relationship from any source is not easy. Usually it is a friend to whom the words are spoken. Sometimes the doctor may decipher an unacknowledged problem. Sadly, rarely does a person (or even more rarely, a couple) openly go along to a marriage counsellor and say 'I want to save my marriage, please help me to do so.' It is often a solicitor who is approached privately and asked, 'What would be my position if…?' Nowadays it may be the mediator who first enables the question to be faced by the couple *together*.

The hardest step is to acknowledge to yourself and then to someone else that your marriage is in difficulties. Most outsiders will not mention it even if they see things that make them wonder. We are not very good at allowing ourselves to be dependent on other people for help. Whereas, in the Western world, dependency is something we think we should grow out of, in more Eastern cultures, accepting dependency as we age is a sign of maturity. We can behave very coyly about asking for help, yet most people view giving it as a privilege. Some of the things people caught up in a struggling relationship commonly say about seeking help are listed below.

Asking for Help

'I'd never tell my parents or they'd turn against him.'

'You see, everyone thinks we're the ideal couple.'

'I've never really talked about it to anyone else – it feels disloyal.'

'I just have to tell someone about it though I cannot believe I am doing this.'

'I'm afraid of speaking about it in case it gets back to him/her.'

Who Seeks Help from Whom?

Only 2 per cent of married people first seek help from a marriage counsellor if they have a marital problem. They will turn first to friends and relatives. (*British Social Attitudes*, Social and Community Planning Research, 1992, Gower, Aldershot).

Only 1 per cent of those who had experienced separation had gone to a counsellor for help, while 60 per cent had gone to family members or friends (National Child Development Study).

The response of the helper

How the person in whom you have placed your trust responds is important. The privilege of being approached for help carries responsibilities. Does the person take up 'cudgels' on your behalf? Do you want them to do that? If you do, are you too frightened to confront the situation yourself? The consequences of recruiting an army may be that your partner will do likewise and the disputes will spiral. If you are really afraid to say what you think to your partner for fear of retaliation, you need to consider carefully the extent of your fear; it may be an indicator of your concerns about your safety.

Alternatively, does the person you approach listen and respond by help-ing you to voice your doubts and disappointments in order to get them into proportion? This may mean either that you try harder to tackle the issues with your partner, or that your disquiet grows until you are convinced that you have to take more definite action. If the latter results, you are beginning to enter the erosion stage.

Your choice of helper will probably be determined by the result you want, of course. The actions we take, sometimes only half aware of our motives, tell us a great deal about ourselves that we may not yet be ready to acknowledge.

The loyalty of marriage

Conventional Anglo-Saxon reserve and strong religious and social conven-tions about divorce and marriage in a range of cultures can stand in the way of asking for help. The feeling that a bond of loyalty is being breached may be a fundamental barrier to admitting a problem. The bond of loyalty is part of the unique nature of a marriage commitment. It is not to be broken lightly. It is the privacy of that bond that does so much to maintain mar-riage. And it is that privacy and loyalty which are so much grieved when a marriage ends. Of course, such privacy and loyalty may also act danger-ously to keep together two people who should part for reasons of safety.

The bond of loyalty is part of the unique nature of a mar-riage commitment. It is not to be broken lightly. It is the pri-vacy of that bond that does so much to maintain marriage. And it is that privacy and loyalty which are so much grieved when a marriage ends.

WHERE TO GO FOR HELP
IN SAVING YOUR MARRIAGE

If you want your marriage to be improved or 'saved', there are two main avenues open to you: marriage enrichment or couple counselling.

Marriage enrichment courses

These courses set out to help you do just that: enrich your marriage. They have developed quickly during the last fifteen years. Some are religious in intention, some are secular. They aim to give couples time and help to come together in relaxed conditions and re-examine their relationships. The courses are conducted in groups, but each couple privately assesses their relationship.

Many people with life-styles that prevent time being given to the care of their marriage have found marriage enrichment courses to be a lifeline. They can replenish and refresh, often in a light-hearted as well as in a deeper vein.

Information about marriage enrichment courses can be obtained from the Directory of Marriage Support Services produced by the Lord Chancellor's Department, Selborne House, Victoria Street, London, or from Churches Together for Families.

If you feel that you are too far apart to attend one of these courses together, or it does not seem your sort of thing, marriage counselling (or couple counselling if you are not married) could help.

Marriage and couple counselling

Marriage counselling ideally involves both partners, though it may begin with one. It can even involve only one if the other partner refuses to attend. This can still help the marriage by enabling that one person to come to terms with their own disappointments, set about making their needs clearer to their partner, or reach an acceptance of the needs of their partner. There are several agencies that provide marriage or couple counselling, some on a nationwide basis, they include:

Relate (Marriage Guidance Council)
Marriage Care (Catholic Marriage Care)
The Jewish Marriage Council
The Tavistock Institute of Marital Studies
The London Marriage Guidance Council

There are other local agencies also, some religious in foundation and intent and some purely secular. Many counsellors offer help on a private basis. It is always worth while checking that they are operating under some structure of accountability. Many individual counsellors, for instance, belong to the British Association of Counselling. Most can be found in the Directory of Marriage Support Services.

The definitions of marriage counselling may differ in some respects but the points made by Relate in a recent leaflet set out clearly what they aim to offer (see overleaf).

Marriage Counselling

For couples thinking about divorce, marital counselling offers an opportunity to:

- consider what is going wrong in the marriage,
- work together towards improving and preserving the marriage,
- understand the situation from the other partner's point of view,
- explore feelings as well as facts,
- focus on points of stress and tension in family life,
- gain an understanding of the family system in which they live,
- explore the realities of staying together,
- reflect on whether the marriage is ended or not,
- weigh up various courses of action,
- gain an understanding of the past in order to prepare for the future,
- work towards reconciliation.

Saving saveable marriages

Many of the debates about divorce in both Houses of Parliament have consisted of expressions of concern lest it be made too easy. Consequently the Family Law Act begins with a clause stating 'the institution of marriage is to be supported'.

Members of all parties agreed with the Government's aim to 'save saveable marriages', so the next clause of the new Act says that 'the parties to a marriage which may have broken down are to be encouraged to take all practicable steps to save it'. There are accordingly provisions in the Act to encourage couples to seek marriage counselling.

These principles and provisions in the Act also sprang from concern about the state of marriage in Britain, which has the highest divorce rate in Europe.

Divorce Rates in Europe (1991)

UK	3.0 divorces per 1000 population
Denmark	2.5 divorces per 1000 population

Following these, in order, are:

Belgium	less than 2 per 1000 population
Luxembourg	" " " "
France	" " " "
Netherlands	" " " "
Germany	" " " "
Portugal	" " " "

Greece	less than 1 per 1000 population
Spain	less than 1 per 1000 population
Italy	0.5 per 1000 population
Ireland	no divorces

(Figures are taken from Factsheet 7, *Families in the European Union*, published by International Year of the Family UK and available through the Family Policy Studies Centre, 231 Baker Street, Lonodn, NW1 6XE).

Risk factors

You may be more likely to divorce if:

- you married under 21,
- your parents were divorced,
- you lived together before marrying, or
- this is a second marriage for one or both of you.

Some people regret ending their marriages but it appears that only in about one in ten couples do both partners regret it.

51 per cent of divorced men would have preferred to stay married.
29 per cent of divorced women would have preferred to stay married.
Only in 10 per cent of divorces did both partners wish they had stayed together.

(Davis, G., and Murch, M., 1988, *Grounds for Divorce*, Clarendon Press, Oxford.)

2

IF YOUR MARRIAGE IS OVER

If your stocktaking leads you to conclude that your marriage is nearing an end, which of you realises this and how you each deal with it will have a profound effect upon subsequent relationships. Some marriages end in mutual agreement. Most do not.

THE LEAVER

For a moment, let us take it that you are the leaver. You will have come to this position gradually and perhaps privately. You may have taken a long time to get here and tried hard to turn away. You may suddenly have become involved in a new relationship. You may be in a torment of guilt as you read this or you may be impatient to get moving.

If you are a woman

Nowadays 72 per cent of those who initiate a divorce are women. This does not mean that you are the first to become unhappy and discontented. You may be the one to make the move because your partner does not see how unhappy he and you both have become.

If you are a woman, you may have become dissatisfied with:

- your relationship
- your own way of life
- your partner's inability to communicate
- his way of life
- his violent reactions when you try to explain your view
- his silence when you try to explain your view
- his lack of time for you
- his lack of time for the children

- his attitude to money
- his attitude to sex
- his attitude to work

You probably tried to deal with your dissatisfaction as you became more unhappy. You may have begun to feel that home is when he is not there or that home is somewhere else. If so, these are devastating thoughts to have and you will have pushed them away. You may push them away now, depending on whether you are going to start this journey or not.

If you turn back now, you could consider seeking help. You may be able to stop the journey if you begin to face some of the things you are dissatisfied with. A counsellor might help you to express them to your partner if you have not been successful in doing so. They are very common issues and they do not mean a marriage is at an end.

If violence is what you fear, you will need to confront its frequency and its effect on you and your children and work out individually with a solicitor, counsellor or the Women's Aid Federation (address in the Appendix) what you should do for your sake and for the sake of your children, as well as for your partner's sake in the long term.

If you are a man

You are, according to research, less likely than your partner to make the first move nowadays, although it was men who made the first move more frequently about ten to fifteen years ago.

If you are a man, you may be dissatisfied with:

- your relationship
- your own way of life
- your partner's inability to communicate
- her way of life
- her violent reactions when you try to explain your view
- her silence when you try to explain your view
- her lack of time for you
- her lack of time for the children
- her attitude to money
- her attitude to sex
- her attitude to work

You probably tried to deal with your dissatisfaction as you became more unhappy. You may have begun to feel that home is when she is not there or that home is somewhere else. If so, these are devastating thoughts to have and you will have pushed them away. You may push them away now, depending on whether you are going to start this journey or not.

If you turn back now, you could consider seeking help. You may be able to stop the journey if you begin to face some of the things you are dissatisfied with. A counsellor might help you to express them to your partner if you have not been successful in doing so. They are very common issues and they do not mean a marriage is at an end.

THE ONE LEFT

For a moment, let us think of you as the one who is left.

If you are a man

If you are a man, it is less likely that you will stay at home with the children – about 10 per cent of men have the resident care of their children – although the proportion has been going up gradually since the early 1980s.

You may feel that you have therefore lost everything: wife, children and home. Research studies show that more men than women regret the ending of their marriage. Research studies also suggest that, in general terms, modern marriage suits men better than it suits women. Depending on the circumstances, you may feel that you have worked hard to maintain the family finances, missing opportunities to be with your family, and you are now cruelly rewarded with losing wife, home and children, and, further, that you will have to pay to maintain your children and even, in some circumstances, your spouse, when the situation has not been of your own choosing.

Alternatively, you may think that it is not fair that she has left when you were trying to maintain the family, when your earnings were too low, or you could not get a steady job. Or you may think that she is being unreasonable in leaving you for someone else simply because she is attracted to him, without taking her responsibilities seriously.

These factors – poverty, overwork, unemployment, sex and affairs – are key factors in marriage breakdown.

If you are a woman

If you are a woman, it is more likely that you will stay at home with the children – about 90 per cent of women have the day-to-day care of their children – although the proportion of men having residential care of their children has been going up gradually since the early 1980s.

You may feel that you have been left with everything – children, all the housework and making ends meet – and with no husband to help. Research studies suggest that, in general terms, modern marriage suits men better than it suits women. You may think that this is because women do more of the domestic work; research shows that they do, even if they are also earning. Depending on the circumstances, you may feel that you have worked hard to maintain the family, missing opportunities of earning yourself, and you are now cruelly rewarded for your efforts by being abandoned.

Alternatively, you may think that it is not fair that he has left when you were undergoing the strain of trying to earn more money by working yourself. Or you may think that he is being unreasonable in leaving you for someone else simply because he is attracted to her, without taking his responsibilities seriously.

These factors – poverty, overwork, unemployment, sex and affairs – are key factors in marriage breakdown.

GENDER DIFFERENCES

The list of things you might be dissatisfied with are the same for both men and women, both for 'leavers' and 'lefts'. However, they may seem gender-biased one way or another. Many pressure points are the same for men and women, but we are likely to perceive them differently. We are becoming much more precisely aware that men and women experience things differently and react differently. We make many false assumptions about each other. According to John Gray's book entitled *Men Are from Mars, Women Are from Venus,* we expect that the other will know what we want and need (when they simply may not) and that they will want or need what we give them, which is what we would want or need (when they actually want something different).

Of course, this is useful to understand if you want to save your marriage or relationship. In fact, it may explain why many relationships grind to a halt or flare into conflict. In the past, those things happened but people did not end marriages, because it was not possible or acceptable to do so.

If you are ending your marriage, it helps to understand how differently you may each react. Some feminist writers in the 1980s suggested that the way men and women perceive themselves actually centres on changes and transitions. Women are more likely, some thought, to see transitions in terms of their responsibilities (to care for others in their family), whereas men were thought more likely to see them in terms of their freedom. In the 1990s, male writers are challenging such views. However, although they are not only to be interpreted in these particular terms, men and women may well react differently to changes and transitions, depending, of course, on how they perceived their lives before.

Theories of gender difference will surely continue to be further explored as one of the key areas of social and psychological study in the future. For example, one study suggests that some men may withdraw from conflict because they seek not to strike out, which is their impulse, whereas women will behave in quite the opposite way and seek to confront an issue because they do not think of striking out. This has a bearing on how we negotiate including during divorce. Such theories are new. We may feel we know a great deal about gender differences but have never been able to think them out consciously before. Such theories may help us to do so.

SHOULD YOU STAY TOGETHER FOR THE SAKE OF THE CHILDREN?

Journalists ask 'Experts' this question as if there were an answer. After all, most children say that they do not want their parents to part. The only answer is, 'It all depends.' It depends, first, on what stage of the marriage breakdown you have reached and second, on how you both behave.

It all depends...

If you are at the 'disillusioned' stage, you will be considering whether the process of dissolution can be reversed. It is at this stage that the most intense struggles and arguments often occur as each partner tries to get from the other what they want in order to sustain the marriage. Children may be hating this struggle. They may be listening to it going on. Many children, or adults reflecting later on their childhood, will describe being in bed listening for the arguments and hating them. You may be able to hide your struggles from the children; this is worth achieving.

Staying together for their sake may depend on:

whether the arguments are so bad that you have to part because of their
   effect on the children;
how far you are able to *protect* the children from them;
how effective the arguments are in achieving what the children most
   probably want: a reconciliation between you.

If you are becoming estranged, into the second stage, you may be considering whether you can live with this, for the sake of the children. Children can live with parents who are distant or 'detached' as long as they are not distant or detached from *them*. It depends on how the adults conduct themselves. Children hate to hear one parent talking disparagingly about the other because they usually have an equal loyalty to both parents. So, again, it depends first on which stage you have reached, second, on how you are both able to conduct yourselves in respect of the children and, third, on whether or not you decide that a detached relationship is better than a divorce.

If you decide to maintain a detached marriage (which, of course, may or may not become more satisfying later in life), you may have to face the fact that marriages in this condition are vulnerable to the next stage, as detachment may lead to the search, overt or unacknowledged, for another close relationship. How will this affect your children?

Your children will be affected by this if they are aware of it. Some marriages continue through this third stage and overcome the intrusion of affairs. There are accounts in some biographies of famous people and research studies of ordinary people who have had affairs, sometimes for years, that describe how the secret was kept from their partner and from their children. The crucial factor is whether parents can preserve the family and their relationships with their children.

If an affair is kept secret from children and they learn about it much later, they may reflect on the 'private life' or 'deceit' of their parents. In many communities, however, it is not possible for an affair to be secret. Many people find such secrecy impossible, morally and psychologically, even if it is socially feasible and acceptable.

No expert can easily proclaim on such dilemmas.

DIFFERENT STARTING-POINTS

A characteristic of divorce is that it is not a well-planned journey. People do not start together with a common purpose. Rarely does everyone involved want to make this journey.

'The Grand National'

For some, the start is like the Grand National of 1994, when there was confusion over whether the race had started or not. The leaders hesitated and looked back, or charged on unaware of what they had left behind, while the rest of the field did not know whether to stay put or to run hard to catch up. You may like to reproduce the chart overleaf and plot where you, your partner, your children and your parents are at this moment. The second chart gives an example for a fictional family.

My Parents	Me	Our Children	Him/Her	His/Her Parents

Start →

My Parents	Me	Our Children	Him/Her	His/Her Parents
X Dad		X John	X James	X X Tom Amy
		X Jenny		
X Mum				
	X me			

Start →

Where is everybody?

Draw four lines lengthwise down a sheet of paper, leaving the middle space wider than the others. Head the first space on the left 'My Parents', the next space 'Me', the middle space 'Our Children', the next 'Him/Her' and the last 'His/Her Parents'.

Draw a line across it horizontally about half-way down and head that 'Start'. Add arrows.

Mark in each person's position at the start of the separation or divorce. They are moving in the direction of the arrows.

When you complete your chart and can see where everybody is placed, you can plan how to assist those who are at different stages. If your partner is further ahead or further behind, one of you has to allow time for the other to catch up. The greater the distance between you as actions begin to be taken, the more resentment and confusion are likely. One cannot act too fast and then expect the other to negotiate in good faith.

The children are likely to be far behind each of you in coming to terms with what is to happen. You will see from the result of research given in Chapter 6 that children are very often taken completely by surprise when their parents divorce. Finally, the rest of your family are likely to be even further behind, unless one of you has confided in them.

3
SEPARATING
'I just walked away'

For many couples, parting is sudden and abrupt, for others long and painful. How and on what basis you part are important for you and your children. If the parting is abrupt, the likelihood is that nothing will be sorted out. This can lead to a pattern of communication that is conducted across a wider and wider gulf, increasing suspicion and missed opportunities for resolving problems in the interests of each partner and the children. If solicitors are contacted they will then find themselves taking on the task of communicating between you via correspondence between them. This is not an efficient way to plan day-to-day matters.

However, if you are able to establish some basis for future communication before parting, many things will become less problematic, such as planning how to tell the children, sorting out who pays the bills and ensuring that everyone has enough money for daily living. Mediators find that if couples come into mediation before they part there is a greater chance of working things out sensibly together. There is more than enough to sort out without creating avoidable misunderstandings.

TEMPORARY OR PERMANENT SEPARATION?

Some couples decide that by giving their marriage a rest for a while they will be able to reappraise their situation. This is a valid option and one that is very likely to clarify the situation for you. Separation alone does not resolve matters *between* you, but it may resolve matters in your own minds. It can help to renew energy if you have become worn down. With that energy, you are more able to make decisions.

Clare and Sean are two people who experienced a temporary separation. Sean had an affair, in what we might now see as the early disappointment stage of the marriage. He, of course, did not have such a clear view. His wife was not only angry and hurt at learning of the affair, but lost her confidence in herself as a result. She thought that motherhood had removed her attractiveness. Sean did not accept this explanation but, when he was confronted by Clare's knowledge of his affair, expressed his view that, with her busyness in caring for the children and keeping her job going, he had been missing her appreciation and the companionship upon which he had always relied. He finished his affair and the marriage continued without a separation.

However, Clare began to seek reassurance about her attractiveness and, feeling to some extent justified, began an affair herself. On discovering her affair, Sean left the house. She then finished the affair and they began to fight about his contact with the children.

This couple came to mediation at this point to sort out different contact arrangements between Sean and the children. The arrangement they had been operating between his departure and their first mediation session involved his seeing the children – and the adults seeing each other – every day. It was in the mediation session that their dependence on daily contact with each other became apparent to both of them. Every time other options were considered, they rejected them. Eventually the mediator asked each of them what was so important about the children seeing their father every day in this way. Sean answered, 'Because it means I can see Clare.' The temporary separation had done its job. He moved back in and they sought marriage counselling to be sure that the tit-for-tat episode would not recur.

MANAGING THE PARTING

For both partners, parting is painful as old bonds are pulled apart and the future glimpsed through the chinks or chasms. The actual parting, the physical separation, is often remembered far more vividly than the legal divorce, which usually comes later.

Here are three cautionary tales of how three couples parted *without* thinking or talking about it beforehand.

Beattie and Jim

Beattie is a part-time teacher living in Richmond; Jim is a businessman who works in London and travels a lot. They have three children at secondary school.

Beattie:
> Well, I did the classic thing of seeing a letter on his desk. I realised it was from a friend who would normally have written to us both.
>
> The feeling of disbelief was so strong that I almost fainted. The doorbell went at that moment so I had to go and answer it or otherwise

I think I would have fainted. My mind then went into overdrive in recalling all the contacts between us and this so called friend until I came to see clearly what I had been blind to. That took most of the day.

I then began to plot how I would hide my state of mind from the children and how I would confront him. I raged out loud, saying, 'How could you?' and things like that.

When he got back, he just said it was true. It was an anticlimax in a way. He just sat down and said he had always meant to tell me but never found the right time. I screamed that there was no right time and he just sat there offering no explanation whatsoever.

I asked him about all the occasions I could think of when I realised that I had been betrayed before my very face. I waited to hear about all the other times behind my back but he said nothing about them. I almost felt sorry for him having to face me and I felt like a harridan, whatever that is.

We went to bed but I slept not at all and eventually went off to another room. I went on retracing everything, giving myself the hardest time of my life and angry that he was asleep. I didn't wake him up, though.

We went through the motions of living. I was either stony-faced or artifically bright or very, very tired. I spent long periods in bed. He kept away and stopped coming home at night except at weekends, when the children would have expected to see him and when we couldn't pretend he was working away.

I said absolutely nothing to the children and neither did he. It was bizarre. Eventually, after about three weeks or so, we went out for meal and he said, in the semi-public of the restaurant (where I wouldn't shout) that he was going to leave, that things had been hard for him and I hadn't seemed to understand and he'd just fallen in love and that was that!

And he packed one morning and left. We didn't discuss at that time anything about the future. I was left to explain to the children. It was unbelievable, like someone else's life I was living.

We even hugged in tears, both of us, when he left – can you believe it? The children were at school at the time, thank God. I don't know why I say, 'thank God'. If there is a God, he was preoccupied at the time.

Then I removed the wedding photograph and got on with work again and went to a counsellor. It was only then when she invited my husband to come in that we began to talk about what had gone wrong. The worst thing of all was the fury I felt for that other woman whose name I can still not repeat. I just call her 'the snake'.

Jim:

I was sitting on the train going to Glasgow, with the bag on the rack, wondering how other people could not see what turmoil was going on inside my head. It was seething and throbbing with the pain of what I had done to her and to the children. How could people not see I was abnormal? Yet I felt like a train myself, out of control. I could not keep away from Diana. I kept telling myself that this was a mid-life crisis but I just seemed unable to be rational about it at all. At other times I thought I was being supremely rational and could justify my actions totally.

I had acknowledged to myself even before I had got involved with Di that things were badly wrong. I blamed myself more than Beattie. I had become a dried up old stick who seemed to be travelling all the time, worrying about the next report I had to write and who I was going to meet and whether I could save things – the job, the firm, the house, the marriage. When I got home I never concentrated on Beattie and the children; not on anything in the house except the plants. I got quite obsessive about the plants.

I found her utter preoccupation with the children and her work and the PTA so excluding that I got more and more distant and dreaded going home and hearing about it all. In fact I had stopped listening ages ago.

It was classic, my falling for the first person who asked me what was wrong. But she does understand. She has been through it herself. She doesn't prattle. She's quiet and I do feel calm with her. She's helped me get my work together. I would never be able to face Beattie without thinking of Di waiting when I got home. Silly that, because but for Di I would still be at home. I'm not sure now where home is, am I?

I realised that we had to have some sort of inquest. I want to be fair about her and the children. I don't want any more rows, with her going on at me all the time; I can't face it any more. Well, I never could, but now I have an option.

I guess I've done the normal thing for men in my position. I know several who've done the same. Stupid, isn't it? They only see their children at the weekends. That is what cracks me up.

Then I got this letter from a marriage counsellor. Well, Di urged me to go. And then I thought, does she want to get rid of me now? She must have thought that I'd perhaps change my mind. She said I had to square things with Beattie somehow and I'd never do it on my own. She was right.

God, I hated it, but I went and I didn't change my mind. I think she was as fed up with me as I had been with her. If I hadn't gone, I guess she might have, except for the children and her loyalty to them and setting them an example. Which, of course, I had done – a bad one.

It was the counsellor who suggested, once it was clear that it was over and we'd said some of the things that had to be said, that we try mediation for the sake of the children.

Ashley and Flo

Ashley works in a Manchester sports shop and Flo is at home looking after Jamie, their young son. They are both members of African Caribbean families.

Ashley:

She left and went back to her mother. I keep going round kind of hoping she'll change her mind. I can't stand being in the house on my own and I know we've got to move. We're behind on the rent anyhow – or rather she says I am! I don't want to go back to my parents. That's the last thing I want and yet I guess I'll have to do it.

I probably pay Jamie more attention now than I did before, when I left it all to her as she was so good with him. That's what went wrong, really. She was so good at it – so fulfilled – that I just felt like a stranger in the house. Don't get me wrong. I love Jamie all right, but everything was 'Jamie this' and 'Jamie that', 'Don't do this because of Jamie', 'Don't do that because of Jamie'....

We stuck it out for about a year and then she just said she was going. Wouldn't even try to get it right again.

Flo:

I just knew I couldn't cope with him around any more. He was never there when I wanted him. He never took any responsibility for Jamie. He worked all right, I guess, but I was never sure what his hours really were. It was me that managed the money all the time, when I got it, I thought I could cope better on my own; why do I bother?

So, I told him one day at breakfast. I had already packed but he hadn't noticed. Typical. I didn't want to do it at bedtime. And I left and went back home. My mum wasn't surprised. Jamie didn't seem to miss him at all at first so I thought I'd got away with it, him being so young. But then Ashley started to come back at all funny times 'to see Jamie', he said. But I knew he was coming hoping that I'd say I'd go back. He asked me every time. But I just knew he wouldn't change. Men are all the same as far as I can see nowadays. Not like my dad, though.

Ashok and Ros

Ashok is a chemist and Ros is a legal executive. Both are from Indian families in Birmingham. They have no children.

Ashok:

Ours was not an arranged marriage. She was not prepared to behave in the way our family expected of her. She wanted to go on with her education instead of accepting her traditional role. If she had wanted everything, she should not have married at all.

When it became clear that she was determined to be wilful, wanting to pursue her own career and not prepared to give me the support I needed to pursue mine, things became unpleasant. I could not let her rule me. Our marriages are not like English marriages. I have seen enough of those go wrong at work. I did not want a marriage like that. I value our traditions. I wanted her to respect my parents. She would not.

Things became worse and worse. Then she just left without any explanation and went back to her parents. To make matters worse, she wanted everything back – even the gold. I had to stand up for what I believed. I now have an arranged marriage and that is much better. We were too young at the time.

Ros:

I just walked away. I made a mistake. It should have been an arranged marriage, then his background would have been investigated. There were no investigations. No family members were interviewed. I thought I knew best. I knew there were stories about his family (his father was violent to his mother in front of the children – he had told me), but I thought, I am marrying him and not his family.

Then he became violent and would not let me continue with my education. I think it is my entitlement. He would say, 'Be a wife and do what I say.' He wanted me to serve his parents meals. I would respect his parents – I respect all old people, it is in my blood – but I would not serve them in the way he wanted me to when I was not allowed to respect myself.

I got nothing, not even the gold I had been given. My father had helped him set up his business but because it was a gift I could not get it back.

I had no financial freedom but I got my freedom and that was what I wanted in the end. He was violent, so I did not pursue it. They said it would cost me a lot of money to pursue it and I might not win, so I just walked away. I feel very sorry for those Asian women who have nowhere to go. My parents took me back and have now arranged a marriage for me.

These three stories are not unusual – the overloaded couple who lose touch with one another at the busiest time of their lives; the young couple not getting beyond the changes brought by a first child; the marriage that occurred without the traditional support of an arranged marriage in the Asian community. All six individuals see the situation from their own perspective and feel aggrieved and even justified as they raggedly part. Nothing was settled when they 'walked away'.

In the rush of a pent-up need for affection, or frustration, or clashing expectations of marriage, the three leavers in these accounts had more energy to escape than to confront their difficulties. The left were indeed left to come to terms with the shock, betrayal, loneliness, helplessness and injustice as best they could. They had little energy for coping.

It does not seem extraordinary to mediators that marriages end so untidily. Cooperative partings are very difficult to achieve and are most easily managed when couples stay together (somehow) until well into the 'detachment' period. However, few couples tend to stay together until that stage is reached. Most divorces happen, under the present law, within six months. All three leavers in the stories above had moved into the 'erosion' stage, whereas the left were only just entering the starting gate.

These stories may help you think about achieving a better parting. It is a challenge, but likely to benefit you and your partner in the future and also your children: many children say they remember a parent leaving as the worst moment of their parents' separation or divorce. Do not set unrealistic goals for yourself, however. You are not likely both to be at the same stage and you cannot totally avoid the pain and mess of breaking a bond.

Nor can you avoid some blaming. During the parliamentary passage of the Family Law Bill, much was made of 'getting rid of fault'. You cannot get rid of faults that have occurred in a crumbling relationship or in conduct that has led the relationship to crumble. Having an affair may be one 'fault'. Being perpetually angry, withdrawn, critical or violent may be others. In divorce petitions under the present law, many accusations are made to get a divorce quickly. When a relationship has deteriorated badly, things that were previously tolerated become unsupportable, whereas some situations, like violence, that should be unsupportable are often endured for too long.

How to avoid the blame game

The 'blame game' that marriage counsellors see so frequently is a destructive and fruitless habitual response to pressures and demands when couples are still together. When they separate, it seems to assume a life of its own, pushing them into justifying their positions in a reciprocal blame game, where each partner gets caught up in accusations and counter-accusations. This can become addictive, so that it is difficult for either to break out. Mediators often see such patterns of behaviour in couples and have to intervene to stop them taking place during the mediation session. Solicitors may experience the blame game at one remove, as they see only one party. They may have a frustrating time (expensive for their clients) trying to parry accusations in letters and telephone calls from 'the other side'. Couples often enlist their solicitors in this dangerous and costly game and will sometimes describe their solicitors as really good if he or she 'takes up the cudgels' for them.

One solicitor attending a seminar to learn about mediation said, 'But what about my reputation? My clients come because I am known as a good fighter.' Some solicitors, however, will be very unhappy to take part in such activities. If they know the solicitor on 'the other side', they may be able to calm matters down. If the other solicitor is the fighting type, they may make frustrating and fruitless efforts to fulfil the tenets of their Code of Practice (see SFLA, p145). They may watch the costs going up, warn their client, but be unable to stop the escalation.

Many bitter extended disputes have the blame game at their heart and end up with judges and family court welfare officers trying to reach a solution. Sometimes they resolve once a court has made a decision and sometimes they rumble on for years. Frequently they are about, or come to be about, the couple's children.

Halting a spiralling conflict may necessitate understanding what is driving it. Sometimes it is a deep sense of justifiable injury. Sometimes it is an inability or refusal to acknowledge one's own part in a situation. Sometimes it is deep pain at loss. 'Grievance' is a strong word, associated with grief. There is no quick remedy for profound emotional hurt; only time and positive experiences heal it. Sometimes divorce counselling can help you to come to terms with any deep grievance that you feel. Sometimes mediation can help by providing a safe opportunity, as part of the mediation process, for the accusations and hurts to be expressed to one another. An amicable divorce is more likely to be achieved if both partners openly acknowledge their strong reactions rather than pushing them aside.

> **Paradoxically, an amicable divorce is more likely to be achieved if both partners openly acknowledge their strong reactions rather than pushing them aside.**

Jilly and Jon

Jilly is a health visitor and Jon is an estate agent. They have two children, aged ten and seven.

This couple managed their situation with great courage. Jilly learnt very abruptly about Jon's affair. Somehow he stayed his ground to listen to her fury and she was generous enough to listen to him as well as venting her fury on him. They described how they spent several dreadful nights in each other's arms, crying for the end of their marriage, until the storm blew itself out. Jilly had little doubt that the marriage was over and had in fact suspected the affair for months but had not faced up to it. These two people managed to express their grief together and focus on the needs of their children. They used their first session in mediation to plan how they would do this.

They prepared for the actual parting and for telling their children. They decided to tell them together that Jon was going to go because they no longer could stay married to each other and that Daddy now loved someone else and was going to live with her. The children knew who the new woman was. They were stunned, but asked questions which both parents tried to answer in a matter-of-fact way. When his seven-year-old son asked why he loved this other woman more than Mummy, Jon made the mistake of saying, 'I'll tell you when you're old enough to understand, at which point his son shouted, 'Tell me now and I don't care whether I understand!'

It was a tough experience for all the family. It was not 'amicable' in the conventional sense of the term. It was rather that this particular couple remained in communication. It must have been very painful, but surely less traumatic for their children than if one parent had left without explanation in the night or while the children were at school, for example. To stay in control in this situation takes courage.

'You can't improve on the truth,' Laurens van der Post wrote in *Venture into the Interior*. He meant 'the interior' in a geographical sense, as he was describing having to tell a young woman of the sudden death of her husband on a mountain in Africa. The bravery and pain involved in telling the truth applies equally to interior journeys.

4

NEW RELATIONSHIPS

'...*the fragile, complex web*
of adult emotional life'

(The Best of Friends, Joanna Trollope)

The ending of your relationship may well become swept up in the turmoil of one partner's new sexual relationship. Research studies based on responses to questionnaires indicate that affairs in marriage are more common than many people suppose.

Affairs

Research studies indicate that between 25 per cent and 75 per cent of adults claim to have had an affair during their marriage. One survey (The Sexual Lifestyles Survey, published in 1994) found that 4.5 per cent of married men and 1.9 per cent of married women reported having more than one sexual partner in the last year. The figure for cohabiting couples was higher: 15.3 per cent for men and 8.2 per cent for women. (One Plus One factsheet: 'Adultery')

If you or your partner have begun a new sexual relationship, this could have occurred at any stage in the breakdown of your marriage relationship. However, the effect of it may vary according to the stage of the breakdown. That will also affect how you deal with it.

STAGES AT WHICH
NEW RELATIONSHIPS MAY BEGIN

Stage 1 Disillusionment

Marriages, with what Robert Weiss termed the 'overload of tasks, emotions and responsibilities', can create a strong wish to revert to a simpler, uncluttered relationship. Some marriages clearly survive affairs and some partners may never know that they existed. If you are both basically content, then such an affair may pass, although it will leave its traces of distrust and trust will have to be rebuilt. If you are both disappointed, uneasy or angry within your marriage, will this outside relationship create new energy to save your marriage or begin the slide into the next stage of marital breakdown? Hiding from the problems in one relationship by beginning another is not a lasting solution.

Stage 2 Erosion

The search for new relationships is more likely to happen when there is growing distance between partners, though it may nevertheless come as a surprise. It may spring from anxiety and loneliness when a marriage seems to be drifting away across a bleak landscape with little communication to light it.

New relationships at this stage will have an effect proportionate to how far the erosion is shared and acknowledged by both; it may be the experience of only one partner. When there is a confrontation, energy may be found to save the marriage.

A couple went for marriage counselling, the husband initiating the request for help in the hope of saving his marriage having learnt of his wife's new relationship. At first, his fury and disbelief were directed as much at her retreat from him as at her relationship with another man. He simply had not read the signs and was angry with himself as well as with his wife and the other man. In the session, they both were very angry and began to express the discontents that had led to her affair. This brought them together again.

New relationships at the erosion stage provoke the wrenching of a bond by one partner against the grip and tug of the other, who may well have been unaware of the distance between them. The struggle of the latter may reawaken the marriage. Many marriages are remade when the partner who is to be left puts up a vigorous fight. Like any animal species, we try hard to recover our lost partner as a component of grieving. (The word 'mourning' comes from an old Norse word meaning 'calling out, searching'.)

Stage 3 Detachment

Logically, it should be most common for a new relationship to begin at this stage of marital breakdown. This may not, however, protect either of you from the distress and grief that may spring up even if you have become quite detached from each other.

Stage 4 The physical separation

The actual separation may be closely related to the beginning of a new relationship by one partner. Turmoil may occur, no matter how much the one who is leaving may try to orchestrate their departure. In *The Best of*

Friends Joanna Trollope gives an account of the strong reactions of adults and children alike to the announcement of a parent's departure. The male character making the move had simply not calculated on the consequences for everyone else and he was engulfed by a wave of reactions from his wife and daughter and friends.

Couples caught up in such storms may suffer rage and jealousy in turn, alternately clinging to and rejecting their partner. These are some of the strongest emotions in human nature. Many people survive and become stronger as a result of previously unimaginable experiences.

Stage 5 Mourning the marriage

This stage of breakdown is a difficult time in which to enter a new relationship. People may be searching for what they have lost and find hasty and inappropriate replacements. Some temporary family changes may take place. If you mourn in this way, trying to find a replacement for the partner to whom you still feel closely bonded, it may be helpful to see these painful aspects of your emotional divorce as part of mourning. Such wounds take time to heal.

Two people, both of whom had been left by their partners and had the the day-by-day care of their children, fell in love. They found comfort in a common grief. What they could not manage was the sheer complexity of the life they created by grouping together not only two abandoned adults but four children, all of much the same pre-adolescent age. The exhaustion of all six people involved eventually caused a split. These two people had been huddling like sheep on a cold night against the wind of change. They were both too much in grief and it was with relief – and a little regret – that they parted. These two people then went on to make positive new relationships at a later stage in their recovery. They had helped each other through the mourning stage and their children were not too damaged by the experience; for them also the pain was in the loss of the first marriage.

Stage 6 Second adolescence

Before you and your ex-spouse have had time to recover, either may embark on one or more relationships, reminiscent of your earliest excursions into sexual life. If it is your ex-partner who is doing this, you may feel a wave of complex reactions: 'Why doesn't he grow up!', 'How embarrassing!', 'Is she becoming a tart or what?' or 'He's old enough to be her grandfather!' To see your ex-spouse behaving in such a way may make you say 'Good riddance' or feel profoundly sad. If it is you who are experimenting with your new-found freedom, you will see yourself in this light only occasionally, perhaps when your children pass comments.

Second adolescence is such a common phenomenon that it is clearly an important part of the recovery process for many people – and thus another stage in the emotional divorce. By separating yourself from your ex-partner in this way you may be reclaiming your own sexuality.

However, some research reports into the effects of divorce on children describe the unsettling effects for children of passing through 'a succession of households'. How you manage what may turn out to be transitory relationships from the point of view of your children is of vital importance to them.

Stage 7 Integrating the trauma

If you are getting over a marriage breakdown, you may feel extremely cautious about entering any new sexual or emotional commitment. You will be getting used to your new identity. Although you may no longer see yourself as half of a marriage, you may not be ready for a new commitment.

One of the things that can occur is that the making of a new bond helps to sever the old one and turn it into a different kind of relationship. You may begin to like your ex-spouse again; you may begin to understand your marriage and how it ended and this may make you feel free of it. A new relationship may form around the new person you now perceive yourself to be.

One writer described the later reinterpretation of a relationship as the 'cognitive thrust', by which he meant that your mind takes you – thrusts you – forward and, with hindsight, you can make sense of what has happened. A new relationship may help you do this as you realise how differently you relate to this new person. However, if you find you are relating to them in exactly the same way as you did to your former partner, and you are unhappy about this, you probably need to try counselling so that someone else can help you with that 'thrust'.

If it is your ex-spouse and not you that is entering a new relationship at this advanced stage, and if you have truly integrated the trauma, you may find that you do not begrudge them their new partner. It is a test of your recovery, of your emotional divorce. If you mind bitterly, you have to accept that you still have work to do – more grief to face. We cannot avoid the grief that is in us. Starting new relationships only when you are able to cope with them, and with their consequences, will be easier for you – and for your children.

Elizabeth went abroad to work after her husband left her. When she returned to this country at retirement age, she had to come to terms with his new life at a closer distance and realised that she had to complete her grieving. She had left to escape it and it was awaiting her on her return. Elizabeth went on a divorce experience course – the oldest person there –

in order to do the work of finishing her emotional divorce. She was a brave woman and helped the other participants greatly.

GAY AND LESBIAN RELATIONSHIPS

One of the most difficult explanations to give to outsiders for the breakdown of a marriage is that one partner has realised that he or she is not truly heterosexual. This is quite common: most professionals in the field of separation or divorce have known a number of marriages end for this reason. For the spouse who is left, the sense of rejection is a complex one, especially if he or she has had no experience of homosexuality in friend or family. The partner who leaves the marriage may have feelings of guilt about not having been open with their partner before as well as about 'coming out'.

Where there are children, the parents will have to cope with many prejudices about the supposed dangers of children growing up with homosexual parents, although there is no evidence that the children of homosexual parents also become homosexual. Children coming to terms with a parent being homosexual and having a partner of the same gender will need well-informed and unprejudiced assistance when they seek explanations.

A mediator was used to assist one family to cope with the ending of a marriage when the mother entered into a lesbian relationship. In this situation the mediator consulted the children, at the request of their parents, about their views of the arrangements the parents wanted to make. The children's grief about the end of their parents' marriage had an extra dimension: how much secrecy would attach to the reasons for the separation and to their mother's future life-style? This could have influenced any decision concerning which parent the children would permanently live with. In this family, however, it was (as in any other family) their deep attachment to both parents and their growing independence in pursuing their own individual outside interests that resolved the issue of where the children would mostly live.

Although the children knew about their mother's lesbian relationship and had to come to terms with it, it did not turn out to be the crucial factor in this case, as many outsiders might have supposed. However, it was important for the mediator to be sensitive to the issue. She had to ensure that any messages she might indirectly give out were respectful and that she took her cue from the attitudes of the family members. When she ended her mediation work with this family, she felt a deep respect for them.

Our sources of dissatisfaction and the way we express them have a bearing on how we conduct the journey. Partners may express their dissatisfactions differently and the way they perceive them will affect the course of their separation. The new divorce law will do away with our 'faults' as *a ground* for divorce, but it will not do away with the sense of grief and grievance we suffer when our marriage ends.

Starting new relationships only when you are able to cope with them, and with their consequences, will be easier for you – and for your children.

5

YOUR NEEDS

ATTACHMENT

It has become a truism that divorce is like a bereavement, but it is no less true for being often said. The experience of grief is gruelling and inescapable. After the parting, you have yourself. You may have a new partner, you may have your children with you, but in some private way you are alone again; your marriage is over and that particular intimacy is gone; the bond is broken.

Bonding, or 'attachment', is a basic building block in personal development. The concept is mostly associated with how a young baby cleaves to its mother. Theories about attachment developed from the work of John Bowlby and have been responsible, for example, for psychological concerns in the 1940s and 1950s about babies separated from their mothers. Then the concept was widened to include a child's other important relationships – with their father, for instance. The creation of an attachment is now thought to depend on the quality as well as the frequency of the close relationship in question; the concept has been revived in the modern notion of 'quality time'.

Attachment (or bonding) is not often associated with adult relationships. Several writers have, however, used the concept to study the ending of close relationships formed in adulthood. Robert Weiss writes powerfully of the loneliness of young adults who have successfully detached themselves from their parents but experience a great inner loneliness until they reattach to another adult.

This theory helps to account for the depth of the inner loneliness and temporary loss of identity that sometimes comes with divorce. Some people may re-experience the loneliness they felt as a young adult, before marriage.

Should you go back to your parents?

Some people, like Flo, actually return to live with their parents in these situations. Conversely, some vigorously avoid doing so. Having detached themselves once, with difficulty perhaps, they do not want to go back. A temporary return to the familiarity of a previous attachment, however, may be one effective way of stoking up, of filling that hollow left by the withdrawal of intimacy from a partner with whom you had expected to live your life 'until death do us part'. Or it may be the only option you can financially afford in the immediate circumstances.

You may get stuck in an old comforting relationship and fail to move on. Alternatively, that relationship may act as a springboard for moving on, either because this is what your parents helped you to do before, or, conversely, because they did not and the adult person you have become strives again to be free.

The possible effects of divorce upon your health

The loss of their relationship may have powerful effects upon the health of both partners after a divorce. Marital breakdown has been found to be marked by 'continuous episodic stress'. The series of life events involved in separation or divorce can adversely affect your health.

A report entitled 'Marital Breakdown and the Health of the Nation' (second edition, 1995) by the marriage research organisation One Plus One, describes a train of health-related responses to such stresses. These may lead to a reduction in immunity and a series of conditions that have been categorised as somatic, behavioural and pyschological. They make up a worrying list, ranging from headaches, abdominal pains and allergies, for example, to increased smoking and drinking and varying degrees of depression, anxiety and anger.

Selected life events from the Holmes and Rahe social readjustment scale (disruption = stress = ill-health)

Life events	*Life change units*
Divorce	73
Marital separation	65
Change in financial status	36
Change in number of arguments with spouse	35
Son/daughter leaving home	29
Trouble with in-laws	29
Change in living conditions	25
Change in residence	20
Change in social activities	18

15–199 = mild life crisis
200–299 = moderate life crisis
300+ = major life crisis

(Extract from One Plus One factsheet, Impact of Divorce.)

How to stay healthy

It is widely recognised in the West, where there has been something of a culture shift in recent years, that grieving people need to express their grief. So, if you are left, most people will understand your need to express your grief to someone. The grief caused by divorce is likely to be mixed with and sometimes buried under anger and disappointment, but the grief is usually there waiting to be expressed. It helps your children if it is not only they who hear you cry. You will need to turn to friends or counsellors who can give you this opportunity.

Jilly, whose controlled separation from her husband was described above, used to call on her friends. She never outstayed her visit, somehow, but went in and simply cried, usually over someone's kitchen table. It seemed quite natural. She offered some apologies, but none were needed. Jilly used a self-healing process. It did not last too long – a few weeks in the early stage of acute grief, perhaps.

Friends and family are crucially important. They may take sides when they hear your story; they may not, especially if they knew you both, but it is *the expression of grief* that matters. Sometimes you may be lucky and find someone else who is going through a similar experience at the same time. In one village, two women were left by their husbands within a few weeks. They became godsends to each other, going out, laughing and crying together. The air was probably thick with vitriol at times.

Many men prefer pubs to kitchen tables, though some men cannot easily express their feelings. In a recent study it was reported that most men confide their anxieties only to their partners. In many pubs there may be one or two men whose wives have left them. Everyone knows their dilemma. It will be rarely talked about, but that pub is their second home – and at times, their first. Television soaps thrive on divorce – it is one of today's recurring themes. Yet the experience of separation is unique to each person.

Actively maintain your self-esteem and your energy

It is essential to recover your self-esteem. It affects how you dress and what you do. Do whatever makes your spirits rise again: laughing, singing, outings with children, physical sports, dancing, making something, listening to something, going somewhere, liking someone, loving someone. All these are active verbs. Time will help but most people will recover sooner if they actively *do* something rather than wait.

Support for the one left behind

For the partner who is left there is bitterness and sometimes rejection to compound their grief. They may also lack energy. Bitterness is the characteristic ingredient divorce introduces into bereavement. It may last for years after a rejection if it is not exorcised and self-esteem is not resurrected.

A woman once wrote to a woman's magazine to express her joy that after 24 years she no longer felt bitter towards her ex-husband for leaving her. She regretted all the years when her energy had been consumed by bitterness.

Many more men than women find that their bitterness at being left by their wife is cruelly compounded by the loss of the day-to-day lives of their children. They often remain angry and hurt for many years.

Support for the one who leaves

The person who leaves may have the advantage of action, but may find it difficult to get support from anyone except a new partner. They may well feel ashamed. One man said, 'They may see me as the man who left. I see myself as the one who let them down.'

Women particularly may feel blame and guilt for doing what is commonly perceived as unthinkable: leaving their children. Some women experience a temporary menopause brought on by the trauma of leaving their children when they felt they had little option at the time. We cannot judge from the outside.

Men who leave are sometimes perceived as taking the typical way out. 'Just thought he could get out, did he, and leave it all to you to sort out?' There are echoes of ancestral voices from our childhood past here. 'Well, that's what you chose to do, isn't it?' the voices may say. The broken bond will hurt until it heals over – unless, that is, you have separated so far along the process of dissolution that the grief has already passed.

There are support organisations for adults on their own and these are listed on pages 218–9.

UNTYING THE KNOTS

Your relationship as a couple is ending. What will your future relationship be? It was Freud who first described grieving as untying all the knots one by one. You must untie the knots that bound you to your partner: this is essential if you are to re-establish yourself as an individual, not half of a pair. You may prefer to wait for them to dissolve like sutures but that will take longer and sap your energy. You cannot escape grieving when you lose someone important, even if this comes as a relief. If you just wait for it all to go away you risk being like the woman who was handicapped by her anger and bitterness for 24 years.

Some marriages do not end because one partner leaves the other but because both partners come to recognise that they are no longer a pair. They may decide to part amicably without the conflict associated with most divorces. They may settle their future arrangements together. One couple realised after their children had left home that they no longer wished to live together. After joint discussion they sold the family house and bought two smaller ones quite near to each other. They kept in touch, sometimes went to the theatre together, and arranged to be together as parents and grand-parents when their children visited. Although they did grieve, their grief was not incapacitating. The children, who had lost the united family home to which to bring the grandchildren, seemed to grieve more. The grand-parents, on the other hand, were actively dealing with their grief and expanding their horizons as a result.

One of the advantages of sorting out the future together is that you can adjust better to your *separate* futures. When you come to negotiate what those futures will be, you can each properly weigh up your own needs and argue them through. You may be able to expand your own range of strengths and skills as you come to realise what you need. You may find that you each take on some tasks that were individually allocated in your marriage.

Taking on each other's roles

After a successful series of mediation sessions, one woman expressed her sense of achievement in learning to live alone and manage her own finances. She said, 'I cannot believe that I allowed myself to feel so useless about such matters for so many years.'

Another man commented:

'We owe them [the mediators] a lot and I certainly owe them a great per-sonal debt, because they were incredibly supportive to me... As a typical male, I think I have been out of touch with my feelings for most of my married life, and it took something like this to bring me in touch with them.'

A support group for people trying to recover from divorce used as an exer-cise, a suitcase and a litter bin placed either side of the door. At the end of each session participants wrote lists on separate pieces of paper headed 'What I leave behind' and 'What I take with me'. They deposited them either in the suitcase for their future journey, or in the litter bin, as experiences to leave behind.

The thread from which your knots were made is still there ready to weave the new relationship you will form with your ex-partner in the future. It is important that the threads of parenting continue to be tightly held. A book entitled *Parenting Threads* produced by Stepfamily, is based on this image.

As with any bereavement, you will recover your energy in time; this is likely to take about two years. The human spirit seeks recovery, although at first we may resist it, because misery can seem safer, more predictable and more under our control. There are many versions of the graph of recovery, sometime it has been called 'the parabola of human experience'. One version is shown below.

The Graph of Recovery

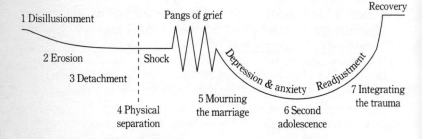

Both partners may experience this graph but at differing times and rates.

___ AVOIDING AND REDUCING BITTERNESS ___

The third principle of the new Family Law Act states that '…a marriage which has irretrievably broken down should be brought to an end with minimum distress to the parties and to the children affected'.

Is this a pious hope? Do the politicians who added it to the Act know what they are talking about, you may wonder? The question to ask yourself is, 'Can we end our relationship with the minimum of bitterness?'

Continuing bitterness can affect your own health and the well-being of your children. The research into the effects of separation and divorce on children shows that their self-esteem and confidence depend to a high degree on the positive outlook of the parent who cares for them day by day. Whether you are that parent or the other, it is in your children's interests that you avoid bitterness and exhaustion.

Unfortunately, we can become addicted to conflict. We tend to be drawn towards it, and find it hard not to keep stirring up the flames. It is like touching a wound to see if it is still there. There is a form of grief that seeks to keep the relationship alive by dwelling on the anger. One function of bitterness might be that it keeps the connection switched on, the attachment maintained. It can be an attempt to ward off the loneliness that waits behind an important broken relationship. But if you remain bitter too long, you will have no energy left for recovery.

Mediation can reduce bitterness

Mediation can help to remove the bitterness. A research study has established that the bitterness was lessened for many couples who used mediation. It seems that the work carried out by a couple in mediation to sort out their future plans together can help to rebuild trust and reduce bitterness.

Reducing Bitterness through Mediation

A male mediation client:
'I think it has reduced the amount of bitterness over a shorter period than perhaps would have been the case – a plus, but not one that I had considered beforehand.'

A woman client:
'Because of the way we have done it we are still quite friendly.'

(Comments from two [unrelated] clients of mediation three years after divorcing.)

DIVORCE COUNSELLING

If bitterness is a problem for you, like the end of a virus, it may need a remedy to shift it. If you experience continuing and continual bitterness, you can ask for divorce counselling in your own right. The following list sets out what Relate consider to be the benefits of the divorce counselling they offer.

Divorce Counselling

For those couples who have decided to divorce or separate, divorce counselling offers an opportunity to:

- cope with the trauma of separation and divorce;
- explore the realities of separating;
- come to terms with the past and understand what went wrong so that previous patterns are not repeated in future relationships;
- individually, to understand and acknowledge their own part in the breakdown;
- work through their feelings of failure;
- prepare for mediation by reducing conflict;
- accept the realities of post-separation parenting;
- accept a new form of relationship to each other after divorce,
- recover from the loss of a partner after divorce.

(Source: Relate.)

6

THE NEEDS OF YOUR CHILDREN

'I can't have both of you, can I?'

There has been a great deal written by journalists about children as the victims of divorce. It is now commonly accepted that separation or divorce are potential 'psychological emergencies' for children. However, there is a growing understanding that it is not the event of divorce that is harmful so much as what precedes and follows it and how it is handled. If divorce is handled well, children can deal with it well.

Not everyone will want to read the facts presented in this part of the book. The evidence is there if you want to read it, but the advice derived from research, suggesting positive actions to take, is picked out so that you can read it and not the detail if you prefer. In the following list there are some very general statements that may give you courage and purpose.

Your children are unique.
They will be very upset for a time.
Children can get over divorce well.
It is very important how you handle the experience for them.

Your children are unique

Every child is unique. If you have more than one child, you know that each will react differently to any event: the visit of a grandparent, a holiday, a change of house. You will usually expect to deal with their reactions differently, even separately, as well as having to deal with them as a group. Their differences make for a unique set of reactions that characterise the special identity of your family. It will be just the same for your children when they have to deal with your separating or divorcing; each child will respond to the experiences in their own unique way.

They will be very upset for a time

Fifteen years of research indicates that separation is very disturbing and upsetting for children for about two years.

Children can get over divorce well

After that, depending on how the separation is handled and what life continues to be like for them, they will recover.

It is very important how you handle the experience for them

For a child, getting over a separation or divorce depends crucially on how the experience is managed by the adults involved. Leaving children in the dark, subjecting them to disappearing fathers and to impoverished and exhausted mothers are the three stereotypical scenarios to be avoided.

—————— LESSONS FROM RESEARCH ——————

The greatest benefit of research studies is their capacity to help you understand what your children may experience so that you can help them through it. Researchers talk to children and parents, and sometimes to schoolteachers, about their experience of divorce. However, it is essential to know how the writers of each piece of research you read obtained their information.

When you read the results of research described in this chapter, you should remember that children change and develop over time and most of the children interviewed or studied were approached at a particular time after their parents' divorce. You will need to think about where your children are in the 'Grand National'. Do they know anything yet? Have they just learnt about your separation or divorce? Have you separated yet? Are they seeing you both? How old are they? Have they been coping with your divorce for a long time? If you have two or more children, are they coping differently, as might be expected? How differently? You might come back and read this chapter again in a few months' time to see how far they have got.

Kinds of research

There are basically four kinds of research into the impact of divorce on children:

1. interviews with children and their parents who have all experienced separation or divorce in the same year,
2. interviews with individuals who experienced divorce a long time ago and were all born in one year,
3. interviews with parents and children who went for therapy following divorce,
4. interviews with children who have experienced divorce compared with children who have not.

Some researchers are currently trying to interview children as they go through the experience of divorce, and this would be a fifth kind of research.

Remember that your children are involved in your divorce *now* which means that their experience may be very different from what it might have been even ten years ago, because divorce has become less of a stigma now for children.

At the end of each research account below there are pointers, giving the main messages. There is a 'health warning' at the beginning and again at the end of this section to remind you that *your* children will be different from any of the children involved in the research reported here.

Warning

Research concerning other people's children will never tell you all that you want to know in order to understand and help your own children. All research studies can do is give you either very general descriptions of many children or very specific descriptions of some particular children.

——— 1 FIFTY CHILDREN IN EDINBURGH ———

In 1981, Ann Mitchell, a remarkable woman from Edinburgh, tracked down 80 out of 112 couples who divorced in Edinburgh in 1976 and who, five years later, had children aged between sixteen and eighteen. She set out to interview the children and the parent with whom they were living in order to find out what the children had understood when their parents separated, what their feelings had been, and how often, and in what circumstances, they had seen the parent with whom they were not living. She talked to 50 people who had been between ten and thirteen years of age when their parents divorced.

The most striking things she found were that:

- far more (two-thirds) of the children described themselves as being upset at the time of the divorce; (or twice as many) than their parents had thought.
- thirty had been upset or angry or both;
- seven had felt relieved;
- thirteen could not remember how they had felt;
- *most said that nobody listened to them.*

Unhappiness

Here are some of the things they said:

'I felt empty.'
'I didn't want my parents to split up.'
'I felt sick and couldn't get it out of my mind that my father had left.'
'My parents were very childish.'
'I didn't want it to happen but in a way I did.'
'I thought Mum and Dad ought to be together, but not Dad the way he was.'

Anger

Just as adults feel angry as one way of grieving for a person to whom they feel attached, so children's grief can come out in anger:

'I am angry for him being so sneaky.'
'My Dad knew he had a drink problem. He should have put a fix to that; he never done anything about it.'
'I was very, very angry, really angry. I'm still angry.'

Often their anger was directed at the parent who had left. Sometimes it was directed at the parent who had stayed with them:

'She keeps going over the same things again and I lose my temper. I get sick and tired of hearing about it.'

Rejection

Even though the parents did not think for one moment that they were leaving their children, the children in many cases experienced the departure as rejection of them:

'I'm always wondering why my mum left me.'
'I still feel hurt that my father left me'.
'I didn't like my mum for a bit because she left me. I was angry with her for deserting us.'

Surprise

One child in six had been surprised by their parents' separation:

'I hadn't expected my parents to split up.'
'Although I knew my mum wasn't happy, I hadn't thought of a breakup.'

Embarrassment

Children hate to be different. Although divorce has become more accepted, this does not mean that children are more accepting of it. One child said he hated 'snide remarks at school'. Another said she felt the need to apologise to her friends about it 'although I am not ashamed'.

Relief

Of those six who had felt relieved, all but one described their parents' arguments. Some of the fathers had drink problems. One child said, 'I dinna like him.' Another took three years to come to terms with her father's departure: 'I've always believed that my father was the greatest, no matter what he done. He left my mum, not me. Now I have a wonderful family life' (living with her mother and seeing her father frequently).

No feelings

Several said they could not remember their reactions, one also commenting, 'I suppose I was upset.'

Wishing for reconciliation

Half the children wanted their parents to get back together, some even years later:

'I'd love them to get back together but I know it can't happen.'
'I've never stopped hoping my parents would come together again.'
'I knew it was my mother's fault, but I wish he would take her back.'

The purpose of the desire to reunite parents may be partly to resolve the split within the child. At one level children may know that their parents will not get together again. At another level they want to keep both parents together in their minds. So they daydream that they are together.

A message from the Edinburgh children appears below.

Message from Edinburgh

- Expect your children to be upset, but do not be too surprised if they do not show it at first.
- Remember that they can feel very isolated if you two are not in agreement.
- Try to listen to them whenever they choose to talk.
- Be aware that they may want someone else to talk to, not just the two of you.

- It could be helpful to reassure them that it is normal to feel unhappy, angry or even embarrassed.
- Assure them that even if they feel rejected, it is not they who have been rejected.
- If they feel relieved, that it is also quite normal if there have been bad arguments.
- Tell them what is happening as well as you can, bearing in mind their age and understanding and taking account of their own very particular characters.

What this research report does not tell us is the reactions of groups of siblings, as only one child was interviewed in any one family. It also does not tell us about the reactions of children who were younger than ten or older than thirteen at the time of the divorce.

2 LARGE LONG-TERM STUDIES OF CHILDREN (COHORTS)

The second kind of research study is of a large number of children born in the same year and followed through at intervals over the following years. Such studies are called 'cohort' studies, because they study a cohort (group) of children. The findings from these studies are wider, larger and taken from longer ago. In one 1991 study, all children born in one week in 1958 were analysed. It is called the 'British National Child Development Survey'. Information was collected when the children were 7, 16 and 23 years old.

Children's life chances

The researchers, Jane Elliott and Martin Richards, stated the following:

> We want to suggest that we should think about the issues related to children in terms of growing up in a divorcing family and the consequences this may have not only in childhood but also those which may continue into adult life. We argue that the divorce of parents can be an important determinant of an individual's life chances.

Elliott and Richards identified three key factors: difficulty at school, the effects of conflict, and low self-esteem.

Difficulty at school

Children from divorced families are more likely than those from families that stay together (or bereaved families) to experience greater difficulty in

reading and arithmetic and more likely to be worried,unhappy and/or disruptive.

The effects of conflict

In separated families, conflict between parents frequently occurred *before*
separation and was associated with both more difficult behaviour and
poorer academic attainment. This was true whether children were still with
both parents or with parents who had separated. The authors commented:
'Conflict between parents tended to erode parent–child relationships.' However, they say that not every divorce is accompanied by conflict.

Low self-esteem

The effects are likely to be greater if a child loses a parent through divorce
than through death. This may be partly due to the presence of conflict and
the difference may lie in the child's self-esteem. The child who loses a parent
through death will be likely to think positively of that parent and hear him
or her talked of lovingly, whereas the child who loses a parent through
divorce is more likely to think negatively of that parent and hear him or her
talked of negatively.

Messages from Elliott and Richards' long-term study

- Expect your children's education and behaviour to be affected for a
  while, but do not be too surprised if it is not.
- Try to reduce the conflict between you, and try especially to keep
  your children out of it.
- Try not to talk badly of your ex-spouse in front of your children.
- Do everything you can to maintain the self-esteem and inner confidence of your children.

_____ 3 CHILDREN IN CALIFORNIA _____

The first study of children and divorce to get publicity in this country came
from California and was carried out at a mental health centre. One hundred
and six children were interviewed from sixty families, one year and four
years (and, later, at ten years) after separation. The study was called 'Surviving the Break-up' and was published in 1980. It made many people
aware of the problem for the first time.

*The most important finding was that most of the children who fared
badly had become the focus of their parents' conflict.*

Age-related effects of divorce

The California research is rich in detail about age-related effects. This will help you to look at your child in relation to the age he or she has reached. But bear in mind that your child and his or her circumstances may mean that his or her reactions are quite different from those described here.

Young children

With children aged under seven, you should watch out for:

confusion
blaming themselves for something they have done
going back to behaviour they have grown out of (toilet training, bed-wetting, thumb-sucking)
possessiveness about toys
increase in sleep problems (nightmares or wakefulness)
separation anxiety (fear of being left, clinging)
greater aggressiveness in play
temper tantrums
difficulty in moving from the household of one parent to that of the other

Some researchers think that young children can cope with the separation anxiety by developing two different worlds and homes. Others warn that some children cannot compartmentalise their lives so easily.

School-age children

With children aged between seven and nine, you could watch out for:

sadness and longing for the parent who has gone
feelings of rejection and loneliness
less co-operativeness (more fighting and teasing)
more difficulty in expressing anger to the departing parent or to the parent with whom they live
divided loyalties
wishing their parents would reconcile (day-dreaming and difficulty in concentrating)

With children aged between nine and twelve, you may observe:

more poise and clarity about what is happening
greater activity as a way of managing their feelings
anger more easily expressed, often directed at one parent

Gender-related factors

In some cultures, parents may treat children differently according to their gender. Boys may become more aggressive, for example; their parents may not know what they do when they are out of the house and therefore may still give them approval. On the other hand, girls may be given more responsibility and this may result in more conflict between them and either parent.

Adolescent children

The older a child is, the more difficult it is to separate out the effects of separation and divorce from what has gone on beforehand. Their peer networks will be very important to them.

You may notice:

their being 'laid back'
withdrawal into themselves or keeping away from home more
shame and embarrassment about sex
loyalty conflicts
greater than usual fluctuations between independence and dependence
worry about finances

Messages from California

- Children's reactions are influenced by their age.
- Young children are not able to express their feelings well in words but will do so by their behaviour.
- School-age children develop a wider range of ways of dealing with the change and loss, but their reactions will depend on how adults treat them, in relation to age and gender expectations.
- In adolescence, greater than normal swings between independence and dependence might be expected.

4 THE EXETER STUDY (1995)

Seventy-six children who had been living with both natural parents since birth were studied and were compared with 76 who had experienced family change. This is the most recent study on the subject. The researchers were Monica Cockett and Dr John Tripp of Exeter, in Devon.

According to this research, *children who went through multiple reordered families had the greatest difficulties.*

Conflict began for more than half of the families at separation – not before – and most children had not expected their parents to separate.

Only a minority of children had been told in advance and only 6 per cent were told by both parents together.

Children wanted to keep in touch with the parent who had left and many non-resident parents felt isolated and missed their children. In nine out of ten cases it was the father who left the home. They did not feel the divorce process took account of their views.

One in four of the children studied had experienced domestic violence.

The Exeter study also found that continuing conflict hindered plans for contact with children; as a result, these were often rigid and irksome for the children. Lack of accommodation also made contact difficult for the non-resident parent; many children wanted to see their non-resident father on their own.

Parents complained about a lack of information about divorce and many said they got help only when things got really difficult; they felt that schools and medical services were not much help. Few of the families knew about mediation.

Messages from Exeter

- Children would have valued more discussion and explanation about the changes in their lives.
- Children who are very quiet and compliant may be 'suffering in silence'.
- Prepare children for introductions to new partners.
- Don't expect your children to share all your initial enthusiasm about new partners.
- Try not to give them too many changes at once.
- Keep them out of your conflict.
- Arrange for the parent not at home to see children individually at times.

__ WEST OF SCOTLAND STUDY – 'TWENTY-07' __

In 1996 a study was published on research carried out in the West of Scotland. Like the Exeter study, it compares different family forms. Greater numbers were involved, as it was a 'cohort' study. A thousand 15-year-olds were interviewed at the beginning and again three years later. Of these, 80 per cent were living with both biological parents, 12 per cent in a step-parent's family and 5 per cent in a one-parent household.

Three perspectives were taken: the form of the family, the amount of conflict in the family and the time spent together in the family. Several aspects of the young people's well-being were estimated: their self esteem, health, academic success, smoking and use of illicit drugs.

The main finding was that the family form was not the key factor in how these young people fared. However, there were some links with some aspects of family life with some of the outcomes. Those living with both biological parents at fifteen were least likely to have used illicit drugs or be unemployed three years later. Young women living with both parents were more likely to leave school with qualifications and least likely to be pregnant by the age of eighteen.

As might be expected, judging from the results of other studies, those young people who reported more conflict with parents (regardless of family structure) were more likely to have health problems and lower self-esteem. They were also most likely to smoke, to have done less well at school and less likely to be students.

However, the newest and most interesting perspective concerned 'family time'. It emerged that those young people who spent more time with the rest of the family fared better on all counts.

Message from West of Scotland

- It is not the form of the family that matters so much as what that family is like.
- Conflict is not good for children, whatever kind of family they live in.
- Try to spend as much time as you can together as a family, no matter what sort of family your children are living in – with one parent, or in a stepfamily, or still with both parents.
- Remember that your children want someone to listen to them and it may not always be you.

(Source: 'The Relationship between Family Life and Young People's Lifestyles', Joseph Rowntree Foundation, April 1996.)

Warning

It must be repeated that research concerning other people's children will never tell you all that you want to know in order to understand and help your own children. All research studies can do is give you either very general descriptions of many children or very specific descriptions of some particular children.

CHILDREN WHO SURVIVE WELL

The glorious thing about many – perhaps most – children is their resilience. We cannot take it for granted, but we can delight in it when it surprises us.

Making a difference

Professor Sir Michael Rutter, a well-known child psychiatrist,wrote an article called 'Resilience in the Face of Adversity', in which he listed the factors that protected or 'buffered' children against being damaged by life. He was struck by the fact that some children, with everything against them, thrived, whereas others, with less to contend with, faltered. He identified the factors he thought made a difference:

1 Help your child to make sense of what has happened.
2 Help your child to act, not just react.
3 Maintain your child's self esteem.
4 Make sure that your children mix with you and with others.
5 One good thing leads to another.
6 Good early experiences help.

1 Help your child to make sense of what has happened

If children can make sense of what has happened to them in a way that they can live with positively, their self-esteem will not be damaged.

One child quoted by Jill Krementz, an American writer, said: 'I guess the main reason my parents got divorced is because they didn't fit together like they should.' He said this at the age of twelve.

In later life, such a child will probably look for someone with whom he *can* 'fit together'.

2 Help your child to act, not just react

Children who tackle life with energy do better than those who give in. It is easy to be judgemental about children who give in. Some children do not have the same energy as others. They may have had little energy at birth, they may have needed a lot of encouragement all their lives, or they may have lost their confidence somewhere along the line. However, if children can act positively, they are likely to do better.

3 Maintain your child's self-esteem

If your children have enough steady and secure relationships to keep them in one piece psychologically, then they will do well. If, for any reason, you cannot stick with them, someone else must. Grandparents, teachers and friends can make a world secure for a child.

4 Make sure that your children mix with you and with others

The quality af attachment depends on the nature and frequency of the interaction between people – the warmth, love, fun, mutual trust and enjoyment. An old piece of research studied the effect of laughter in families and (not surprisingly) found it to be an important factor in distinguishing between families that coped well with life and those that coped less well. Your children will not want to lose closeness or fun with either of you. Ways to maintain contact are discussed in Part 2.

5 One good thing leads to another

Dealing successfully with stress once makes it easier the next time. Children who cope with one adversity may be in a stronger position to cope with further stresses.

6 Good early experiences help

Each child is unique, not only because of his or her personality but because of what has already happened to them. If you gave your children a good start they will be well set up to cope with adversities.

This is a positive note on which to end. There are many opportunities for us to put things right for our children and for others to help where we cannot.

CHILDREN'S EXPERIENCES

Grief

Clare Winnicott, a social worker famous in the 1960s, wrote that children should be allowed to suffer as much as they are able. This seems a hard doctrine. Children have their own cut-outs and can change the subject very rapidly and in a very matter-of-fact way, but the moment when they express their suffering to you is precious and should be treasured. They need to grieve as far as they are able.

Being out of step with each other

It is not unusual for parents and children to be out of step with each other. You may have had time to make your decisions; your children have no choice and need careful telling, time and information. If you are ahead in the 'Grand National', you have the opportunity to take care of them as they begin their journey through your divorce. Helping your children – and doing it well – is very difficult, but it is possible. Even if you feel you have made a mess of your relationship, you can succeed as parents.

If your children are living with you, try to be positive. The positiveness of the parent with whom a child lives after divorce is a key factor. If they are not living with you, keep in contact. Even if adolescent children want to stop seeing you for a bit, keep in touch in another way because, in the long term, they will want you again. One day, perhaps, they will want you to be there as grandparents to their children.

Only children

Do siblings have a slightly easier time? Sophie, the daughter in Joanna Trollope's fictional family, remarks that when there are only three people in a family everything becomes a big deal – 'even where the spoons are put'. An only child can feel very lonely when he or she is the sole recipient of great adult news. Grandparents, cousins, friends and their parents can be helpful in spreading out, diluting the intensity of the experience. A children's counsellor can sometimes be a confidante, hearing the kind of comments that siblings can say to each other but cannot say to either parent, such as 'Why don't they grow up? They are always telling me to.'

Sibling groups

One family of four girls, whose parents had separated and came to mediation, illustrates how different siblings can be. In this family the older sister took charge of the three younger girls. She got some reassurance from her new-found power and responsibility. The next sister was quiet and beautiful and was consequently treasured by everyone. She derived comfort from adult appreciation inside and outside the family. The next youngest was wild and tomboyish, always into scrapes. She experienced thrills, spills and disapproval, yet she expressed the frustration of her sisters and was a line of communication between the two households. However, she missed out on affection. The youngest cried a lot. They all thought she had missed out on cuddles, so they often cuddled her. This child was likely to have difficulty in being allowed to grow up.

In another family who sought mediation an elder boy carried a lot of responsibility and was harassed to distraction by its weight and anxiety. His little sister crept along beside him wherever he went and couldn't let him go anywhere without her. This both comforted and frustrated them as she always cried when he left her.

More Words from Children:

'I think that if parents are going to divorce and not scar their children for life, they should keep them out of what's going on as much as possible.' (Fifteen-year-old girl quoted by Jill Krementz in *How It Feels when Parents Divorce*, Victor Gollanz, London, 1985)

'I was nine when my parents separated and it was a total shock to me. In fact, when my father and older sister told me, I thought they were joking.' (Fourteen-year-old boy, Krementz)

'I just go up to my room and try not to listen when the shouting starts.'

7

TELLING THE CHILDREN

In Joanna Trollope's novel *Best of Friends* the breakdown of a marriage is not handled well. The husband miscalculates when he tells his wife and their sixteen-year-old daughter that he is leaving. The following extracts from the book sum up the untidiness of the end of a marriage and the splitting up of the family.

Husband:

He had totally, cruelly blundered with Sophie whom he had supposed…to be, at sixteen, beyond the security-craving dependence of childhood and well into comprehension of the fragile, complex webs of adult emotional life.

Wife:

He said…that he just couldn't bear me any longer.

Sophie:

I can't leave Mum. I mean, we can't all just walk out on her.

Grandmother:

I could crown them for what they are doing to that child.

Telling the Children Together

- Try to tell them carefully and together if you can.
- Be sure that you do not argue while telling them.
- You may have to explain different kinds of love.
- You are almost sure to have to answer the why? question.
- Telling them together can prepare for your future relationship as parents.
- Do not expect that you will have done it once and for all.
- Tell them what is going to happen next.
- They will worry about you.
- Try not to feel hurt by their reactions.

Try to tell them carefully and together if you can

It is better to tell your children together if you can. Your children may feel more secure if you do this, as Jilly and Jon (see p. 35–36) found out. Plan it together first in a calm way. Discussing anything important calmly is diffi-cult enough; to tell your children that their parents are separating is surely one of the hardest tasks in family life. That is why so many parents do not do it together and some not at all.There cannot be one right way. Each person, each couple, will have to do the best they can. A mediator can help you to plan this.

Be sure that you do not argue while telling them

You would be wise to promise each other that, while telling the children, you will not argue with one another about the ending of the marriage. You will have to work out what explanations you can honestly give without provok-ing each other into arguments about the whys and wherefores in front of the children.

You may have to explain different kinds of love

There may be nothing much you can say about those 'fragile, complex webs of adult emotional life' that your children will understand. Self-justifying explanations are not helpful. Over-simple explanations that do not credit your children's intelligence are only marginally better. To say 'We do not love each other any more' may well make any child, of whatever age, fear that the security of family life itself, and your love for them, are equally fragile. You will have to couple any such simple explanation with an assurance that parent–child relationships are not the same as husband-and-wife relation-ships. Always add: 'It does not mean that we could or would ever stop loving you.' An explanation about different kinds of love might include saying that you have known them from their very beginnings whereas you have known each other only as adults; this makes for a different kind of bond.

You are almost sure to have to answer the why? question

Every statement you devise will have to allow for the usual question: 'Why?' Children of different ages will want different kinds of answer – few actually want to hear complex explanations.

They want to learn that you have not suddenly become irresponsible, irrational and unreliable.

You should be able to tell your children that you have thought about your separation long and hard. You may have to explain that you are not agreed upon it. It would be good to say that you have tried hard to make things better, but that you could not succeed. You may have to say that you thought your relationship would last for ever and made serious promises to each other that it would last, and that you are very sad that it cannot, no matter how hard you try. You could tell them that living together makes you both very unhappy.

Say that you are not giving up easily – people have unhappy times, and they often pass. But you do not think this will pass, so you have had to come to terms with it and you now both want to behave wisely and make sure that you are putting their needs first for the future.

Telling them together can prepare for your future relationship as parents

If you can support each other while doing this, it will help you and your children prepare for your future relationship with them as parents, not partners.

Do not expect that you will have done it once and for all

Children might find it odd to be sitting together talking with you. You might do it over a meal if this is usual in your family. However, and wherever, you tell them, they will drop the odd comment and ask the odd question in funny places and at funny times, like children normally do about other matters of importance to them.

You will probably decide not to tell your children at bedtime – whatever age they are – as they will then be alone all night with the new knowledge. However, it may be at bedtime that they say the most important things to you. It was at bedtime that one eight-year-old girl said to her father, 'I can't live with both of you, can I?' A boy said to his father at the school sports day, 'I don't expect you will see me next year.'

Tell them what is going to happen next

Some parents decide in mediation to postpone telling their children until they have some idea of what arrangements they will make for them. Their odd questions remind us that children will have unexpected worries of a practical nature, based on their understandable lack of knowledge or on their own limited experience.

One child said, 'I expect I shall have a foster mother.' The only relevant experience he had was of a child at school who had joined the class because he had gone into foster care when his parents separated. Another said, 'Will Daddy have to sleep on the pavement?' because he had seen a homeless man near King's Cross Station on a visit to London and had been told that he had no home of his own.

It is better to tell them, for example: 'Mummy is going to stay in our house with you and I am moving to live in a flat in Lenster Road and will see you often.' Take care, even then! One child had a very strange idea of what a flat was. 'Won't you have any furniture?' she asked, as in her imagination she saw only a bare floor.

They will worry about you

Judith Wallerstein, who conducted the first Californian research on children and divorce, often quotes a child who immediately rushed to the fridge in her father's new flat to make sure there was food in it. Your children will worry about your physical needs being met, as well as their own. Comments like, 'But you can't cook' or 'You can't change light bulbs' will be as much about your survival as about theirs.

Teenagers may try to be worldly wise. 'I expect you've got someone else' may conceal disapproval but will also be an attempt to show that they can cope with such things now.

Try not to feel hurt by their reactions

Don't allow your hurt at your children's reactions to stop you listening to them. They may be very damning and angry and rejecting at first, when they learn what is to happen. If they say, 'What about us? Have you thought about us?' when you have been thinking of little else for a month, it might make you bridle, but always remember that they are suffering too. If you could have prevented their pain, let us hope that you would have done so. You are suffering and they will discover this as the days and weeks go by. You are the parents, however, and trying to focus on their suffering is part of your responsibility, even though there are times when you feel you cannot carry it.

The major differences between this and other hard experiences lie in the fact that you are the ones who are making it happen. Your children, of whatever age, will find this difficult to understand. It may be the first thing that you have ever done that is perceived by them as for your good rather than theirs.

Telling them on your own

While are reading this book, you may be aware that things have already gone too far. There is no way that you can tell your children what is to happen together, as it has already happened. Someone has left. There may have been a sudden, even violent, end to the relationship and you have left, or been left, for that reason. Or one of you may have gone, having said nothing to the children and leaving nothing settled.

Portray your partner in a positive light

Children will fear that it is they who have been left. They will want eventually to think well of their other parent, or at least to understand them. Bear this in mind as you tell them.

There is no point, however, in telling untruths. Children will spot them and you will make them begin to doubt their own reactions and endanger their trust in you. Be honest. However, you need not give them all the adult detail and explanations.

You may have to manage on your own – and this may be the story of your life. The best you can do is not to say dreadful things about your partner. It may help to invent a sort of pub scoreboard in your mind: chalk up every small, unobserved triumph, each time you might have said something vicious but refrained from doing so: 'Your father left for his own reasons, to do with me and him. It had nothing to do with you.' (Give yourself ten points!) 'Your mother tried very hard to make things work, but felt she had to go and leave us to it and we shall do our very best to make it work.' (Ten points!)

Telling the children on your own

- Try to convey a positive picture of the other parent.
- Be honest.
- Keep a score of your successes.

If there is domestic violence

You may have to explain the breakdown of your relationship to your children unilaterally if you have no choice but to leave for the sake of your safety, and theirs. In the case of domestic violence, the priority must be safety.

Should you try to excuse or explain the violence so that your children do not blame their father? Many mothers try to do this, but forget that their children have to come to terms with what they have seen and that they are also afraid. You will not want to make violence acceptable in their eyes. Honesty is a good policy: give a factual account of your actions to protect yourself and them, and offer them opportunities to express their views and understand what has happened in their own way.

8

YOUR CULTURE: KITH AND KIN

'A plague o' both your houses'
(William Shakespeare, *Romeo and Juliet*,
Act III, Scene i)

> I hardly recall any occasion as a child when I was alone. In African culture, the sons and daughters of one's aunts or uncles are considered brothers and sisters, not cousins. We do not make the same distinctions among relations practised by whites. We have no half-brothers or half-sisters; my mother's sister is my mother; my uncle's son is my brother; my brother's child is my son, my daughter.
>
> (Nelson Mandela, *Long Walk to Freedom*)

In the wonderful old phrase 'kith and kin', kin means 'family' and kith, 'friends'. These are Anglo-Saxon words and belong to a past era, when our kith and kin had strong, clannish elements to them. Yet we all understand what these old words signify in our lives, regardless of our particular ethnic culture.

For Africans, African Caribbeans and Asians, for example, kin ties are usually very strong. By comparison, some white Britons may seem to have lost many of their kinship ties, particularly in terms of their influence on family decisions. Visits back home may not be as regular as in some British-Caribbean families, where adult children may still be expected to go back home for a Sunday meal. Kinship ties may not be as visible in cities as in some rural areas, where everyone went to the same school and knows who is 'so and so's boy'. Small towns still generate an acute sense of class and culture, based on which end of town you live and which school you went to. Urban life makes keeping in contact difficult, but for most people, the ties are still strong and it is usually members of the family who are contacted when things go wrong.

Many people want to be free of such constraints on their behaviour. Cities offer anonymity – who knows whether or not you have separated or are married? Perhaps only play-groups and schools know how many 'real' parents a child has, whether it is their father who fetches them and whether their mother is single, married or separated.

In whatever cultural context you live, there will be a kith and kin element in your separation or divorce. The question to ask is, are your kin a source of support, as they were for Nelson Mandela, or a source of conflict, as in the story of Romeo and Juliet? Can you help your kith and kin network to support you so that you do not end up crying 'a plague o' both your houses'?

TWO CAUTIONARY TALES

Kin and conflict

A young couple, Kim and Alan, had separated and had one child. They could not agree with whom Sam (aged six) should live or how often he should see the other parent. They each had a solicitor and battle was waged in correspondence for months. Kim and Alan stopped speaking to each other and Sam became unhappy at school.

At last the solicitors referred them for mediation.

The mediator, David, asked a few questions and discovered that the two sets of grandparents lived in the same street, around the corner from the mother and the little boy, and that Alan was living with his parents. David began to realise that pleasing the grandparents was very important in this family. He suggested that they might be consulted as part of the mediation and asked a female colleague, Linda, to come in to help.

The two families lined up on opposite sides of the meeting-room table, with the young couple nearest David's end of the table and the grandparents near his colleague.

After a few carefully chosen words, the mediator sat back and asked them all a question. Within minutes both sets of grandparents were on their feet threatening each other across the table. He interrupted them but, although they stopped and looked at him briefly, they immediately resumed the battle. David and Linda exchanged glances. Then Linda achieved a temporary silence by banging a large glass ashtray on the table. In the half-minute space, she invited the grandparents to step next door with her so that she could hear them better. They followed at once, carrying on their argument as they went. They continued it in the other room, only slightly more quietly.

Meanwhile, David had a very useful conversation with the parents of the little boy, finding instant common ground between them in their embarrassment and frustration with their parents' aggressive behaviour!

In a few minutes, they had sorted out the arrangements for Alan to see his son and both agreed that the little boy should stay with his mother in the family council house. They even went so far as to say that if they could get a house exchange away from their parents, they might try to live together again.

The mediator then invited his colleague and the grandparents back in and, in a period of stunned silence, the two parents proceeded to tell both sets of grandparents what they had agreed.

What had taken place in the next-door office had not mattered one whit, except in so far as it allowed the young couple to reassume their parental responsibility and put the needs of their son first. Their plans included arrangements for the kind of contact he could have with both sets of grandparents.

This is an example of kin at their worst, as far as separation and divorce are concerned. Whatever the rows were about, they were only marginally about the grandson, except in so far as to whose family he now belonged!

Kin and support

Another family had separated into two households, each with a parent and a new partner. The conflict in this arrangement was between the two women – the mother of the children and the father's new partner. The children moved between the two households with great caution, dreading the notes they would be asked to deliver. Every time a note was opened, there was a mighty row. Things got so bad that, one day, one child, a girl of ten, ran away to a grandmother. The two sets of parents exchanged angry telephone calls, each blaming the other, and telephoned their solicitors to resume the fight for residence and contact.

Meanwhile, the grandmother telephoned her counterpart grandmother. They jointly arranged for their granddaughter to be collected by her mother at the other grandmother's house. They then sorted out what contact would take place between all the children and the parents and grandparents, often using their own homes as neutral places.

The grandmothers' good relationship with each other and with the children safeguarded the children, preventing them both from running away and from being further caught up in the conflict between the two parental households. They were the ports in the storms of those particular children's childhood.

_____ KIN _____

If you had a Church of England wedding, the vicar would have said, 'In the presence of God *and before this congregation* [Mary and Mark] have given their consent and made their marriage vows…'. The congregation are witnesses. They play a part. They have an interest. For all cultures, the invited guests are very important.

Who came to your wedding? There were two sides, 'Bride' and 'Groom'. How was the invitation list devised? How many kith were you allowed, or was it a 'kin only' wedding?

How will those 'kin', and any subsequent kin, learn of your separation or divorce? Will your parents ring round? Will both sets of parents talk to each other about it? What will they say? How will all the relations respond in each family?

As you begin to answer these questions, you will get a picture of your kinship network and the effect of your divorce upon it. Will you lose touch with half of your kin? Will they create conflict or bring support? Is there anything you can do to ensure that they are given the right opportunity to offer their support, and that any conflict does not spiral, involving the whole kin network?

As part of their training, National Family Mediation mediators create a 'street' of kith and kin, so that they can become aware of how much the 'nuclear' family is affected by, and affects, the other families linked to it and how these linkages can be helped to redeem rather than inflame broken family relationships. As the trainee mediators play out their roles, it often becomes apparent that children can so easily be neglected, when the kith and kin eagerly get down to the business of fighting.

Grandparents

The Children Act was influenced to some extent by grandparents' concerns that their grandchildren may lose touch with them after the divorce. There is provision in the Children Act for parties other than parents to seek contact orders or seek parental responsibility in addition to that automatically held by parents. Grandparents can therefore approach the court. They can also approach a mediator.

Unless your children are living with you (in which case they will continue to see your parents, much as they used to), they stand to lose half of their kin – the whole of the right or left side of the church! The Exeter Study showed that this happened with over half of the Exeter families interviewed.

Unlike marriage, divorce is not marked with a ceremony. The two sides do not come together to express their solidarity as kin networks, yet they are needed even more when parents part. Much grief and loss can occur if steps are not taken to reconnect kin in a new way.

This is best done co-operatively, of course. Family mediators can help parents to include contact with grandparents in their plans. Belonging to a wider family is an important element of your children's lives; research is being carried out into just how important this can be for children's well-being.

While research studies indicate that the role grandparents play is a helpful one, in a small study carried out into 27 families who sought help, ten saw grandparents as causing additional stress. Only four families felt positively helped by grandparents. (However, as these were families seeking help, the absence of helpful grandparents would have made it more likely that they would seek outside help.)

What can you do? Agree to deal with the situation openly and as cooperatively as possible. Waiting until Christmas may be a good idea if it is close, but although sending a Christmas card which simply omits one partner's name may seem an easy way out, it does not help your wider family to approach you with any confidence that they can support you. It imposes a silence on what has occurred and this may also give your children a message that such things are not to be spoken about.

KITH

Friends can also be lost at divorce. On whose side are they? It is very difficult for them not to take sides and to stay in touch with both of you. It is also hard for you to remain in contact with your spouse's friends, or your joint friends, without aggravating conflict between you. Strange jealousies and competitions can develop: 'You have taken my friends,' 'He never liked her before; now he's talking to her to spite me.'

Again, remember your wedding. That congregation who were 'here present' will want to know what has happened. Who will tell your friends? Is there a formula you can use or is it a battle to see who can set out 'the truth as I see it' first?

Kith and conflict – another cautionary tale

Two couples, the Kings and the Taylors, became very friendly. They lived almost next door to each other. Their children were the same ages and attended the same school. Then Ann Taylor became very ill. All three of the other adults cared for her. While this was going on, Max Taylor spent a lot of time with Brenda King, the mother of the second family. Before long they had drifted into a sexual relationship built, initially, on compassion. Paul King, feeling excluded, confided in the sympathetic school secretary – and, yes, there began a second affair.

Soon the children began to be teased by pupils in both classes at school. 'Your mum and dad have swapped.' 'Your dad is going out with Mrs Fox!'

The children began to avoid each other's company and gradually fell out altogether, dodging each other on the way to school, moving places in the classrooms and not playing together in the playground. They stopped going out in the evenings. The boys stopped going to the Cubs and the girls to dancing classes. They became recluses, and unhappy ones because the atmosphere in both houses was tense. One mother was dying, aware of the affair. The other mother was comforting her friend's husband at night, while her own husband was frequently at the house of the school secretary, Mrs Fox.

The children's needs were not given much attention. Neighbours were not neutral about the circumstances of the affairs, particularly in the light of Ann's tragic illness. The children suspected any kindnesses shown to them as traps or bribery, to enable questions to be asked about their parents' behaviour. School was a daily torment to the children and the staffroom talk was frequently about them and the role played by the school secretary.

The story could go on and on – you can finish it any way you like. In reality it was settled slowly by Ann's death and the repartnering of the other adults. The children had to acclimatise themselves to their new households and families.

Kith and support – a happy story

Russell hurriedly left his wife for another woman, unable to face the consequences of his actions. His wife, Jean, was left with three young children. The children were sad, angry and bereft. They were hard on their mother and silent about the matter with their father, knowing that he was unable to deal with it. They avoided the topic when they went out with him on Saturdays.

Neighbours and friends rallied round the family. They called in frequently, had the children to stay and invited the wife out. However, one particular set of friends became particularly uncomfortable, feeling that they were taking sides. Instead of dropping out of the picture, ignoring Russell or gossiping critically about him, as others were prone to do, the husband telephoned him and invited him out for a drink. He kept in touch with him and, with his friendship for Russell and his wife's closeness to Jean, they were able, as a family, to support the children and both adults through the experience. Eventually they even encouraged them to go for counselling. Although this really happened, hardly anyone apart from those involved knew about it.

Some pointers about keeping in touch with kith and kin are set out overleaf.

Kith and Kin after Divorce

1 Tackle the future family relationships co-operatively between you and avoid splits and unnecessary losses.
2 Try to arrange that kith and kin become supports for your children and prevent them from becoming part of any conflict between you.
3 Communicate in good time, and co-operatively where necessary, with relations, neighbours, friends, work colleagues, bosses and schools, so that they help you to help your children.
4 Understand each other's family traditions.

CROSS-CULTURAL DIVORCE

In many marriages the partners come from different cultures. Therefore, any separation will also be cross-cultural. Dissimilar expectations can contribute to difficulties both in relationships and when they end. There are particular problems if the couple come from different ethnic communities or different countries of origin. The wish to 'go home' when a marriage ends is very strong, given the separation from the family that may have occurred as a result of marriage. This can create:

fears of abduction,
loss of contact between parents, grandparents and children, and
misunderstandings.

One such situation was only partly settled by mediation. A couple, one from Africa and the other from a Caribbean island, had met as students, married, moved to England and had two children. They struggled hard to keep their marriage together, with less and less success. It then entered a bitter and destructive stage. The parents realised that the children were suffering. The Caribbean father chose to 'go home'. The children did not want to move if it meant they could not stay in their schools, but they were very close to their father. His solution was to disappear, without explanation, as he feared that it would be too painful to say goodbye.

The mediators (two in this painful situation), having been present when the parents reached their decision, agreed to consult the children. The children's view was that they should wave their father goodbye as he boarded the aeroplane. This is what took place. The mediators enabled the parents to face the pain with their children in a subsequent session and make plans whereby the children would maintain contact with their father in various ways.

Another situation had a very successful outcome. The two parents were from different African countries. After separation, the father wanted to take the children 'home'. This filled their mother with fear of an abduction. In mediation it was discovered that to this father, who had come from a matriarchal country, it was totally unacceptable that he should remove the children from their mother. The children would return to the UK and to their mother: his family would expect and insist upon this. Because the mother came from a country with a patriachal tradition, she had feared the worst. The problem was resolved amicably – almost with laughter.

Mediation and different cultures

Attitudes of different communities to divorce vary whether they are religious communities – for example, Muslim, Hindu or Christian – or ethnic communities – Chinese, African, Caribbean, Punjabi, Gujerati, English rural or English urban, for example. How individuals expect to resolve disputes within their own religious or ethnic community varies. In relation to mediation, the important factor is the extent to which the community perceives mediation as a helpful process in the resolution of disputes.

Mediation can be useful in any community. It is potentially less culturally specific than legal process. Legal process is usually very culturally specific, with well-developed cultural conventions. Mediation could become useful to many different communities because it is a process people can use as they choose. The mediator must be sensitive to the culture of the family and anti-discriminatory in their own approach. When mediation works between or across cultures it is because ways of listening and understanding have been found.

SCHOOLS

The Exeter study indicated that parents do not often see schools as sources of help for their children at the time of their separation or divorce. However, from the children's point of view, many teachers and headteachers are the ones who look out for them and give them opportunities to discuss what is happening at home. They make allowances for lapses in concentration and for homework not being done as carefully as usual.

Some teachers hear about a parent leaving only by accident – from what a child writes in an essay or in a diary, perhaps. Headteachers or teachers may be caught up in a conflict over which parent should be sent reports or attend a parents' evening. Sometimes they have to try to sort out arguments at the school gate. The lesson here is to inform the school, by joint agreement, and make arrangements so that both of you can keep in touch with your children's progress.

YOUR CHILDREN'S FRIENDS

Children will usually know what is happening to a classmate and friends are probably the greatest comfort, in a matter-of-fact way, for many children. Adolescent children can be very supportive, especially (but not exclusively) if they are girls.

If you are alone with your children after a separation, you may find that you also derive support from your children's friends and from their parents. Again, this is likely to be forthcoming if you are able to deal with the events in a straightforward manner.

On a final, lighter note, the parents of one teenage girl decided to remarry each other a year or two after they had divorced. She was overheard saying to her best friend, 'I don't want anyone to know. It is so embarrassing!'

PART 2

How to Work It Out

9

WHAT IS FAMILY MEDIATION?

'We gathered up our differences and threw them in the air and gave them to the wind that shakes the barley'

(From the folk-song 'Elsie Marley'.)

HOW TO ACHIEVE A FAIR AND AMICABLE DIVORCE

Achieving a fair and amicable divorce requires consideration of your needs, your partner's needs and your children's needs and working out how you are going to meet them, financially and emotionally. Although this sounds bland and straightforward, it is actually a struggle to overcome strong emotions in order to meet your responsibilities in a constructive way.

Such a goal challenges you to establish a relationship with your ex-spouse that will serve as a sound basis for continuing to meet your responsibilities as parents, not partners. If your children come to feel at home in both of your homes, you will have achieved a great deal. If they feel comfortable about moving from one to the other without fear of upsetting either of you by doing so, you and they will be doing well. If you have energy and confidence to begin another phase of your own lives, even if not straight away, you will have avoided the worst effects of divorce.

Reaching this goal will mean that you focus less on winning your separate battles than on finding common ground: a win/win, not a win/lose, outcome. You may not (nor should you) throw all your differences in the air until you have thoroughly examined them, but you will try to resolve them in order to put them aside – to give them 'to the wind that shakes the barley'.

Mediation is the route, above all others, that aims to help you achieve this goal. Most of this chapter will therefore be about how mediation can help you to work things out directly, face to face.

You will learn how an outside solicitor can help you by advising you from the sidelines of the mediation.

You will also learn how many family solicitors try to help their clients achieve a similar goal, by negotiating for you with your partner's solicitor on the basis of your instructions. This process can achieve a fair and amicable outcome. As it is less under your control, you will have to choose your solicitor wisely. He or she will need to be in sympathy with your goals.

If you can resolve matters by neither route (mediation or negotiation through your solicitors), the court will settle matters for you. The role of the judge and the family court welfare officer is discussed in this part of the book, as is the new procedure being tried out for financial dispute resolution.

HOW FAMILY MEDIATION WORKS

Family mediators are there to help you negotiate together face to face.

Mediation belongs within an ancient tradition of resolving disputes by discussion. The tradition is sometimes called 'Alternative Dispute Resolution', or 'ADR'. It is an alternative to law courts, in which people are usually represented by lawyers. In some other countries, for example, Africa and China, mediation has long been used as a way of resolving disputes. The Quakers have also traditionally used mediation as a way of resolving arguments among Friends. UK culture may have done so once before we became so dependent litigation.

ADR, in general, aims to be informal, 'friendly' or 'amicable', in the sense that it tries to re-establish a business-like or a friendly relationship between people after the dispute is over. Mediation, with the same broad aims, involves the presence of a third party, a mediator, to assist those who are in dispute (or who want to avoid a dispute) find common ground and make their own agreed decisions.

Mediation is therefore of especial value where those involved need to get on with one another, perhaps because they cannot avoid one another entirely, or because their future depends on their getting along together. For example, they may be neighbours arguing about a fence or about noise, none of whom wants to move house. They may be managers and workers who, although in dispute, cannot actually get anything done without each other. If either side wins too well or loses too badly or nothing is resolved, the relationship is not going to get back on to an amicable footing.

Particularly because of the needs of children, mediation is thought to be valuable in separation and divorce. Sometimes couples without children may be able to break off contact entirely (although this is really likely only if the people move a long way from each other), but if you are parents, it is your children who stand to lose most from your doing so. Parents have to re-establish some sort of continuing relationship with each other on a business-like, friendly basis. Not to do so risks creating the sort of loss, conflict and tension that damages children.

Mediation in separation or divorce further recognises that such personal matters may be very difficult to resolve without outside help. You both know each other very well, which has advantages and disadvantages when you are negotiating. Each may feel that the other always wins; or one or both may get heated very quickly and be unable to stay calm enough to talk anything through to a conclusion. You also know how to wind each other up. Without a mediator, one of you might go out slamming the door behind you rather than stay to resolve the problem. Mediation can keep you working at the problem in order to find a mutually acceptable solution. One client made this comment: 'When we were sitting on opposite sides of the kitchen table it all got very abusive. It's hard to be objective about things when you're so emotionally involved.' Couples who cannot manage on their own often benefit from mediation.

However, the mediator does not make the decisions. You do. The mediator does not negotiate. You do. The mediator's responsibility is to ensure that there is a safe environment and a fair process. From a fair process comes a fair outcome.

Nevertheless, because family mediation is a private process, in that it goes on in a pleasant room with the door shut, rather than in a court room with officials and the public walking in and out, it may not be suited to everyone.

IS MEDIATION FOR YOU?

Mediation is based on the following:

1 Common, not opposing, interests
   Mediation may be effective if what you have in common seems more important than your differences.

2 Full exchange of information
   To be effective, all the relevant information needed to make decisions must be shared, so that a range of options for those decisions is likely to become clear. By the time your proposals are seen by a judge, a serious view would be taken if you had not disclosed all the relevant information. This means that you have to be prepared to trust your spouse to be honest and thorough and negotiate in good faith.

3 Win/win rather than win/lose
   Decisions made co-operatively should result in each side benefiting rather than one winning and the other losing. You will therefore have to enter mediation prepared to negotiate and not just to get everything you want.

4   Future focus
    Mediation focuses on the future. You will wish, at times, to discuss the
    ending of your marriage, as this has a bearing on the future, but gener-
    ally the mediator will be looking with you towards the future, not the
    past.

5   Private ordering
    There is privacy and confidentiality in mediation because you are
    making your own decisions. The court will eventually look over what
    you propose, but it will be your proposals that it examines to make sure
    that they are fair. You will have to feel comfortable about taking this
    responsibility and be prepared to try to work together, respecting and
    making use of the confidentiality of your discussions.

6   Commitment to joint decisions
    If you make thorough decisions yourselves, you are more likely to keep
    to the arrangements you make than if they are made by an outsider.
    You must be ready to honour what you have decided and not think
    that you will go back on it later, unless there is a very good reason for
    doing so.

If any of these ideas appears relevant to your situation, you could consider
mediation as your route through divorce.

When mediation may not be suitable

The factors that could make you hesitate to use mediation are:

1   Fear of being in the same room with your partner, even with the pres-
    ence of a mediator

2   Fear that your partner would set out to cheat you or to conceal from you
    information that would make any decisions you reached unfair or
    invalid.

3   Fear that you could not keep your end up in the negotiations because
    your partner would bully, threaten or intimidate you.

Many begin by having these fears and then find that they were groundless.
However, you may conclude that, even with a mediator present whom you
could grow to trust, you and your partner would argue and fight too much
to be able to talk issues through to a decision. Bear in mind that you may be
able to overcome these fears with the mediator's help. No one will force you
to mediate, though – it is your choice.

MEDIATION PRINCIPLES

Because mediation is private, family mediators must have strong guiding principles to ensure a fair process and a fair outcome. They must work to a code of practice and follow some clear principles. These are set out below. They are included in the Code of Practice of the UK College of Family Mediators (see page 209).

Mediation Principles

Voluntariness

Impartiality

Confidentiality

Flexibility

Family mediators come from a variety of background professions, including law, social work, counselling, education and health. It is vitally important that they undergo mediation training and operate under a regulatory body. National Family Mediation (NFM) was one of the three founder bodies of the UK College of Family Mediators and our mediators have worked to a code of practice since 1985, now gathered up into the new Code. All college mediators are trained to observe this Code for the protection of their clients and to maintain a high and ethical standard of practice.

PRINCIPLES IN PRACTICE

Voluntariness

It is important to the mediator that you and your partner should enter mediation voluntarily. Sometimes, the Press has wrongly published news stories saying that mediation is or will be compulsory. NFM mediators, however, believe strongly that mediation must be voluntary for three reasons:

- because forcing people to negotiate face to face when they do not choose to do so is to coerce them into a situation in which they will not feel in charge;
- because voluntary entry prevents people from mediating who are too wary of their partner or ex-partner to negotiate freely on their own behalf and in their own interests,
- and because research shows that agreements last and have greater benefit to you and your children if *both* of you enter willingly.

Mediators aim to treat people with respect. Voluntariness is therefore fundamental to a family mediator.

Impartiality

Impartiality means that the mediator must not take sides. Mediators, of course, have their own beliefs, views, thoughts and feelings and are caring people, but they are acting in a particular professional way which requires them to ensure that each person and each person's views, wishes and feelings are treated with equal respect.

Family mediators may very well begin by telling to you that if you do not perceive them as impartial you should say so at once. It is important to the mediator that you feel that the process is being conducted fairly from the beginning. It is sometimes difficult to face an impartial mediator when you actually want the mediator to support your view of the situation. However, the mediator is not there to judge who is more right or whose wishes or will should prevail, but to help you talk and listen to each other's point of view to see if you can find a way through to a mutually acceptable course of action.

Confidentiality

Mediation offers a private opportunity for you both to discuss the consequences of the ending of your marriage. It is important that you should feel free to say what you think and feel. The mediator will not tell anyone else what you say in mediation. They will ask you to treat what is said as confidential.

This is because of the freedom it gives you to say what you like and to explore ideas without having them thrown back at you later. Any negotiation is a gradual process in which a range of different thoughts and ideas can be pursued until the best ones emerge. 'It isn't finished until it is finished.' For example, no one should be able to hold you to something you once said, but about which you later changed your mind.

The mediator will not pry into your private lives. They will not take private notes or report to anyone about what you have said (unless there is a safety issue). The session is for you and the mediator takes the cue from you. Any questions are to help you define what the issues are and what information you need to make decisions. If a mediator writes anything down it is to aid you in gathering information for your negotiations. (They often write it on a flip chart, so that all of you can see it.)

Because your freedom to discuss whatever you choose is fundamental to a mediator, they will ask you not to use what your partner said against him or her later on (if, for example, you go to court because you have not been able to agree in mediation), but to honour the process and take from it what you both agree as the outcome.

If you are unable to agree and a judge is later asked to settle the dispute, the judge will not ask you, or the mediator, what you said in mediation but only what you did or did not agree. This understanding is established in law and is called 'privilege'. It means that the court grants you 'the privilege' of not having to tell the judge what was said in mediation. A judge will only have a right to ask what you agreed at the end or to see any written agreement you made. You can waive the privilege if you both want to. If you gather factual information in the process of mediating finance and property issues, on the other hand, that can be passed on to solicitors and to the court.

Safeguards in Mediation

There is an exception to this principle of confidentiality. If either of you reveals that your child or children are at risk of harm from either of you or from anyone else, the mediator has a responsibility to ensure that the safety of the children comes first and report to the Social Services Department if a child is at immediate risk. They will tell you that you should inform the Social Services Department. They will check up that you do and if you do not they will do so. The law set out in the Children Act states that the interest of the child is paramount.

Similarly, if either one of you threatens the other, or reveals that harm has been threatened or done to either of you, the mediator will stop the process to ensure your safety. In some ways the mediator is no different from anyone else in that all citizens have to pay regard to the law. In other ways the mediator is different, because they invite you into a private situation to talk about family matters that may have become explosive. There must therefore be some rules to ensure that all are safe.

Flexibility

This sounds an odd principle to go with the other three. It means that the subject-matter of the mediation is for you to determine. It is a flexible process because, unlike in a court of law, there are no set procedures. You do not have to speak in strict rotation, for example. Mediation does not have a fixed order like a court or a tribunal or the Houses of Parliament or even a meeting conducted by a chairman with a secretary taking minutes. It is a private discussion which can flow in many ways and must be conducted flexibly enough for all differences and possible solutions to be fully aired and explored. Each mediation is therefore unique.

10

PREPARING FOR MEDIATION

There are four aspects of separation and divorce that you will need to consider in planning your future lives:

> your own needs,
> your children's needs,
> the part played by your wider family and community,
> financial costs and needs for the future.

Whether you manage your own divorce, use solicitors to negotiate for you or use mediation, you will need to understand how these aspects should be worked out in relation to each other. For example, what you decide about money affects your children; what you decide about the family home affects your future lifestyle; what you decide about your children affects their relationship with their grandparents. The extent to which your own and your children's needs are met will influence the way everyone copes with the situation. Everything is related.

In All Issues Mediation these aspects are worked on together. Which ever route you follow through your divorce, they will have to become integrated or people's needs may not be met. An adversarial or separate approach to resolving problems always risks creating gaps and conflicts in meeting everyone's needs.

In preparing to negotiate, whether you negotiate for yourselves in mediation with a solicitor's occasional support or whether your solicitor negotiates for you, it is helpful to ask yourself the following questions:

1 What are my preferred outcomes?
2 What is my 'bottom line' (i.e. my basic sticking point)?
3 What might I accept in between 1 and 2?

You can discuss these with your solicitor before you begin any negotiation. This means that you try never go below your bottom line and do not expect to achieve your preferred option in every aspect. Negotiation is about what takes place between the extremes in the middle area.

The facts comprising the legal and economic aspects of divorce are set out in Part 3. You will be able to refer to them as and when they affect your situation.

A time and a place to think

It may help to give yourself some thinking time to sit and read this section, with a pen in your hand, and list all the things in it that apply to you. Refer to Part 3 as you go.

Setting aside a place in the house where you keep all your papers and lists could be helpful. Some people may be lucky enough to have their own desk at home. It is more likely to be a drawer that no one else touches, which you can keep orderly and lift out on to the table when you work. You will need to collect documents and papers if you are to divorce. You can do this together; at some point you may need to do it separately. In mediation or for solicitors you will have to produce certain documents to verify the facts and statements that the court will ultimately check, for example, marriage certificate, pay slips and letters from pension companies. (These are dealt with in more detail in Part 3.)

Document cases and files can help you to become organised. Winston Churchill apparently described his writing desk as being like a spaniel, always pleased to see him when he got home. Your writing area may become a safe place quietly awaiting you when you make time to sit down and consider how your life has been and will be spent. It will help you to stay in control.

APPROACHING A
FAMILY MEDIATION SERVICE

It will be clear by now that a mediator cannot mediate with only one person. Mediation requires at least two people to be present with the mediator. Those two people must be able and willing to sit together and talk. For this reason mediators take care to clarify a number of points before their clients begin mediation. In NFM Services they may arrange what is called an 'intake interview'. Other family mediators (see Useful Addresses) may begin differently.

Usually one of you will telephone the Family Mediation Service first. The person answering the telephone will establish some basic facts of the situation. Are you contemplating separation or divorce? Are you already separated or divorced but have an issue or issues to resolve? If the answer is 'yes', you will be usually be offered an 'intake interview' in which you will be told the basic facts of mediation. It will be stressed that both of you will need to attend, although not together in the first instance. You will be told something about the principles of mediation and that mediation is confidential and that the mediator has no direct contact with the courts or anybody official.

Mediators will explain that mediation is not an alternative to legal advice (which you may well need from a solicitor and to which each person has an individual right), but it is an alternative to legal representation, that is, to solicitors negotiating *for* you or courts making decisions for you.

The staff of the Family Mediation Service will be particularly careful, even at this early stage, to be sure that there are no grounds for concern about anyone's safety if you come together. They will also ensure that members of staff do not begin to take one person's side. They will help you to decide if mediation is suitable for you both.

They will explain that if you think you would like to use a mediator, either you can ask your partner to come, or the Family Mediation Service will write and ask him or her to come. Many people say, 'Oh, they won't come.' However, experience shows that many more people do come in response to an invitation than their partners might suppose.

Comments from Mediation Clients

Christine:
Basically, we had a problem, not on the…children side but on financial issues, division of the property, and because of the emotional energy we were feeling it was very difficult to do that on our own…so the idea of a third party was most appealing.'

Gordon:
I think it is true that before that stage when it was to do with the marriage and personal problems and the divorce, I think my wife would be much more eager to go to the Mediation Service than I would. When it came to specific problems we were finding it increasingly difficult to talk about them. I was equally as keen.'

Before an appointment, the Services will send a leaflet to each of you, or to both if you are still living together, to read beforehand to try to ensure that you understand what mediation can offer.

ALTERNATIVE HELP

If mediation is not what you want, the Service can give you other information and assistance in deciding on another form of help, such as marriage counselling, divorce counselling or legal advice.

Marriage counselling

You may be more suited to marriage counselling, if either it is clear that you want to try to save the marriage or it is unclear whether or not you want to end it. Mediators can help people decide whether this is what they really want and and give them a contact number.

Divorce counselling

You may be so distressed that you need counselling even if you do not believe that your marriage can be saved. Divorce counselling may be what you want. If so, you will be referred to the right place, usually Relate.

Children's counselling

You may be worried about the effect of the separation or divorce upon your children, although you are not in disagreement with the other parent. You may want to use the mediator to help you talk through your concerns about the children together. Or you may decide that your child or children might benefit from counselling directly themselves. Children often want someone outside the family to talk to and to listen, as we have seen.

There are some counselling services for children. If there is one in your area, the Mediation Service will know of it or may be running it themselves (see page 221). If they run a children's counselling service, it will be separate from any mediation you undertake so that, in counselling, your children's needs are seen in their own right. Counselling gives a child someone to listen to them in confidence in order to help them sort things out in their own minds. The importance of this was emphasised in Part 1, Chapter 6.

Legal advice

The Mediation Service does not act *for* people but *between* them, so the mediators cannot act to protect your individual interests. They can give you information, but they cannot give you advice. Therefore, you are likely to need legal advice.

Legal advice is given by solicitors whose specific job it is. You may need a solicitor to give you legal advice urgently (for example, if there is a worry about someone's safety or about how your partner is handling your finances). The Mediation Service will clarify such issues with you and show you a list of solicitors, usually those who are members of the Solicitors Family Law Association.

Welfare benefits

You may need advice about benefits, in which case you would be referred to the local Citizens' Advice Bureau, who specialise in this area.

Safety and protection

If there is danger to anyone, the police, the Social Services Department or the Women's Aid Federation Helpline might be required (see page 224).

Information meetings under the Family Law Act

Once the Family Law Act comes into force, you will have to attend an information meeting before you make the necessary statement of marital breakdown which will start off the divorce. This will give you an opportunity to learn about your options and about how the new law will work. At the end of the book there is more detail about the Family Law Act. This will not apply until about 1999.

In future, if you want legal aid, unless it is already obvious that mediation is clearly not suitable in your situation, you will also be required to attend an intake meeting with a mediator to see whether mediation is suitable.

THE FIRST CONTACT

Let us assume that these other services are not required at this point and that you want to use mediation. You have been offered an appointment and you and the mediator think it is suitable for you both.

Some mediators begin by briefly seeing each person separately. This might mean either giving them each a separate appointment or giving each person a separate slot at the beginning of their first joint appointment.

The Family Mediators Association, for example, ask their clients to complete some forms before they attend a meeting in which they are asked to give some basic financial information and state what issues they hope to resolve. NFM Services usually leave this until after they have met the couple so that everybody is clear what is to take place.

The prior, separate contact is used for specific purposes:

- to help each of you prepare for the negotiation you are about to enter,
- to clarify what issues you want to resolve and what you want to achieve,
- to establish that you each understand that you will be negotiating for yourselves with the mediator responsible for a fair process,

- to establish, if you have been referred by the court, for example, that you are nevertheless entering mediation voluntarily,
- to establish that there are no grounds for fear for either in your coming together.

_____ EXAMPLES _____

Jim and Beattie

Let us imagine that Jim and Beattie, the first couple described in this book, chose mediation.

Jim telephoned the Mediation Service after he got to his hotel room in Glasgow. The co-ordinator of the Family Mediation Service asked him how he might help.

Jim: 'My wife and I have been in marriage counselling, but the marriage is over and I have left. The counsellor advised us to come for mediation to sort out what we do about the children and the house. Can you help?'

Co-ordinator: 'Has your wife also agreed to come to mediation?'

Jim: 'Yes. I said I'd arrange it, but I've been very busy.'

Co-ordinator: 'Shall I explain what mediation offers?'

Jim: 'All right, but I haven't got long. I'm telephoning from a hotel in Glasgow and I have to go out to meet my team almost immediately.'

Co-ordinator: 'Shall I first send you and your wife some information? I could also make an appointment if you are both agreed upon mediation. The mediator would want to see you separately first briefly to make sure that mediation is what you both want and that it is suitable for you.'

Jim agrees, and gives the co-ordinator his own address and that of his wife.

In this case, the Service co-ordinator feels under some pressure from Jim. He is careful, however, to ensure separate appointments so that Jim can take time to prepare himself and that Beattie has a chance to weigh up for herself whether mediation is what she wants and can prepare her agenda. The mediator is on fairly secure ground, however, because the couple seem to have decided as a result of marriage counselling to come for mediation.

Flo and Ashley

In this situation the co-ordinator who answers the telephone asks Flo some questions but is careful to make a separate appointment each for Flo and Ashley before the two attend together to be sure that each is making their own decision about the suitability of mediation.

Flo: 'Can I see a mediator?'

Co-ordinator: 'In what way do you think a mediator could help?'

Flo: 'Well, I've gone back to my mother with Jamie – he's three – and my ex keeps coming round and bothering me. Every time we talk we row.'

Co-ordinator: 'Have you discussed mediation with him?'

Flo: 'No.'

Co-ordinator: 'Have either of you got a solicitor?'

Flo: 'Well, I haven't.'

Co-ordinator: 'When did you leave?'

Flo: 'About two months ago. We've got nothing sorted out about the house. We just row when he comes to see Jamie.'

Co-ordinator: 'Are these bad rows?'

Flo: 'It depends what you mean by bad.'

Co-ordinator: 'Does it come to blows or to shouting?'

Flo: 'I yell at him all right, but he's never hit me, if that's what you mean.'

Co-ordinator: 'So you think you could both sit down and talk?'

Flo: 'Well, I could. That's what I want to do.'

Co-ordinator: 'We would arrange to see you each separately first. Will you ask him if he is willing to come or shall I write to him?'

Flo: 'Can you? I think we'd row if I asked him. If he had a proper letter he might come.'

The co-ordinator agrees to write a letter but also goes on to suggest that Flo discusses mediation with Ashley so that he will expect a letter. She gives Flo the opportunity to consider whether the bad rows she mentions are such that mediation may not be suitable. Flo gives a reassuring answer indicating her own confidence. The next task is to pave the way for Ashley to come; he may be reluctant. The mediator will offer them separate appointments first.

FROM ARGUMENT TO NEGOTIATION

A researcher in America called Gottman has analysed arguments between couples and believes that all arguments go through a series of moves:

> finding a place,
> building up an agenda,
> tackling the issues,
> negotiating a solution.

Mediation helps couples to turn an argument into a negotiation. Respect is paid to each person's views, needs and differences. Though each may begin by thinking the other wrong, mediation respects the view each person holds. Negotiation, as distinct from an argument, ensures that each person has an opportunity to put forward their own view and to listen to that of the other person. Negotiation gives people the satisfaction of having their say and being listened to. The disagreement is thoroughly explored. Towards the end of negotiation, people can feel more relaxed and relieved and begin to negotiate, bargain, or make a deal, perhaps. For example: 'I won't do this if you don't do that.' Sometimes they apologise for misunderstanding each other; sometimes they agree to differ; sometimes they find common ground and decide there is nothing left to argue about (give their differences to 'the wind that shakes the barley').

11

THE MEDIATION PROCESS

The mediation process has an innate structure. It has a beginning, a middle and an end. Mediators think of it in five stages:

establishing whether the couple wish to enter mediation and explaining the process ('engaging');
establishing the agenda,
exploring the issues
generating options
reaching agreement.

The Mediation Process

1 *Engaging the couple* into the mediation process by ensuring their voluntary entry.

2 *Establishing the agenda* by identifying the issues to be resolved or already in dispute.

3 *Exploring the issues* by discussing the facts and differences fully.

4 *Generating options* by thinking of different ways that might resolve the issues.

5. *Reaching agreement* by choosing the options that best resolve the issues to the satisfaction of both.

These stages make up the flexible structure the mediator will use. It has a logic and a momentum. If you both want your divorce to be amicable and fair, mediation will give you a chance to have a good discussion and see it through to a satisfactory conclusion.

A COUPLE IN MEDIATION

The following series of illustrations will help you visualize a mediation process. Our imaginary couple are called Karen and Pip.

1 Engaging in mediation

In the first picture you will see that Karen is the one making the move (being the leaver) and suggesting mediation. She looks very cheerful. Whatever has gone wrong between them has left Pip feeling puzzled and depressed, whereas Karen seems energetic and determined to divorce him. However, she gives him some consolation, as she would see it, by saying that she wants the divorce to be amicable. This may be wishful thinking on her part, of course. She may dread rows and be hoping that they might manage the change without too much hassle and expense.

Pip is unlikely to see the consolation that Karen offers as in the least consoling. He may feel pushed into a situation he has not chosen. He may well be resentful as well as hurt and confused and feel that he has no power over his own life any more.

2 Establishing the agenda

They arrive in mediation with different goals and expectations. Pip is bitter, feels he has not deserved what is happening to him and stands to lose everything: children, home, money and his whole way of life. To counter this, he imagines himself with the children, protecting them from his irresponsible wife. He sees her as soundly and justifiably defeated by his commitment to his children and his very rightness. Any deals to be done are his deals and he must win them.

Karen, on the other hand, sees herself managing alone with the children and doing it generously and well. She imagines Pip, rather more cheerful than he appears, popping in on regular trouble-free visits to her children. She sees herself keeping them happy and occupied and relatively unaffected by the split. The natural rightness of her having the children with her is without question in her mind.

They are not approaching mediation from the same angle. However, they can agree about the agenda – to resolve all the issues and get everything sorted out – even if they do not agree on how they want the issues resolved. The mediator will have to begin to construct a process with them that gives each of them a chance to gain some control over what is happening. She may well use a flip chart to list the issues so that they can see what they want to tackle.

3 Exploring the issues

Having got the agenda agreed (children, house, money) the mediator helps the couple to explore each of these issues bit by bit. In this picture they have got down to work. Often – and probably in this case – reaching this stage was not as trouble-free as it might seem. The issues 'on the table' (as a mediator would say) may look as if they might be tackled logically, but the thoughts, expectations and fears 'under the table' will mean that the discussion goes through some stormy moments. Karen is anxious to get started on her dream picture; Pip is set on his. They are quite different pictures. The mediator is not likely to have an easy time either. (By the way, there may not be a table quite like this in every mediation room.)

Let us imagine a small piece of the dialogue.

Mediator: 'Shall we begin by discussing the first item on your agenda – the arrangements for the children? Who would like to begin by saying something about the children and what they might most need in your view at the moment in this situation?'

Karen: 'Well, they are really coping very well. Pip hasn't yet moved out but they know he is going. Mind you, his depression can't be easy for them to put up with. It is not easy for me either, I can tell you. I think we need to sort things out quickly so that they can get on with their lives.'

Mediator: 'What do you both think you need to achieve for the children?'

Karen: 'Joe is eight and Jenny is six and they need to know where they are going to be.'

Mediator: 'So how would you each see their lives being organised?'

Karen: 'Well, they would have to stay with me. Pip would never have the time or the energy to keep up with all that they do. That's been part of the trouble. He works all the hours that God gives and then comes home exhausted and irritable. He's worn me down.'

Mediator: 'So you see the children living with you?'

Karen: 'Of course, but I do want to be amicable. I do want them to see a lot of Pip – if he can find time, of course. I am not going to get married again, you know.'

Mediator: 'How do you see the situation, Pip?'

Pip: I don't know how she can sit there so smug and cheerful. She has ruined our lives by going around with someone else. She imagines that things will all go on as if there has been no damage done to anybody. I'm crucified and the children are very worried and upset.'

Mediator: 'Do you have an idea about what you would like to see happen?'

Pip: 'Karen to come to her senses and call this crazy plan off.'

Karen: 'I told you I will not call it off. You seem unable to hear me say that it is over. I am worn down with it and so are the children.'

Mediator: 'It seems that you are not agreed at first base whether the marriage is over or not. Is that something that should also go on the agenda?'

Pip: 'I think it should, but I have little hope that she will change her mind. If she is determined to end the marriage then she should go and I will stay at home with the children. I am not seeking to leave.'

Mediator: 'Well, you both have very different pictures of what should happen.'

Karen: 'That is typical. We have had different ideas for years.'

Pip: 'We may have different ideas, but what about our children? I want to continue to be a real father – I must keep my job and I must have a home for them.'

Karen: 'OK. I want them still to have two parents too. I don't want to shut you out of their lives. I will have to work too, though, as two homes will cost more than one. But I am their mother and they must stay with me and we must sort things out together. That's what we are here for.'

Mediator: 'Perhaps it would help you to get to work by talking about the children. What have they been told? How have they responded? What makes up the lives they lead and how might they be best cared for by both of you?'

The mediator summarises what Pip and Karen have revealed so far and searches for the first common ground: their concern about the children. She could have started with the end of the marriage, and they will almost certainly return to this, but she is looking for a place to start that might produce some listening. If this is achieved, they may then be able to talk constructively and seriously about the ending of their marriage instead of sniping angrily at each other, which is what their fear and nervousness seem to be making them do now.

Between the third and fourth pictures a lot of work will have been done. From occupying totally different positions, the couple are helped to put their competitive solutions to one side for a while in order to discuss the children. Pip's fear of losing the children is expressed. He owns up to deep feelings of failure at having lived and worked in such a way that he has allowed a gulf to open up between him and his wife.

Karen begins to be more honest about her real feelings of loss and disappointment. She expresses regret for the failure of their marriage and is sorry for Pip but repeats, albeit in a softer tone, that it is too late. She feels too detached from him. She is already seeing someone else although she insists that it is not serious. The mediator learns that Pip has known about this other relationship for some time and has been depressed about it. They do not accept the suggestion of marriage counselling, both saying it is too late.

However, they talk about the children with real feeling now. The mediator may be able to summarise their deep and shared commitment to the children. They may reach an agreement about what will work best for the time being, or they may agree on the longer-term arrangements whereby they both see a great deal of the children, for almost equal amounts of time, perhaps. However, they will have to work out a lot of details before they reach a final agreement.

Sorting out arrangements for children usually takes between two and four hours in one or two sessions. It is hard work, but it will have satisfied the couple if they have discussed the children thoroughly. They may find that they can talk without shouting and getting hurt, and that they can agree on what suits the children best. This is often arrived at by a discussion conducted *from the children's point of view.*

Sometimes parents feel that they are not getting a clear message from the children, either because the children are afraid of taking sides or because they seem unwilling to talk to either of their parents. In some situations, the mediator may suggest consulting the children on behalf of their parents and bringing back their views to discuss in the next session.

4 Developing the options

Karen and Pip discuss options about the children with the mediator. They talk about each child in detail individually – what each is feeling and how each is reacting. At this point couples often find themselves in agreement, in that they are thinking the same thoughts and having the same worries about each child. They will begin to consider what will work best for each child; what does each child need and want? How much do they have the same needs and how do they differ? Do they want to be together with each parent or do they sometimes want a parent to themselves? What are their daily routines?

Gradually it may become clear where the children should live and who has time to do what with them. What seemed like an all-or-nothing scenario is now more varied, individual, interesting and particular to their own family life. It will not fit either of the dream pictures the couple had when they started – Dad with the children or Mum with the children – but each of them will be with the children in different ways and at different times. The arrangements will be worked into a plan which gives the children the continuity and predictability that children usually want and thrive upon.

As a plan is constructed, it will become clear where the children will most easily spend most of their daily life, what is the most realistic arrangement for them: where they should mostly sleep and eat, how they can continue their other activities and maintain their close relationship with each parent.

The plan is entered in a weekly diary. Sometimes it is complicated, sometimes simple. Sometimes the mediator writes it down for them; sometimes a problem is resolved so simply that nothing needs to be written down.

5 Writing down a settlement

Pip and Karen have reached a settlement and this is written down. As you have seen, this couple settled all their issues in mediation. They concluded with a Memorandum of Understanding.

Some couples use mediation for children's arrangements only. If they want some things written down in detail, it might take the form of a 'parenting plan'. A sample parenting plan is shown in the following chapter.

12

MAKING ARRANGEMENTS FOR YOUR CHILDREN

MEANINGS OF THE TERMS USED

'Making arrangements for children' means just what it says: making practical arrangements for this child or these children to live their lives in a predictable way, keeping in touch with both parents and being looked after by them when they are with them. The central purpose of arranging for the child to remain in contact with both parents is to maintain the attachment for the child.

The court uses the word 'contact' or 'residence' only if it has to make a Section 8 order (see pages 201–4, the Children Act). The courts no longer use the words 'custody' and 'access'.

The 'custody battle' of Paula Yates and Bob Geldof featured below show how hard it is for parents (and journalists) to find out how the law now operates. In this example, two famous people go to court to sort out the arrangements for their children. The Press sees it as a 'custody battle'. In fact, it seems that they left court with a simple solution, the details of which they had worked out for themselves and which must have been similar to what they had been doing before the proceedings began. But when a highly public crisis arose, they seemed to have no other way of handling it than going to court. Perhaps, they could have achieved much the same result, and at much less cost to them both, with the help of a mediator.

'TIMESHARE CHILDREN'
(*Daily Mail*, 10 October, 1996)

Paula Yates and Bob Geldof ended the battle over their children at the High Court yesterday.

The divorced couple agreed to continue sharing custody of Fifi, 13, Peaches, six, and four-year-old Pixie. Geldof had been 'awarded temporary custody' last week, following a police raid which uncovered what were believed to be drugs at the Chelsea home of Miss Yates and her lover, INXS singer Michael Hutchence.

A solution came after a four-day court hearing in private before Mrs Justice Hale. A joint statement was authorised by the judge: 'Two concerned parents came to court to do what each of them believed was right for their children,' it said. 'They have resolved matters in a way which they both believe to be in the best interests of their children. Bob and Paula have agreed that they will continue to share the care of their children.'

MAKING PLANS FOR CHILDREN

Making plans for children means considering very practical things as well as managing everyone's relationships and feelings in a changing situation. The needs of the children must be paramount. Each child has slightly different needs and you will have to try to meet these as specifically as you can within the bounds of your situation.

Mediators usually offer to write down the plans parents agree to make. The way these are written down varies greatly from one mediator to another and from one family to another. They are tailor-made.

Parenting plans

Some families like to construct a detailed plan. A parenting plan, for example, is a kind of mini (rather than Magna) carta for the future family. An example of one such plan is given on page 106. A parenting plan could be shown to the children by their parents for their views upon it before it becomes permanent. This will depend on the ages of the children. It then can be sent to solicitors and thence to the court to become the basis for a consent order; or, if you are separating and there are no court proceedings, it is simply your 'consent' – your own agreed plan. No arrangement with children is ever completely permanent, of course, because children change and their life-style changes and so may yours.

Stability and flexibility

Other plans will need to be made from time to time. As long as it is appropriate, a plan can give some stability. Before long, flexibility will also be required. The relationship between children and a parent who does not live with them needs to be very individual and interesting and right for those particular people. There is sometimes an assumption that, after divorce, a father (most frequently) gets to see his children for two hours on a Saturday afternoon, often in McDonald's! This can become very unrewarding for everyone after a while. Time spent with your children deserves careful

SAMPLE PARENTING PLAN

We, John and Mary Godden, in ending our marriage, are resolved to work together to ensure that we help and support each other to care for our children, Joe and Jemma. We have therefore made the following plans for Joe and Jemma after our separation. We, as parents, recognise that things do change, that children can get upset, and sometimes may misbehave. When they get upset or if there are behavioural problems we take responsibility to discuss this together.

Homes – Mary will stay at 54 Beatrice Road with the children and John will live in a flat at 25 Hawk Road. We will continue to sort out financial arrangements for this with our solicitors (or family mediator) and we intend that John will furnish his flat so that the children will also feel at home there.

Money – We will work out a fair way of sorting out the financial cost of looking after the children with our solicitors.

Everyday arrangements:
- Mary will see that Joe and Jemma get to and from school, but will ask John for help when she needs it.
- Joe and Jemma will stay with John at the flat every other weekend and John will take Joe to football every Saturday. On the weekends when Joe is with him, he will wash Joe's kit.
- Mary will take Jemma to the music club on Saturday mornings.
- John will take both children to the swimming club with him on Wednesdays as usual. If there is ever a problem in doing this we will contact each other during the week in good time to make fresh plans.
- Pop and Nana Godden will invite Joe and Jemma for Sunday lunch at the weekends when they are with John, and Nana and Granddad Finch will visit them at Mary's as often as they do at present.

Holidays – We wish arrangements for Christmas and Easter holidays to be flexible. We should like to have some special time

each with the children on these occasions. This year, Mary will have them with her on Christmas Eve and Christmas Day and John will have them overnight Christmas Day and Boxing Day.

During the summer this year, Mary will take them to Wales with Nana and Granddad Finch for three weeks in August and John will take them to Eastbourne for the last week of July and have them with him at home for the last week in August.

Pets – Moggy (the cat) will stay at Beatrice Road, although John will look after him, by arrangement, whenever Mary, Joe and Jemma go away on holiday.

New partners – If either of us intends to live with another partner, we undertake to inform the other and meet to discuss how we can together support our children in adjusting to this major change in our children's lives. We undertake that we will seek to ensure that, in the event of other adults entering their lives, the children's precious relationship with each of us will be protected.

School – We wish to share all the information from school and will continue to make joint decisions about their schooling and any other decisions about welfare. Mary will notify the school of this.

Medical and dental treatment – Except in an emergency, we will make mutual decisions about and medical or dental treatment.

Changes – We agree to notify each other at least one week in advance of any changes in any arrangements we have made. If any dispute arises that we cannot resolve ourselves, we will return to the Family Mediation Service to sort it out.

Signed: _____

Date: _____

thought. It must suit every person involved and be able to change from time
to time as the children grow and change.

If the arrangements are made in mediation and everyone is satisfied
that contact can take place, but conflict needs to be kept to a minimum, they
may be written down, very briefly, carefully and sparingly. For some families, the plan will therefore be very short and very specific and may take the
form of a jointly agreed letter to solicitors written by the mediator, in consultation with the parents, at the end of a session. An example of one such
statement of agreement is given below.

A Short Statement of a Plan

Marian and Rod have agreed that Rod should collect Jerry and Della
from Marian's home at 2 p.m. on Saturdays every fortnight, beginning
on January 25th. He will take them to the Mile End Contact Centre and
bring them back by 6 p.m. This plan will be reviewed at Whichway
Family Mediation Service in a month's time.

Behind such an agreement may lie months of struggle and argument.
Maybe the Contact Centre is being used because Marian is not prepared to
let Rod take the children anywhere where there are no other adults she can
trust. If Marian has experienced some abuse, the supervision available at
the Contact Centre will make her feel more comfortable. It will also make
Rod's contact with his children more relaxed, because the centre will provide
activities for them to do together. Marian's safety must be assured. Sometimes contact is not in the children's best interests because it puts a mother
and her children at risk. In these situations, mediation is not suitable.

Straightforward written plans

Sometimes nothing much needs to be written down, because the parents
and children have agreed things easily between themselves and want the
mediator to write down the plan only as a sign of what they have succeeded
in planning.

Some plans need to be written down in diary form because they are very
complicated, owing to the sheer number of activities to which the separated
parents must accompany their children. A plan for such a routine might
simply be stuck on the fridge doors of the two parental homes.

Is contact always appropriate?

Some couples are in very bitter dispute about their children when they come
to mediation. The Family Law Act endorses the desirability of contact by
stating:

the welfare of the child will be best served by

(i) his having regular contact with those who have parental responsibility for him and with other members of his family.

(ii) the maintenance of as good a continuing relationship with his parents as is possible.

There can be no hard and fast presumption of contact, however. In some circumstances this may not be in the best interests of the child. If this is the case, a court will have to decide. See chapter 16.

Contact Centres

If a court decides on contact but wants it to be carefully watched, a Contact Centre can be very useful. Contact Centres are also useful when there is simply nowhere for the visiting parent to go or when some reassurance is necessary.

Contact Centres have been set up over most of the country in the last ten years by voluntary groups, by the Probation Service or both to provide a safe and pleasant place for parents to meet their children. The resident parent can bring the children to the Centre and the visiting parent can then spend time with the children with the resident parent able to leave knowing that the children will be safe and that the time spent will be interesting and as enjoyable as possible for the children. There are staff on duty and plenty of toys and games for all ages. There are also facilities for making meals and drinks.

What helps settle disputes?

The exchange of information between two people who have become newly receptive to what they hear is the simple ingredient that settles most disputes. The process of mediation facilitates this exchange and helps people to listen and therefore to negotiate. Negotiation does not mean giving in. It does not even mean compromise. It means talking and listening and, in the process, seeing a way of reaching a solution.

Our imaginary couple in mediation, Pip and Karen, began to listen to one another; they didn't pursue their own desires at each other's expense.

Here is a simple example of how the clouds can roll away in discussion. Lisa and Dave had been separated for some time. Dave had left his wife with the care of their daughter, Becky, and formed a new partnership. Becky and her father had a very close bond, which he had maintained by visiting very regularly, encouraged by his ex-wife. Then Lisa's father died. She began to find the visits difficult and suddenly stopped them, saying that they upset the little girl. There was a gap of several months. Dave went to his solicitor. A bitter correspondence began and attitudes hardened. Dave's solicitor suggested mediation.

The Mediation Service asked them both to come in to separate meetings. Neither was hopeful that discussion would succeed; the husband said his wife was irrational, she that he was unreliable. However, they agreed to come together.

The session was not easy. Dave was pleading and accusatory; Lisa was closed and critical. Then, during the discussion, she referred, as if in passing, to the impact of her father's death upon Becky. Dave said, 'I'm sorry about that.' Lisa retorted that he hadn't said so at the time. He replied that he had not known what to do and thought that he would not be welcome at the funeral. Lisa said that he might have said something. Dave then told her that he had felt very sad as he had liked her father very much. Lisa began to cry, and Dave said it must have been difficult for her. After a longish silence she said, apparently changing the subject in an unconnected way, that perhaps they could try this Saturday for him to come and see his daughter.

What had happened was that Dave acknowledged Lisa's loss. It seemed, though it was never directly said, that this is what she most wanted to hear. It unlocked the dispute.

CONSULTING CHILDREN

The Family Law Act includes a section that requires mediators to encourage parents to consult their children about their 'views, wishes and feelings'. The European Convention on the Exercise of Children's Rights proposes rights for children who are subjects of court proceedings 'to receive all relevant information; to be consulted and to express his or her views; to be informed of the consequences of any decisions'. An extract from the United Nations Convention on the Rights of the Child is set out below.

The United Nations Convention on the Rights of the Child

The UN Convention on the Rights of the Child states in article 9, paragraphs 1–3:

9.1 States Parties [i.e. those countries that sign up the Convention] shall ensure that a child shall not be separated from his or her parents except when competent authorities determine that such a separation is necessary for the best interests of the child.

9.2 In any proceedings, all interested parties shall be given an opportunity to participate in the proceedings and make their views known.

9.3 States Parties shall respect the right of the child who is separated
     from one or both parents to maintain personal relations and direct
     contact with both parents on a regular basis except it is is contrary
     to the child's best interests.

Families vary in how much every member's views are considered in reaching decisions. Some families plan and talk over almost everything together;
some families only discuss certain things with everybody there. The ages of
the children are an important consideration. Giving them an opportunity to
express their views does not mean that they have to be asked questions that
lie outside their responsibility. They should not be asked, for example, with
which parent they wish to live unless they are almost grown up. It is a
parent's responsibility to decide this. Apart from the fact that they probably
neither know nor fully understand all the relevant factors, children will be
reluctant to reject (usually) either parent. Their voices should be heard, but
they should not be given adult responsibilities. A fine line? Maybe, but an
important one. There is growing emphasis in family law on taking 'due
account of the views expressed by the child'.

Mediators consulting children

Sometimes parents find it hard to be sure what their children want or feel
and the mediator may offer to consult the children on their behalf. Sometimes it is the parents who ask the mediator to do so.

Whichever way the idea arises, mediators will be very careful to proceed
with great respect for the children, the parents and their own family style of
communication.

The two parents in this example, Jack and Barbara, came to mediation
long after they had separated. They found it very difficult to be in the same
room as each disagreed with everything the other said. They would stop
and say, 'You see how we are together.' They explained that the arrangements they had made for the children had once worked fairly well, but the
wife said she could no longer keep them up.

The arrangement was for their two daughters, Rachel and Sarah, to
spend alternative nights at each home. One parent would take them to
school each day and the other would collect them. This way they did not
have to meet and did not row and the children saw them both equally.

As they could not agree on an alternative, the couple suggested that the
mediator (Clare) should see the two girls. Clare was rather cautious, not
wanting to put the children into the midst of a conflict by asking them to
resolve a problem that their parents could not resolve. What if they suggested something the parents did not like, or that one liked and the other did
not? The mediator talked over her reservations with the parents.

In the end, Clare agreed to write to the children asking them to come in to discuss how the arrangements were working from their point of view.

The two girls came in. The mediator explained carefully that they were not to make decisions, but that their parents wanted her to consult them about the arrangements because they wanted to know what they thought, as it seemed to be getting difficult to keep them up.

Rachel asked, 'Did you see them together?'

The mediator said she had.

'Was it all right?' said Sarah.

'Well, they do find it difficult to agree on things,' replied Clare cautiously.

The girls looked at each other.

'They're awful together,' Rachel said gloomily.

'We spend the same time with each so that they don't argue,' sighed Sarah.

'Does that work out for you?' asked the mediator.

'There's too much rushing about,' answered Sarah.

'We never know where our things are,' her sister added.

'But we want to see both of them a lot,' continued Sarah.

'So you'd like your parents to find another way in which you can see them both a lot, but not changing every day?' Clare asked them.

'Yes, but be very careful how you put it,' said Rachel, 'as they might get cross with you.'

The mediator worked out with the two girls what she would say to their parents. She told them she was probably not too afraid of them getting cross with her, but asked how they coped with their parent's anger. They said it was all right if they kept them away from each other!

In the subsequent session with the parents, both seemed rather humbled by Sarah's comment about 'too much rushing about'. They suddenly began to work together without blaming each other. They altered the plans to a less punishing schedule that still avoided the adults having to meet.

In another family, a sixteen-year-old daughter, Tracey, stayed with her mother, Christine, after a period of disruption in which each parent had left the home in turn and then returned. Finally Christine had left for good. Then Tracey decided to live with her father, John, leaving her younger brother, Paul, behind with their mother. This resulted in John not seeing Paul for two months. Christine said Paul did not want to go and that John was stopping Tracey coming to see her.

The parents came separately to an appointment with a mediator. The mother admitted that she feared that Tracey preferred her 'stepmother'. She was angry with Tracey and desperately wanted her to come voluntarily to see her. She realised that Paul wanted to see his father but did not want to feel she had 'given in' by letting him go. In his appointment, John said that he could see no problem here. Tracey could please herself, whereas he had applied to the court to stop his ex-wife's contact with Paul.

They both came into mediation. The mediator asked a colleague to come in also. The mistrust between the couple was very clear. Furthermore, it emerged that as each had only access to one child's view, they could only imagine what the other parent was saying to the other child. However, although neither trusted the other, they were both committed to being fair to both children. The mediators suggested that they consulted the children. They encouraged the parents to express and face their worst fears if the children were to be consulted. The mediators explained that what the children said would be confidential and the mediators would only tell the parents what the children agreed should be passed on, the only exception being if the children led the mediators to believe that they were at risk in some way. The children's safety was always paramount. The parents agreed to their children being consulted.

The mediators wrote to the children to invite them to come in together, saying that each child could have some time alone with the mediators. They added that what they said would be confidential and that their parents had agreed that it should be.

The children came separately, waited anxiously for each other and were then extremely pleased to see each other. The mediators left them alone together for while to catch up. Then the mediators saw them together. They both said they were fed up with their parents. They could not believe that after all this time there were still problems. 'Nine whole months!' one of them said. They asked the mediators to tell their parents to stop criticising each other, to stop trying to persuade them to live with one or the other and to let them visit each other. They said that they loved them both but were happy where they were.

This was a difficult message for the mediators to pass on, but they did – and the parents accepted it with relief.

Nowadays more mediators offer the opportunity for children to be involved in discussions about plans made for them where it seems appropriate. They are careful to avoid giving children a responsibility that is inappropriate, however.

These comments were made by a mediation client to a researcher three years after mediation:

> 'I wish there had been an opportunity somewhere in the process for my daughter (aged twelve at the time) to have been involved in negotiations involving her. I know this is not always appropriate but my daughter would have liked to feel that somebody was interested in her feelings and I think she would have benefited from some sort of discussion involving her.'

COMMON PROBLEMS IN MAINTAINING
CONTACT WITH CHILDREN

The Children Act endorsed a view that had gained support during the 1980s: that contact with the parent who left the home was the children's, not the parent's, right. How that contact should be maintained need not be constrained by conventional notions. Courts now rarely make orders that tie children and parents to set times and places. The aim is for the relationship to flourish as naturally as it can under the circumstances.

Most separated families eventually reach a working arrangement that is not rigid but has a pattern upon which everyone can come to rely but is not afraid to alter when necessary. Small children need to see parents frequently and regularly in order to maintain the attachment. Older teenagers seem to be able to go no longer than about 6 weeks before feeling the lack of contact as an aching pain. (Students away from home are susceptible to this sort of pain.) Between these extremes is a wide range of possibilities. It is easy to be flexible if you live near each other after divorce. It is much harder if there are distances involved and children have to go for long periods without physical contact. Telephone calls, letters and cards can reassure children that you are not forgetting them.

The more rigid arrangements become, the more this indicates that there is conflict between parents, barely kept under control. The Exeter Study showed that rigid arrangements that were conditioned by parental conflict were often restrictive and onerous for children. It is worth keeping an arrangement firm to avoid conflict, but it is also worth trying afresh to resolve the conflict. An upsurge of conflict sometimes arises from a change in circumstances which has increased suspicion, such as a new partner or a job change. Making a fresh opportunity to communicate can often correct misunderstandings.

There will be changes and difficulties. You may need to devise a code of conduct for contact. Sometimes ground rules are written into parental agreements in mediation. Common difficulties to be overcome may include:

- children who, depending on their ages, do not want to go on an arranged visit because they

  are afraid of being bored by a routine outing that is no longer rewarding,
  do not want to leave their resident parent (i.e. separation anxiety),
  want to go somewhere else with their friends instead,
  want the parent all to themselves and do not want to share them with siblings,
  are embarrassed at being seen on a contact visit by their friends,

do not want to be with their parent's new partner or their children,

realise that the visiting parent is in a new relationship and is not going to come back and fear that they will be ignored,

realise that the resident parent is in a new relationship and believe that unless they stay and keep an eye on it, they may be ignored.

● children who cry when they return because they

miss their parent when they drive away (i.e. separation anxiety),

are afraid that their parents will row when they meet,

dread their resident parent asking them questions about the visiting parent's new life-style which they have been told not to answer.

● parents who annoy one another because they

expect the other parent to buy essential clothes during the visit,

turn up late,

cancel at the last minute,

buy expensive toys that are not essential,

ask the children leading questions about the other parent's life-style,

bring up controversial issues on the doorstep.

Understanding what is going wrong with contact arrangements can usually produce a simple remedy once strong emotions are recognised and overcome. Understanding and overcoming the emotions of both adults and children is the hardest part, especially if they have reached a high pitch.

Understanding what is going wrong with contact arrangements can usually produce a simple remedy once the strong emotions associated with any of these scenarios are recognised and overcome. Understanding and overcoming the emotions of both adults and children is the hardest part, especially if they have reached a high pitch.

Parents can feel fraught at change-over times for a wide range of reasons which may vary, even from week to week, according to what is happening in their own lives and how confident they feel about managing the demands and anxieties of their own altered circumstances. Such fluctuations may reduce your confidence in your usual capacity to manage your children's feelings and behaviour.

For children, separation anxiety – which occurs, at times, at all ages in different forms – is often mistaken for some other problem. Parents can blame each other for what is upsetting their children at a change-over time, sometimes overlooking the obvious fact of the child's acute insecurity at that moment. In addition to the ordinary problems of parting that occur with most children at some points in their development (for example, leaving a parent to go off to childminders, school, college or even – perhaps especially – their wedding), contact visits remind children of the family that once was. It takes time and the predictability of a reassuring routine for them to overcome this, still feel loved and secure and accept the new situation. Children are likely to need a lot of reassurance for their anxieties. This can be necessary at all the points of change that follow your separation and divorce. It is particularly likely to be needed when parents start new relationships.

At the same time, the children are growing and changing; when they are old enough, consideration must be given to their views, as to how they can best stay close to their visiting parent and continue their own interests.

Parents often make simple changes to contact arrangements after recognising that new emotional and practical issues have arisen. They may ask their mediator to witness or record these alterations.

Postscript: contact with violent parents

In the UK we are more likely to allow or encourage contact where there has been violence than, for example, in Denmark. This is being reconsidered by many to ensure safety for mothers and children, as, if there has been violence, it is quite likely to occur at times of contact. (See Chapter 16)

13

ALL ISSUES MEDIATION

INTEGRATING FINANCE, PROPERTY AND CHILDREN

Increasingly, couples are choosing to use mediation to settle all the issues involved in separation: finances, property and children. If you are interested in doing this, the mediator will give you an information sheet setting out how the process of All Issues Mediation works (see pp. 117–19). It continues in the same order as any mediation, identifying what needs to be tackled, thoroughly exploring the issues, thinking of options and choosing the most workable.

Other mediators and organisations may work in slightly different ways.

Our imaginary couple, Karen and Pip, wanted to sort out everything in mediation. Let us imagine that they now move on to using mediation to sort out their finances and their house. Having talked this through with them, their mediator would ask them to read and sign the Agreement to Mediate to ensure that they agree to its conditions (see p. 120). She would also hand, them the Financial Information Sheets (see p. 121).

Let us suppose that Pip and Karen have very little money. They proceed to gather the information they need to work out their future. Although Pip is a skilled mechanic and has worked hard, he has done very little shift work recently. He has been babysitting while Karen worked part-time in the local pub. Pip is earning £909.49 a month. He brings in his payslips to prove this. He is part of a sharesave scheme in which he has £600. The car is worth £700. However, he does have a pension that will bring a death-in-service lump sum of £42,903 and a pension with a current transfer value of £7,638. Documents to establish these figures are produced.

Karen's bar work pays only £3.01 an hour and she works for fourteen hours a week, which adds up to £182.60 per month. The house is worth about £45,000 and they have yet to pay off £30,400 on the mortgage. The equity therefore is £14,600.

When they work out what they will have to live on in the future, they

6 INFORMATION ABOUT THE MEDIATION OF ALL ISSUES

When two people decide to separate, there are usually a number of other decisions that have to be made about such issues as:

- How to separate
- What to say to the children
- Who will live where
- The distribution of money and property.

Mediation provides an opportunity for you to consider these matters together and, with the help of a mediator, to decide jointly what you think are the best arrangements for you and your family.

1. How does it work?

A trained mediator will meet with you both for a series of sessions, in which you will be helped to:

- Make a list of all the matters you wish to consider
- Collect the necessary information
- Talk about the choices open to you
- Negotiate with each other in order to reach decisions which are practicable and acceptable to you both
- Discuss how you can consult your children appropriately about arrangements you decide to make.

2. What does the mediator do?

The mediator's job is to act as an impartial third party, helping you to exchange information, ideas and feelings constructively so that you can progress towards joint decision-making. However, the mediator has no power to impose a settlement; responsibility for all decisions remains with yourselves, since you will know better than anyone else what is right for your family. What the mediator will *not* do is to advise you about which option is best nor can the mediator protect your individual interests. That is the role of your solicitor and we therefore advise you to engage a solicitor so that you can be advised about the personal consequences for you of what you agree.

3. How many meetings will there be?

That depends on the number and complexity of the issues, and the amount of co-operation which already exists between you. However as a rough guide you should anticipate between four to six sessions of approximately one and a half hours to two hours each.

4. How much will it cost?

Details of charges are given on a separate sheet.

5. Can mediation cover all the issues?

Yes, we offer mediation on *everything* – children, property, maintenance, etc. – arising from the break-up of your relationship.

6. Can anyone mediate all issues in a Family Mediation Service?

Yes, but everyone's circumstances are unique and it may occasionally be appropriate to refer you elsewhere.

7. What are the issues concerning the children?

The major decisions affecting the children are likely to be:

- Where they will live.
- What arrangements will be made for them to spend time with each parent and other relatives.
- Special provision, if any, which might need to be made about such matters as education, religion and health.
- The level of financial support required to meet their needs.
- How they can be appropriately consulted.

The mediator, whilst understanding that you may well have quite different views on some or all of these matters, will help you build on your relationship as **parents** so that you can focus more effectively on your children's needs.

8. How will money and property be tackled?

You will be asked to provide details of anticipated income and expenditure (as far as this can reasonably be predicted), and an estimate of the value of your assets.

This means:

a) making a list of all the money you usually earn or receive over a given period of time (weekly, monthly, etc.)
b) making a reasonable estimate of what you would expect to have to pay for (on the basis of your outgoings during the previous twelve months)
c) considering the housing that would need to be available to each of you, and how this might be financed
d) estimating the market or replacement value of major items – car, furniture, electrical goods, etc. – to be divided in some way between you.
e) providing details of any property, savings, investments, insurance policies, pension rights and other capital assets in which either of you have an interest.
f) identifying loans and debts for which either of you are liable.

9. What about the Child Support Agency?

If you are on certain benefits, the C.S.A. will calculate and collect child support. Otherwise you are free to make your own agreements. However each of you is entitled to apply to the C.S.A. at any time for them to calculate the formula. This can therefore ensure the kind of figure the C.S.A. would be likely to determine and can assist your decisions.

10. Using this information, you will be helped to negotiate on such matters as:

The family home – who should live there, should it be sold and, if so, when and how should the proceeds be divided? (In the case of a rented home, should the tenancy be changed or transferred?)

Maintenance & Child Support – how much should each contribute towards the living expenses of the children (and possibly of the adults)?

Possessions – how should these be shared between you?

Future benefits – does one person need to be compensated for the loss of pension rights, endowments, etc?

On all these issues, the eventual outcome will depend very much on your views about:

- what is 'fair' (which may not necessarily mean a 50/50 split)
- what is realistic
- what best meets the needs of all members of the family, particularly the children
- how your circumstances might be expected to change in the future.

11. A contract for mediation

If you both agree to mediation, you will be asked to sign an Agreement to Mediate which includes a declaration that you agree to be open and honest with each other and not do anything which might pre-judge the outcome of the discussions. If either of you feels the other is not 'playing fair' you are free to withdraw from mediation at any time, The mediator also reserves the right to withdraw from mediation if it becomes clear, for whatever reason, that further progress is unlikely to be made through mediation.

12. Is mediation confidential?

Firstly, mediation is *confidential* and secondly, courts are likely to regard the discussions as *privileged*.

Confidentiality
The agency will not voluntarily disclose to outsiders any information obtained in the course of your discussions without first obtaining your permission (unless it appears there is a risk of significant harm to adult or child).

Privilege
What you *say* during mediation cannot be used later in Court as evidence against you. *Facts* disclosed during mediation, however, are regarded as open.

We will also ask each of you to agree that all discussions during mediation take place solely for the purposes of attempting to reach a settlement and are on the basis that they are both confidential and will not be referred to in evidence in any court proceedings or affidavit about the same issue.

Any factual information provided by either of you in the course of mediation, in relation to financial matters, will need to be verified by you or your solicitor.

If agreement is not reached, the facts disclosed by each of you are available for your solicitors.

It is also part of your agreement to take part in mediation that financial information and any documents produced to verify such information may be used subsequently in Court, although the information and documents will be strictly confidential.

13. Will we have anything in writing?

Towards the end of the series of meetings, a 'Memorandum of Understanding' will be drawn up which is a statement of everything you have proposed during, mediation. You will be advised that you should consult your solicitor on the contents. He or she will advise you on the personal consequences of what you have jointly agreed. The Memorandum will also state any issues on which you have not been able to agree and which may require further negotiation by your solicitors or perhaps a decision by the Courts. However, the Memorandum will not refer to the way either of you responded during mediation.
The Memorandum itself is not legally binding, but is intended for your solicitors to use in preparing a legally binding agreement, where appropriate.

14. Can any arrangements we make now be changed later?

Some Court Orders, particularly those of the 'clean break' kind, will have a once-and-for-all effect as far as capital assets are concerned. This is one reason why it is advisable that you have your own solicitor to advise you. Nothing is binding at this stage. Other Orders, such as those relating to the amount of maintenance paid to spouse/children, may be changed at a later date on further application to the Court. The Court may also be prepared to consider an application to change an Order relating to the children if the original circumstances have altered significantly. Where no Court Order has been made in respect of a particular issue, the arrangement may be varied by agreement between the two of you at some later date.

15. Can the Court impose arrangements different from those agreed?

The final authority always rests with the Court. However, in practice the Court is unlikely to disregard an agreement freely arrived at unless:

a) it is patently unfair to one of you,
b) it is clearly not in the children's best interests, or
c) the facts on which the discussion was based turned out to be incorrect.

16. What happens if we cannot agree on everything?

You may well have reached a certain level of agreement which can be written down and the areas still outstanding can be clarified. You are then able to instruct your solicitors to negotiate a final agreement on your behalf. Ultimately if you cannot agree, the Court may have to make the necessary decisions.

You will receive a more detailed explanation at your first joint meeting with the mediator, when you will also have the opportunity to raise any other issues or concerns you may have about the process.

This Information Sheet is produced by National Family Mediation.

7 AGREEMENT TO MEDIATE

We have decided to use mediation in order to arrive at a Memorandum of Understanding as set out on the Information Sheet.

1. By signing this agreement, we express our sincere intention to attempt to:

   a) be fair to each other throughout the process
   b) leave fault and blame out of the negotiations
   c) be co-operative in resolving disagreements
   d) consider our individual needs, the needs of each other and the needs of the family as a whole
   e) work for the least possible emotional and financial upheaval for all concerned.

2. During the course of mediation we agree:

   a) we will make full, frank and true disclosure of finances and provide all supporting documentation.
   b) we will not transfer, charge, conceal or otherwise dispose of any assets except for the purpose of providing for living necessities and expenses in the ordinary course of business.
   c) we will not make any further charges under any charge account for which both of us are legally responsible, unless mutually agreed upon.
   d) we will communicate with the mediators about issues in mediation only during sessions, unless we agree otherwise.

3. We agree to pay the Family Mediation Service according to their scale of charges.

4. If one of us is unable to keep a scheduled appointment, she/he must notify the other and the Service at least 24 hours in advance.

5. We agree that all communications (except the disclosure of finances) to which the mediators are party are made solely for the purpose of attempting to reach a settlement and are made on the basis that the communications both (a) are confidential and (b) will not be referred to in evidence in any court proceedings about the same issues. They will not be used in affidavits. Financial disclosures are made on the basis that they are confidential, must be disclosed to our solicitors and may be used in evidence in Court.

6. We acknowledge that we have been alerted to the advantages of having separate solicitors to whom we will refer at the end and during the course of mediation when appropriate.

7. If a Memorandum of Understanding is prepared, we acknowledge that it is not a binding agreement unless and until we have legal advice upon it. We will instruct our solicitors to prepare a legally binding document based on the Memorandum of Understanding.

8. If difficulties should arise in consultation with the solicitors, we will notify the mediator of the need for further discussions.

Signed: _____

Date: _____

Signed: _____

Date: _____

This document is prepared by National Family Mediation.

9 FINANCIAL INFORMATION SHEETS

INTRODUCTION

Working out your financial futures with a focus on the needs of your children requires a sound estimate of what you will need and a thorough reckoning of what your income and assets are or could be. The mediator assists you to carry this out by using three sheets, which together help you to gather the financial information needed for the mediation process:

A. Your Income (worked out on a monthly basis)
B. Your Estimated Future Expenditure (on a monthly basis)
C. Your Assets

The mediator helps you to find ways *together* of bridging any gap between what you think you will have and what you think you will need. That is the essence of using mediation to settle finance and property issues:

1. You must each fill in a separate form in your own right.
2. As far as possible, round up or down to the nearest pound.
3. Once the form is completed (in so far as you are able to do so), you should obtain photocopies.
4. One copy should be given to your partner/ex-partner, and the others are for the mediator(s).
5. The mediator's copy should be forwarded a few days in advance of the next mediation session.

You may need to produce documents to prove the statements you make about income, assets, debts and liabilities. Your solicitor and the court will eventually also require at some point to see these documents which are attached to your Memorandum of Understanding. These relate to A. and C. above. In summary, they are:

Salary/wages
• Last three pay slips.
• Form P60.
• If self-employed, recent sets of accounts, tax return and tax assessments for previous 3 years.

Your home(s)
• Valuation of house.
• Mortgage: details of building society, bank or other lender.
• Details of endowment mortgage.
• Details of any other property owned or if rented, tenancy agreement or rent book.

Savings
• Copies of recent statements and passbooks showing balances.
• Details of stocks, shares and unit trusts with current valuations.
• Income from investments.
• Details of any valuables.

Pensions
• Details of any occupational pension, superannuation scheme.
• Copy of rules of scheme and an up-to-date statement.
• Details of any other life policies.

Maintenance
• Details of any payments *made* to former spouse and/or to children of previous relationship.
• Details of children's maintenance *received* from former partner.
• Copies of all court orders or maintenance agreements.
• Details of any regular provision to or from someone else (e.g. deeds of covenant from grandparents.)

New partner's finances
If you and/or your spouse are cohabiting on a long-term basis with someone else and/or have plans to marry, give details of that person's financial circumstances.

Debts
Details of all money owed either individually or jointly.

get quite depressed. There is a gap between what they will have and what they will need that they cannot close. One option is for Karen to go on Income Support and give up her job. Pip would not be there in the evenings to babysit, anyway. If Pip rents a flat somewhere, it would cost him about £45 a week and there is the mortgage to pay, too. Another option is for Karen to work for more than sixteen hours a week and her mother to babysit, which she has agreed to do. This would take her off Income Support and she could go on to Family Credit. They discover that this would produce more income and would not affect either their Housing Benefit or Council Tax benefit.

They choose the latter course because it gives Karen work which she enjoys and makes them both feel that they are able to cope independently. Karen also plans to look for a better job in an office when her daughter, Jenny, goes to the junior school.

Karen's income on Family Credit

family credit	£46.45
children	£23.50
earnings	£55.69
maintenance	£75.00
Child Benefit	£10.80
	£8.80
	£220.24
£15 of maintenance disregarded	£15.00
TOTAL	£235.24 per week

Karen's income on Income Support

Karen	£47.90
children	£16.45
	£16.45
Child Benefit	£10.80
	£8.80
CSA (estimated figure)	£80.00
Lone Parent Benefit	£6.30
TOTAL	£186.70 per week

Although Karen offers Pip a share of the equity in the house, he declines, after taking advice from his solicitor, because he prefers to keep his pension intact and only pay her regularly what he is obliged to by the Child Support Act. In the end they come out with the following balanced arrangements, worded as a Memorandum of Understanding.

Memorandum of Understanding

Without Prejudice and Confidential

We, Karen and Pip Thompson, have reached the following proposals in mediation. We have attempted to balance our mutual interests with what we each need for the future and have tried to put our children's needs first.

We have tried to produce a settlement that is fair, both now and in the future. We intend to divorce after two years' separation. We will part two weeks from the date of this Memorandum of Understanding

We have calculated child support using the formula and these approximate figures were used during mediation but have not yet been verified by the Child Support Agency. We acknowledge that this is our responsibility and not that of the Whichway Family Mediation Service to find out the exact amounts which would be payable.

We intend asking our solicitors for advice on how to turn these proposals into a legally binding document. The Memorandum is without prejudice and does not create a legally binding agreement between us.

Background
We were married on 13 November 1985 and have two children Joe (8 years) and Jenny (6 years).

Health and Education
We plan to share information about the children's health and school progress and Karen undertakes to keep Pip regularly informed, including his being able to go with her to school meetings with their class teachers. Karen will tell him when they have any illnesses other than ordinary colds.

Gifts
We will co-operate over birthday and Christmas gifts as we always have.

Income
Karen has been earning £42.14 a week from part-time work in a public house. By the completion of mediation this has been increased by adding Saturday evening shifts to £55.69 per week (see documentation attached). Pip works as a mechanic and earns £903.49 per month.

Child Support

Karen has applied for Family Credit and this triggered an automatic application to the Child Support Agency. It is expected that Pip's allowable housing costs will be negligible as he has decided to move into his parents' home. His maintenance for the children is estimated to be about £80 per week, using the DSS booklet. (As Pip's parents live about 13 miles away, this figure may be reduced if his travel costs are allowed.)

Until the Family Credit application and child support have been processed, Pip will pay £75 per week by direct debit into Karen's account with Barclays Bank.

The Family Home

The former home, at 4, Cedar Avenue, Wilbarston, has been valued at £45,000 (based on a professional assessment which we both accept as a similar house in the same Avenue has just sold for £43,750). This is subject to a mortgage of £30,400, resulting in equity of £14,600.

It is our aim to have the house made over to Karen's sole name and for her to be responsible for the mortgage. Karen's parents, who own a property, are willing to stand as guarantors for the mortgage. Pip would have no further interest in the equity of the house. This will be balanced by Pip's pension.

We have agreed that we will return to mediation when the divorce goes through and when Pip moves back to his parents.

Overall Divisions of Assets

These are to be divided as follows:

	Karen	*Pip*
House	14,600	
Bank	547	
Sharesave		600
Car		700
Pension		7,638

Pip will retain the sharesave to help towards the cost of a replacement car.

Dated 6 March 1996

By the end of the mediation process, the relationship between them become very much more amicable, partly as a result of Pip feeling reassured that Karen will keep him closely in touch with the children and is not planning to remarry straight away, and partly because he is very relieved that, with her parents' support, she will take over the mortgage so that the children could stay in the home. He is therefore happy for the children to stay with her and they make arrangements for him to see the children regularly.

AN ACTUAL CASE

The following example involves a real couple, Tricia and Mike (not their real names) who first came to mediation to resolve a disagreement about the children and then went on to sort out all their plans in mediation.

Tricia worked as a general practice manager and Mike in a senior administrative post with the Waterbridge Hospital Trust. They had been married for sixteen years and were still living together. They had been for marriage counselling to Relate a year ago. Tricia was sure that the marriage was over, but Mike was not. They had three children: Christopher, aged fourteen, Rebecca, aged eight, and Laura, aged seven. Christopher was very aware of his parents' unhappiness. There was no adultery involved; Tricia had just become very unhappy.

They had been unable to agree on who should care for the children and where they should live and were in some despair when they first met the mediator. Both saw themselves as living with their children, much as Karen and Pip had begun by doing.

Stage 1: Engaging the couple

The mediator saw Tricia and Mike separately for a short session in which she explained mediation and established that they both wanted to use it.

Stage 2: Establishing the agenda – identifying the issues; telling the children

In the very first session they discussed what they should say to the children and when and agreed to do so together. They thought that Christopher's needs were different from the girls' because of his age and understanding. They planned to tell him first on his own. They would then tell the girls.

The grounds for the divorce

They decided that they did not want to fight about the grounds for the divorce and thought that they would wait two years to divorce but would try to settle everything else they could as soon as possible. At present they were living separately in the home; they were sleeping separately and had set aside the dining-room as a living-room for Mike. This had made Christopher very unhappy. The household was sad, they said. They were worried about Christopher's behaviour, which was getting difficult. He was becoming disruptive at school as well as at home. He and Mike were getting into frequent rows. Both Mike and Tricia felt responsible and were clear that they had to sort things out before they got any worse.

Other issues

The mediator discussed All Issues Mediation with them. They were pleased to learn that they could try to settle everything together using solicitors only to advise each of them, not act for them. They were both very afraid that if they did not work things out together they would get into a worse state of disagreement. They said they were anxious to get out of the misery that their lives had become but wanted to achieve an amicable and fair arrangement.

The mediator talked them through and gave them the NFM Information Sheet and Agreement to Mediate. They wanted to sign it straight away, but she advised them to read everything first and think carefully about what they would have to do before they signed. They did however take away the budget forms to begin to collect the information in a form that they could use in mediation. They seemed very relieved to be able to do something practical and together. Mike was especially depressed and was worrying about how the money would go round, something he had always taken as his responsibility.

They both thought that they had been stuck for a long time, hoping that things would improve. They now wanted to shift into action and welcomed guidance and a specific course of action.

Stage 3: Exploring the issues

When the couple returned for the second mediation session, Mike had worked out all of his information on a computer. He felt more energetic now. He had wanted to work out Tricia's details also, but she had been able to say that she intended to do it herself, telling him that she would have to start learning how to manage on her own. This had frustrated Mike, who wanted to sort everything out in one go, but the mediator was able to slow him down and give Tricia space and time to do her share of the work.

The session was spent looking at their income and assets, the mediator transferring what they had written on their sheets on to a flip chart so that they could read the information together. They could then see what information they had not collected and began to identify what documents they needed to bring in to verify what they had said.

They began to feel more confident now that something concrete was being done. The mediator gave them 'homework': to find and bring in the required verification.

They returned for the next session with their estimated expenditure partially worked out. Mike used his computerised version as a basis. They worked out some expenditure items by splitting them between them. The mediator transferred their expenditure prediction totals and income totals on to a flip chart:

	Income (monthly)	Expenditure (monthly)	spare/gap
Tricia	£895.00	£786.27	+£108.73
Mike	£1,248.50	£1,590.00 (adjusted)	−£341.50

Many couples have a worse deficit than Mike. In mediation he adjusted his expenditure needs downwards. The conversation between them in relation to their expenditure was acrimonious at times, but it helped them to envisage the future in practical terms. Inevitably, this stage is often a low point in the process. This is when conflict could well escalate and the mediator needs to keep the momentum going.

Stage 4: Developing options

Some possible ways of working things out began to emerge. With the mediator's help, Mike and Tricia turned their attention to the children's needs, particularly Christopher's, as they were at present. They realised they needed to know more about how he was thinking about the future. Between this session and the next they consulted Christopher and learnt that he was adamant that he wanted to stay in his own room. In the end Mike and Tricia decided that Christopher needed his father very much at the present time. They talked with the girls about how they would view this. They said that as long as they could see Christopher frequently and both homes would belong to all of them, they felt comfortable about Christopher staying with their Dad. Mike wanted to sort out his relationship with him and give him more time. The bond between them was strong and they both thought that Christopher was very disturbed by their own relationship breakdown. They decided that Christopher would live with Mike. They therefore took the unusual step of separating the children because of their unique circumstances, and particular ages, and because they would all live near to each other.

In practical terms, Mike and Tricia's Memorandum of Understanding indicates some of the content of their negotiations. The mediator suggested that they should both go out and see what other accommodation might be available that would suit Tricia and the girls.

By the next session Tricia had found a house that would be suitable for her and the girls. The couple began to work out their budget to see if they could afford to buy this house. Mike and Tricia wanted to split their pension and the only way they could do so at the time was for Tricia to have a share of Mike's pension when it became payable. They were keen to 'earmark' a proportion of Mike's pension fund to implement when Mike retires. They worked out that his pension could accumulate over 25 years and that they had been married for 12 of those years. On that basis, they agreed to split the pension in half (half each) for those years that they were together (12th of its eventual value whatever that was), i.e. half of 12/25, which is 12/50. They were therefore 'earmarking' a proportion for Tricia in the future. In legislation that came into effect in July 1996, after Mike and Tricia divorced, they could have 'earmarked' more easily by working out the proportion based on the current transfer value of the pension. They would ask their solicitors' help to pursue this proposal. The Family Law Act will make it possible to split pensions at the time of divorce (as explained in Part 4) and the Government has said that this should be possible by the year 2000.

Stage 5: Reaching a settlement

The energy released by their joint problem-solving resulted in a marked improvement in Mike and Tricia's states of mind and in their relationship with each other, which got on to a more equal and business-like footing. They said the children were much happier too. Their Memorandum is set out below.

Memorandum of Understanding

Without Prejudice

Tricia and Mike Malone

Introduction

We have been in mediation at the Waterbridge Family Mediation Service. This Memorandum of Understanding summarises the outcome of our mediation. It does not create a legally binding agreement between us. We have both taken legal advice from our solicitors and now intend to ask them to apply to the court for an order based upon this Memorandum.

Throughout the mediation we have tried to balance our own interests while putting the interests of our children first. The outcome is a compromise which has regard to the contributions we have each made over the years but particularly focuses on our needs in the future.

In the course of the mediation, we have established various priorities and objectives. These include being fair to the children above all, devising arrangements which allow us both to be parents to them and facilitating financial independence and security for us both in the future and after our respective retirements.

Background Information

Mike was born on 15.7.46 and Tricia on 31.9.47. We were married on 4.08.78. There are three children of the family, Christopher, born 5.3.81, Rebecca, born 4.2.84 and Laura, born 2.12.85.

Schedule 1 to the Memorandum sets out details of our income and assets, which we accept are accurate and which we used in mediation.

Schedule 2 lists the documents we used in mediation, of which we both have copies.

Schedule 3 shows the division of our capital assets before the mediation and the proposed division as a result of it.

We have agreed to divorce by consent after two years' living apart.

Arrangements for our Children

We have consulted with Christopher, who is 14, over arrangements for his future care. He is attached to his room and home and we feel that he will be most secure if he stays with Mike at 55, Britannia Road. Rebecca and Laura will live principally with Tricia in her new home.

We wish to continue to work together as parents, aiming at sharing child care equally. We feel there should be flexible contact for the children within a framework of staying contact for the girls combined with regular day visits or staying visits if he wishes for Christopher. We aim to meet regularly to talk about the children, probably once a month.

We understand that we can both make wills for proper provision for the children. It is intended that if one of us dies the surviving parent should look after the children.

Our Finances

We have agreed that a broadly equal division of our capital assets would be appropriate. However, Mike recognises that he has a much better pension provision than Tricia and wishes to make arrangements which reflect this. We both understand that legal advice will be needed to secure the payments to be made to Tricia by Mike out of his pension.

The family home, 55, Britannia Road, Suttonby, we agree should be transferred to Mike on payment by him of £30,000 to Tricia. This is to take place by 4th February 1996. Mike is to raise this additional sum on the former matrimonial home. We calculate this to be one half of the equity in that property.

Tricia intends to buy a property for £63,000 with a completion date of 4th February 1996. She will invest £25,000 of the sum received from Mike in the purchase of her new home. The balance of £5,000 will be spent as legal costs and the costs of removals and particularly furnishing the new home.

We estimate the value of the house contents to be about £9,000. We agree that this should be shared equally, i.e. £4,500 each.

Tricia is to receive her share mainly in cash together with agreed items from the house, Mike will make over £2,000 by 4th February 1996 and the rest within a year. We have agreed the enclosed schedule for sharing the items in the house.

Other Capital Assets
We will each keep our own cars. We have two joint accounts with the Nationwide Building Society which we intend to use to cover some of the joint costs incurred in the divorce.

Pension
Neither of us will claim maintenance for ourselves from the other prior to Mike's retirement but:

1 Mike will make arrangements to ensure that Tricia receives 12/50 (1/2x12/25) of any lump sum payable by way of death-in-service benefit.
2 Mike will pay 12/50 of his monthly pension to Tricia by way of maintenance.
   Note This proportion represents a half share each of 12 years' value [their marriage lasted 12 years] of a pension that could potentially accrue over 25 years.
3 Both Tricia and Mike will revise their wills in consultation with each other.

Schedule 1: Financial Information

Income

	Tricia	Mike
Income	£895.00	£1,248.50
Child Benefit and Lone Parent supplement	£134.40	

Capital assets at the beginning of mediation

	Joint	Tricia	Mike
Family home	£85,000		
Mortgage	£25,000		
Balance	£60,000		
Nationwide account	£4,000		
Insurance policy		£4,214	
Nationwide 100 units		£400	
Cars: Peugeot			£4,200
Mini		£2,000	
Pensions		£2,179	£52,000

Schedule 2: Documents used

Pay slips
Building society books
Pension information
House valuation
Surrender value

Schedule 3

Assets after mediation

	Joint	Tricia	Mike
House		£63,000	£85,000
Mortgage		£38,000	£55,000
Balance		£25,000	£30,000
Nationwide account	£4,000		
Insurance policy		£4,214	
Nationwide 100 units		£400	
Cars		£2,000	£4,200
Pensions		£2,179	£52,000
Incomes		£895	£1,248.50

Tricia might well have made the comments that another woman client made after mediation – both had been through a process that made them stronger:

'It gave me peace of mind where I'd been afraid and it freed me to concentrate on the children and on looking after myself. I don't think I'd have been able to deal with it as well as I did if I hadn't gone there.... It's left me free to concentrate on the children, learn to do finances, look after the house and adjust my identity to being a single person and things like that.'

9a INCOME SHEET   *Tricia*

You will need to provide the following information as fully as possible. This is the kind of information courts require as well as being necessary to your mediation. If you are unable to reach agreements, this information will still be needed.

You need to base the income on what you received over the last twelve months (weekly can be multiplied by 4.3 to convert to monthly). You can discuss with the mediator if you would both prefer to use all weekly figures.

1. Salary/Wages (gross) (attach pay slips & most recent P60) £ [   ]

   LESS:

   2. National Insurance £ [   ]

   3. Income Tax £ [   ]

   4. Pension Contributions/Private Plan £ [   ]

   5. Other (e.g. Union Sub., Option Share Schemes) £ [   ]

   TOTAL DEDUCTIONS: £ [   ]

6. **Net income from main employment** *rising this month* £ [895]

7. Part-time employment £ [   ]

8. Bonus/commission (not included in above) £ [   ]

A.2. OTHER INCOME

1. Child Benefit £ [122.12]

2. Family Credit £ [   ]

3. One Parent Benefit £ [   ]

4. Income Support £ [   ]

5. Other State Benefits £ [   ]

6. Child maintenance from former spouse £ [   ]

7. Dividends or Interest Received £ [   ]

8. Income from Property £ [   ]

9. Income from Trusts & Shares and any Pension £ [   ]

10. Other income, e.g. Fees, casual payments, royalties, etc. £ [   ]

    TOTAL: £ [   ]

11. LESS Likely Tax Liability £ [   ]

12. Total Net Monthly Income £ [   ]

13. Total Fringe Benefits (value at) £ [   ]

GRAND TOTAL NET MONTHLY INCOME: £ [1017.12]

9a INCOME SHEET *Mike*

You will need to provide the following information as fully as possible. This is the kind of information courts require as well as being necessary to your mediation. If you are unable to reach agreements, this information will still be needed.

You need to base the income on what you received over the last twelve months (weekly can be multiplied by 4.3 to convert to monthly). You can discuss with the mediator if you would both prefer to use all weekly figures.

1.	Salary/Wages (gross) (attach pay slips & most recent P60)	£	**1,190.00**
	LESS:		
2.	National Insurance £		
3.	Income Tax £		
4.	Pension Contributions/Private Plan £		*worth £52,000*
5.	Other (e.g. Union Sub., Option Share Schemes) £		
	TOTAL DEDUCTIONS:	£	
6.	**Net income from main employment**	£	
7.	Part-time employment	£	
8.	Bonus/commission (not included in above)	£	

A.2. OTHER INCOME

1.	Child Benefit	*Child Allowance*	£	**58.50**
2.	Family Credit		£	
3.	One Parent Benefit		£	
4.	Income Support		£	
5.	Other State Benefits		£	
6.	Child maintenance from former spouse		£	
7.	Dividends or Interest Received		£	
8.	Income from Property		£	
9.	Income from Trusts & Shares and any Pension		£	
10.	Other income, e.g. Fees, casual payments, royalties, etc.		£	
	TOTAL:		£	
11.	LESS Likely Tax Liability £			
12.	Total Net Monthly Income		£	**1248.50**
13.	Total Fringe Benefits (value at)		£	
GRAND TOTAL NET MONTHLY INCOME:			£	

9b MONTHLY EXPENDITURE *Tricia*

Each of you needs to fill in a separate sheet for your future expenditure needs in your own right. If you are not yet separated, fill in the sheet as if you were. The aim is to arrive at a reliable picture of how you could each manage once you are apart.

Try to be realistic, by not over or under estimating your expenses. Most people have to make adjustments to their standard of living when they separate but it is better to make those adjustments when you have all the financial details in front of you.

Any estimates that you make now may well be amended in the course of mediation. Entering figures now does not commit you to that amount; they are starting figures.

To assist you there is a detailed list of the whole range of items most families spend their money on. This can guide you to arrive at the broad figures listed under the headings

1–8, that will be the ones eventually used in the mediation process.

The broad totals you need are as follows:

1.	Accommodation	239.23
2.	Utilities	115.43
3.	Financial commitments	27.00
4.	Transport	55.00
5.	Household expenses	154.36
6.	Personal expenses	25.50
7.	Recreational expenses	24.50
8.	Children's expenses	145.25
		786.27

You will find a schedule below setting out all the things you might need to consider when working out these totals.

Detailed List of Expenditure Items

1 Accommodation *monthly*

Mortgage/rent/service charges	£ 225.61
endowment premiums (collateral policy)	£
building insurance	£ 8.84
contents insurance	£ 4.78
repairs and renewals	£
other	£

2 Utilities

council tax / cty charge	£ 33.10
water/sewerage/rates	£ 7.24
gas	£ 22.00
electricity	£ 25.00
solid fuel/oil/paraffin	£
telephone	£ 19.00
other	£ 9.09

3 Financial Commitments
(list where appropriate)

bank and other loan repayments	£
HP and Finance Houses	£
clubs/mail order catalogues	£

credit and store cards	£
pension contributions	£ 27.00
(not included on the Income Sheet)	
insurance premiums	£
investments or regular savings	£
maintenance to a former spouse	£
legal aid contributions/ solicitor's fees	£
other fees (e.g. re house sale)	£
mediation fees	£
other	£

4 Transport

vehicle repayments	£ 36.00
insurance	£
road tax	£
maintenance and MOT	£
servicing/AA/RAC/breakdown	£
repairs	£
petrol/parking	£ 19.00
public transport	£
savings for replacement	£
other	£

5 Household Expenses

	Super-market	Other
general household items	£	£ 6.00
(including renewals/		32.00
decorations/repairs)		2.00
groceries	£ 107.50	£
fruit/vegetables	£	£
meat/fish	£	£
milk	£	£
pet food	£	£
vet bills, etc.		£
cleaning/gardening		£
dry cleaning/laundry/ shoe repairs		£
TV/video rental/license		£ 6.86
removal costs		£
other		£

6 Personal Expenses

clothes	£
hair	£ 1.00
toiletries/cosmetics	£
newspapers/periodicals	£ 5.00
dental	£
opticians	£
other health expenses	£
tobacco	£ 4.50
alcohol	£
gifts	£ 15.00
charitable giving	£
stationery/postage	£
other	£

7 Recreation

holidays/outings	£ 15.00
sports/hobbies	£ 9.50
cinema/theatre/concerts	£
meals out	£
entertaining	£
video rental	£
other	£

8 Children's Expenses

Childcare:

childminder/nanny	£
nursery/playgroup	£
babysitting /*childcare*	£ 80.00
other	£

Education:

travel to school	£ 9.50
school meals	£
school trip	£
school uniform/ sports gear	£
extra tuition	£
support to students in Further and/or Higher Education	£
other	£

Recreation:

clothes	£ 26.25
shoes	£ 15.00
clubs	£
sports equipment, etc.	£
magazines	£
travel costs	£
gifts	£ 7.50
pocket money	£ 7.00
toiletries/hair products	£
meals/food	£
nappies	£
dry cleaning	£
shoe repairs	£
other	£

Monthly total £786.27

9b MONTHLY EXPENDITURE *Mike*

Each of you needs to fill in a separate sheet for your future expenditure needs in your own right. If you are not yet separated, fill in the sheet as if you were. The aim is to arrive at a reliable picture of how you could each manage once you are apart.

Try to be realistic, by not over or under estimating your expenses. Most people have to make adjustments to their standard of living when they separate but it is better to make those adjustments when you have all the financial details in front of you.

Any estimates that you make now may well be amended in the course of mediation. Entering figures now does not commit you to that amount; they are starting figures.

To assist you there is a detailed list of the whole range of items most families spend their money on. This can guide you to arrive at the broad figures listed under the headings

1–8, that will be the ones eventually used in the mediation process.

The broad totals you need are as follows:

1.	Accommodation	602
2.	Utilities	152
3.	Financial commitments	11
4.	Transport	227
5.	Household expenses	257
6.	Personal expenses	193
7.	Recreational expenses	67
8.	Children's expenses	148
		1590

You will find a schedule below setting out all the things you might need to consider when working out these totals.

Detailed List of Expenditure Items

1 Accommodation

Mortgage/rent/service charges	£	510
endowment premiums		
(collateral policy)	£	70
building insurance	£	14
contents insurance	£	8
repairs and renewals	£	
other	£	

2 Utilities

council tax	£	60
water/sewerage/rates	£	
gas	£	26
electricity	£	22
solid fuel/oil/paraffin	£	25
telephone	£	
other	£	19

3 Financial Commitments

(list where appropriate)

bank and other loan repayments	£
HP and Finance Houses	£
clubs/mail order catalogues	£

credit and store cards	£	
pension contributions	£	
(not included on the Income Sheet)		
insurance premiums	£	
investments or regular savings	£	11
maintenance to a former spouse	£	
legal aid contributions/		
solicitor's fees	£	
other fees (e.g. re house sale)	£	
mediation fees	£	
other	£	

4 Transport

vehicle repayments	£	
insurance	£	
road tax	£	51
maintenance and MOT	£	
servicing/AA/RAC/breakdown	£	
repairs	£	
petrol/parking	£	51
public transport	£	
savings for replacement	£	125
other	£	
		227

5 Household Expenses

	Super-market	Other	
general household items *(including renewals/ decorations/repairs)*	£	£	30
groceries	£	£	
fruit/vegetables	£	£	
meat/fish	£	£	
milk	£	£	
pet food	£ 215	£	
vet bills, etc.		£	
cleaning/gardening		£	
dry cleaning/laundry/ shoe repairs		£	
TV/video rental/license		£	7
removal costs		£	
other		£	5

6 Personal Expenses

clothes	£	30
hair	£	
toiletries/cosmetics	£	4
newspapers/periodicals	£	
dental	£	14
opticians	£	
other health expenses	£	9
tobacco	£	
alcohol	£	60
gifts	£	40
charitable giving	£	
stationery/postage	£	28
other	£	8

7 Recreation

holidays/outings	£	30
sports/hobbies	£	37
cinema/theatre/concerts	£	
meals out	£	
entertaining	£	
video rental	£	
other	£	

8 Children's Expenses

Childcare:

childminder/nanny	£	80
nursery/playgroup	£	
babysitting	£	
other	£	

Education:

travel to school	£	10
school meals	£	
school trip	£	
school uniform/ sports gear	£	
extra tuition	£	
support to students in Further and/or Higher Education	£	
other	£	

Recreation:

clothes	£	53
shoes	£	
clubs	£	
sports equipment, etc.	£	
magazines	£	
travel costs	£	
gifts	£	
pocket money	£	
toiletries/hair products	£	5
meals/food	£	
nappies	£	
dry cleaning	£	
shoe repairs	£	
other	£	

Monthly total £1590

9c ASSETS AND LIABILITIES *Tricia*

State whether owned or leased by husband or wife or jointly. Give date of purchase, purchase price, how financed, how much contributed by each and copy of lease if appropriate.

1 MATRIMONIAL HOME:

Value   *85,000*

Less Mortgage(s)   (1)   *25,000*

                    (2)   _____

Add Endowments (surrender value)   _____

                        Capital Balance: *60,000*

2 OTHER PROPERTIES:

Description:

Value: _____

Less Mortgage: _____

                        Capital Balance: ▬▬▬▬▬

3 BANK ACCOUNTS: (home and abroad)

Bank	Branch	A/c No	Balance	Date
i. *Westminster*		*Tricia's salary in this working account*		
ii.				
iii.				

4 BUILDING SOCIETY A/CS:

B/Soc.	Branch	A/c No	Balance	Date
i. *Nationwide (joint)*				
ii.				

5 SAVINGS A/CS:

Name	A/c No	Balance	Date
i. *Halifax*			
ii.			

6 INVESTMENTS:

(stocks, share option schemes, unit trusts, etc.) as at   (date)

Name	Size of Holding	Value
i. *Invest UK Income Fund* *100 units*		*about £400 (each unit 4p)*
ii.		

Please detail any existing Trusts for which you/your spouse/your children will be beneficiaries:

i. _____

ii. _____

7 LIFE INSURANCES:

	Company	Policy No	Maturity date & value	Surrender value
i.				
ii.				

8 PENSION PLANS/SUPERANNUATION: *intending to go on superannuation scheme*

	Company	Maturity date	Lump sum (£)	Annual pension at (age)	Transfer value of fund (if known)
i.	*Scottish Widows*		*£7–11k*	*60*	
ii.					

9 CARS AND OTHER VEHICLES/CARAVANS/BOATS:

	Description	Outstanding loan	Net value
i.			
ii.			
iii.			

10 VALUABLES (Jewellery, antiques, collections, etc.):

	Description	Market value
i.	*to keep own*	
ii.		

11 OTHER ASSETS (including contents of home, any premium bonds, etc.):

i.	*Post Office*	*£17*
ii.	*To divide contents of house*	

OUTSTANDING DEBTS (if not already included):

12 BANK/FINANCE HOUSES: _____

13 OTHER LOANS: _____

14 HIRE PURCHASE: _____

15 CREDIT/STORE CARDS: _____

16 LEGAL COSTS: _____

17 OTHER (including any court orders or tax liability if self-employed) _____

TOTAL: _____

18 Any expectation of inheritance or of receiving other capital in the next few years (please detail):

9c *ASSETS AND LIABILITIES* *Mike*

State whether owned or leased by husband or wife or jointly. Give date of purchase, purchase price, how financed, how much contributed by each and copy of lease if appropriate.

1 MATRIMONIAL HOME:

Value			*85,000*
Less Mortgage(s)	(1)	*25,000*	
	(2)	_____	
Add Endowments (surrender value)			_____
		Capital Balance:	*60,000*

2 OTHER PROPERTIES:

Description:

Value:　　　　　　　　　　_____

Less Mortgage:　　　　　　_____

　　　　　　　　　　Capital Balance:　_____

3 BANK ACCOUNTS: (home and abroad)

Bank	Branch	A/c No	Balance	Date
i. *Giro*				
ii.				
iii.				

4 BUILDING SOCIETY A/CS:

B/Soc.	Branch	A/c No	Balance	Date
i. *Nationwide (joint)*			*Personal savings*	
ii. *Abbey*			*c.£1,000*	

5 SAVINGS A/CS:

Name		A/c No	Balance	Date
i.			*advance on expenses*	
ii.			*at work £1,085*	

6 INVESTMENTS:

(stocks, share option schemes, unit trusts, etc.) as at　　　　　　　　　(date)

Name	Size of Holding	Value
i.		
ii.		

Please detail any existing Trusts for which you/your spouse/your children will be beneficiaries:

i. _____

ii. _____

7 LIFE INSURANCES:

	Company	Policy No	Maturity date & value	Surrender value
i.				
ii.				

8 PENSION PLANS/SUPERANNUATION:

	Company	Maturity date	Lump sum (£)	Annual pension at (age)	Transfer value of fund (if known)
i.			*52,000*		*see documents*
ii.					

9 CARS AND OTHER VEHICLES/CARAVANS/BOATS:

	Description	Outstanding loan	Net value
i.	*Vauxhall*		*4,500*
ii.	*Honda*		*900*
iii.			

10 VALUABLES (Jewellery, antiques, collections, etc.):

	Description	Market value
i.		
ii.		

11 OTHER ASSETS (including contents of home, any premium bonds, etc.):

i.

ii.   *to divide contents now c.£9,000*

OUTSTANDING DEBTS (if not already included):

12 BANK/FINANCE HOUSES:

13 OTHER LOANS:

14 HIRE PURCHASE:

15 CREDIT/STORE CARDS:

16 LEGAL COSTS:

17 OTHER (including any court orders or tax liability if self-employed)

TOTAL:

18 Any expectation of inheritance or of receiving other capital in the next few years (please detail):

CONSENT ORDERS

The Children Act encourages parents to make their own arrangements. If you do so, your solicitors (and later, the court) can see them and decide that, as a result of such an agreement, no court order is necessary as far as the children are concerned. As explained earlier, the Children Act states that the court will make an order about the children only if the judge thinks that it is in the best interests of the children that an order be made. Most judges, faced with arrangements made by parents, will make no order other than 'a consent order', which is based on the plan put before them. Mediation is a sound way to be sure that the court has reason to be satisfied.

A Memorandum of Understanding in which you have settled all issues, can, after you have received legal advice be drafted by your solicitors into a legally binding document. This will be used by the judge as the basis of a consent order – providing he or she is satisfied, of course.

DOES FAMILY MEDIATION WORK?

Family mediation has been researched several times in the last ten years to see how effective it is. NFM's work from 1985 to 1989 and from 1990 to 1993 was studied by Newcastle University. There were very positive results over-all, with most couples reaching agreement.

A long-term study has just reported on a revisitation of the couples in the 1990–93 sample. Just under half had responded to a questionnaire and the researchers were able to contact more than half of those three years later. This last study concluded that it is *the reaching of agreement* (overall or on children's issues) that creates the best environment for future co-oper-ation between parents.

The specific benefits of All Issues Mediation (like Tricia and Mike's), measured over three years, are set out below.

Benefits of All Issues Mediation after Three Years

Couples are:
- More likely to feel that mediation had helped them to end the marital relationship amicably, reduce conflict, maintain good relationships with their ex-spouses and carry less bitterness and resentment into their post-divorce lives.
- More content with existing child care arrangements and less likely to have disagreement about child contact.
- Less likely to have sought help from outside the family with problems experienced by children.

- Able to reach agreements which had survived the test of time.
- Glad that they had used mediation.

Client Comments

'Mediation helped me not to be flattened by my wife.'

'It helped my ex-partner understand what I was entitled to. It made him realise I was not being unreasonable and therefore helped the general situation.'

'At the worst time of the post separation period my wife and I were able to meet and not scream at one another and I thought that was quite impressive. It didn't come from us, I am sure.'

THE ROLE OF SOLICITORS IN MEDIATION

Some couples use mediation to make arrangements for their children, but use solicitors to sort out their finances. This can work well if the finances do not cause many problems. However, sometimes there are arguments about the house or the money that undermine the agreement the couple might reach about their children. There are therefore advantages in mediating the whole package. If you use mediation for all issues, your solicitor's task is to support you: to advise you before you begin; to answer your personal questions from time to time; to look at what your joint proposals from your own individual point of view, and to draft your proposals into a binding document that the court can then turn into a consent order.

When NFM began to mediate all issues a researcher interviewed the clients and their solicitors. According to this study, the clients found those solicitors helpful who offered them moral support and advice while they went through mediation. This was a new role for solicitors. Mediators cannot advise people individually, so a solicitor is a very important protection.

THE COST OF MEDIATION

The cost of mediation varies, depending on which mediator or Family Mediation Service you choose or is available in your area. NFM Services currently charge about £25 an hour per person for mediating children's arrangements and a sliding scale for mediating all issues, according to people's earnings. The Family Mediators Association have standard fees, of £60 per person, per hour. With the new Family Law Act, legal aid will become available for mediation. At present a solicitor can apply to the Legal Aid Board for a referral for the mediation of children's arrangements and the Family Mediation Service is then paid £23.35 to make a report on the outcome for the solicitor. Mediation is not yet granted full legal aid.

Including an intake interview, children's arrangements usually take about 4–6 hours or one or two longish sessions of two and a half hours. All Issues Mediation takes about six sessions not including intake. Mediation is always likely to be cheaper than separate solicitors as the two people involved sit together working things out directly, instead of two solicitors working separately with separate clients.

Legal advice is needed as well as mediation, particularly for All Issues Mediation, because court orders on finance are irreversible, but mediators have found that clients do not usually need very much advice as the main business is conducted in mediation. The solicitor checks the Memorandum that the couple have produced in mediation, ensures that their client is happy with it from their own individual point of view and then drafts it into a legally binding document for the court to check and approve. If the mediation process does not resolve all matters, the practical work done can be passed on to the next stage – to solicitors, barristers, and the courts – and is never wasted.

═ A FINAL WORD ABOUT COMMUNICATION ═

If you have no children you may not choose to keep in touch with each other but will feel restored if you end on good terms.

If you have children, maintaining regular contact with your ex-spouse will benefit your children. If you cannot yet imagine achieving this, mediation may be able to establish a way of doing so.

The mediation process takes you through the issues step by step. As the future begins to unfold in a practical way, your approach towards your own future goes through a similar transition. Instead of becoming fearful, competitive and distant from each other, as you work together, a way through will gradually open.

One very experienced mediator talks of this *unfolding* characteristic of mediation as its most distinctive and positive feature. Mediators have come to understand that the progression of this process can heal as well as resolve. We trust the process.

14

NEGOTIATION BY SOLICITORS

QUESTIONS ABOUT USING SOLICITORS IN DIVORCE

Do you need a solicitor?

You may consider that you do not need a solicitor. Books are available to help you handle your divorce without help. There are do-it-yourself packs on sale which take you through the procedures step by step. There is a book by Jeremy Rosenblatt called *How to Do your own Divorce* in the same series as this Guide which contains all the divorce forms and a lot of matter-of-fact, helpful guidance. There is also the excellent *Which Guide to Separation and Divorce*, which advises that you may not need if a solicitor if:

> you both agree on the divorce,
> you agree on how to share your property,
> you have no children,
> you do not have much in the way of property,
> you are not in dispute about maintenance or child support.

However, if you are seeking to resolve financial issues, mediators will usually advise you first to seek the advice of a solicitor to ensure that you have not overlooked anything. Many people who do not use a solicitor regret it later.

How do you choose a solicitor?

It is wise to choose a family solicitor who handles a fair amount of divorce. If they belong to the Solicitors Family Law Association, they have a Code of Practice which encourages them to look for agreement and adopt a non-adversarial style.

If you think you would be eligible for legal aid, you will need to choose a solicitor who does legal aid work in family cases. Ask whether the solicitor has a legal aid franchise to do family work. That should be a further guarantee of quality.

Do you qualify for legal aid?

If you qualify for legal aid, the Legal Aid Board can pay any solicitor's fees in the form of a loan which is paid back later out of the proceeds of the financial settlement. There are more details about the Legal Aid system on page 194.

There is a scheme for initial legal advice called the Green Form Scheme (because the forms are green). As things now stand you will be eligible for the Green Form Scheme *for initial advice* if your disposable income has been less than £72 in the last 7 days and if your disposable capital is not more than £1,000 (1996). The income of your spouse is not included but if you have separated and live with a new partner, your partner's income and capital will be included. (For further details, see page 195.)

The following section tells you how solicitors can help you. It outlines the advice they can give you initially and the work they will do if they go on to represent you. This division of work is reflected in the way the legal aid system works.

What initial advice can your solicitor give under the Green Form Scheme?

Under the Green Form Scheme, a solicitor will be able to give you advice about, for example:

- whether you have the grounds for divorce,
- the procedure for getting a divorce,
- drafting the petition or replying to a petition, if one of you starts divorce proceedings,
- what arrangements you might make for your children about where they will live and how they will see the other parent and anything else covered by the Children Act; this can include a small extension to contribute to the costs of a referral to a mediator for sorting out the arrangements for children (the Child Support Agency now deals with financial support for the children and a solicitor cannot give you advice on this under the Green Form Scheme unless there is a legal problem),
- maintenance for you or your spouse and what you might consider doing about the home,
- how to register a charge on your home if only your partner's name is on the deeds (if you are married, this is straightforward; if you are not, you definitely need a solicitor to advise you what you should do)

- whether you should take action and what action you can take if you suspect that your partner could be getting rid of or selling family belongings or possessions,
- whether you should ask banks and building societies to freeze any joint accounts so that no money can be drawn,
- an injunction (if you are being harmed by your partner),
- applying for full legal aid.

What can a solicitor do under the Civil Legal Aid Scheme?

This scheme is available for legal help with applications to the court. The actions your solicitor can take on your behalf include:

spousal maintenance (not child support),
property orders,
lump sum orders,
arrangements for children,
domestic violence.

Your solicitor will apply for legal aid for you. You will need to complete an application form and a statement of your financial circumstances and, if you are working, you will have to verify your earnings by sending in payslips, etc.

The limits are based on your disposable income and assets but are higher than for Green Form advice. Your disposable income is your annual income, net of tax and National Insurance contributions. However, it includes Child Benefit and maintenance. If your disposable income is then less than £2,425, you should be eligible. How disposable income is calculated is set out on page 196.

About 70 per cent of women and about 11 per cent of men get legal aid in the first instance.

Can you use solicitors for some issues and mediation for others?

Many couples use mediation to sort out their arrangements for the children and solicitors to sort out their financial matters. This, as mentioned earlier, can work very well. It works best if the solicitor is a member of the SFLA and understands mediation. It works well if you are not in disagreement about financial issues. It works less well if disagreement regarding your finances undermines the improved communication you achieve regarding your children.

It is still the most usual way of using mediation. However, the mediation of all issues, with the advice and support of solicitors, has received very good approval from those clients who have taken part in research studies in this area.

What can solicitors do if they represent you?

The steps your solicitor would take if you ask them to represent you are the same whether you pay or receive legal aid. You should always ask in advance how much everything will cost, as letters and telephone calls, including when you telephone to ask how things are going, will all be charged to you.

If you are eligible for legal aid, your solicitor will be able to represent you from the date of the Legal Aid Certificate but not before, unless you pay privately.

If you ask a solicitor to represent you, they will help you to:

- apply for legal aid for you, if you are likely to be eligible,
- work out what you want to do,*
- decide whether you have the grounds for divorce, if you are the petitioner,
- begin the proceedings (see page 199),
- sort out what your options are,*
- explain what a court might decide,
- work out what you want to propose to your spouse,
- negotiate with your partner's solicitor by telephoning and writing letters for you,
- check out your partner's responses to your requests (if you are the petitioner),
- check out your partner's requests and advise you how to respond (if you are the respondent),
- track down items that you or your partner may have not fully disclosed and help you understand the documents which are disclosed,*
- prepare your statements (affidavits),
- send all the forms and information to the court,
- go to court for you and/or with you.

* Mediators will also help you jointly with this.

How much do solicitors cost?

Costs vary according to the part of the country. Solicitors in London and the South East usually charge more than in the North. They also vary according to the experience of the solicitor. In some large firms the most experienced solicitor can charge over £250 an hour, whereas a younger colleague may charge £100 an hour. There is no simple answer, as the solicitor has to weigh up the cost of considerable overheads (for storage of documents, for example, not only for attractive offices) and of those times when they cannot charge. Solicitors will usually charge for everything they do, whether it be telephone conversations, correspondence, preparing documents, actual consultations or going to court. If they are partners in the firm they will usually have a target sum that they have to earn.

What if your solicitors take a different approach from one another?

Those solicitors who are members of the Solicitors Family Law Association (SFLA), will know that, if your partner's solicitor is also a member, they will both be helping you to find a settlement.

However, if either of your solicitors is not an SFLA member, they may be inexperienced in family matters and may take a 'get as much as you can' approach. If this is your approach, you probably will not be reading this book! If it is your partner's approach, but not yours, he or she may not agree to mediation (at least at first).

If your solicitor takes his or her cue from you (and they should), i.e. to try for an amicable process and outcome, they may be able to talk to your partner's solicitor and agree a common approach. The other solicitor may be able to explain to your partner the benefit of such an approach, emotionally as well as financially. They then may refer you both for mediation, or negotiate for you, using a settlement-seeking approach.

However, there are times when 'the other side' (as they are typically called) do not co-operate. What do you do? There is no easy answer to this, except to ask your solicitor to negotiate as best they can, seeking a settlement but also guarding and promoting your interests as vigorously as the other solicitor does for your partner.

In the Family Law Act solicitors will have to tell those clients who receive legal aid about the benefits of mediation. If there is no obvious reason why mediation is unsuitable (for example, domestic violence), they will have to refer legal aid clients for an appointment with a mediator to see whether mediation is suitable. This will give a further opportunity to consider the benefit of co-operation. If the clients choose not to use mediation, they will get legal aid for representation. Mediators, as was explained earlier, will always seek to ensure that entry into mediation remains voluntary.

What happens if mediation of finance and property fails?

If you use mediation to sort out all issues and you cannot succeed in reaching agreement, you will not have to start again from scratch with your solicitors. The information you have collected will be available to them. Your solicitors will be able to look at the factual information afresh and work out, in consultation with you,what settlement you might achieve with their help.

In mediation, it is not the *factual* information that is confidential and 'privileged'. It is rather the *discussion* that is private, including any proposals either of you might have made. You cannot be legally bound simply by what you *say* in mediation, and any proposals you might have made in mediation cannot subsequently be used in court against you. Further, any agreements you reach in mediation are not legally binding until you have been separately advised upon them and they have been turned into a legally binding document for the court. If you have not been able to reach agreement, the solicitor will start again, but with the benefit of the work you have done.

For this reason, you do not run a risk, by mediating, of giving your partner an unfair advantage over you if you do not reach agreement.

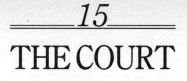

15

THE COURT

COURT HEARINGS

Many people imagine themselves in court being cross-examined by a judge in a wig. This does not happen in family cases, which are called 'private proceedings'.

Most judges nowadays hold 'preliminary hearings' or 'directions hearings' to sort out the issues in the case before a full hearing takes place. They may set a timetable for work to be done. This will happen under the Family Law Act, where matters are expected to be sorted out within a set period of time before the divorce is granted. Judges will often try to avoid a court hearing in order that better ways of settling matters are tried first.

You will be asked to attend a preliminary or directions hearing at the judge's room at the court. The judge will not be robed, but in their ordinary clothes.

Many people find this an anticlimax, as they come expecting some judgement there and then, whereas the judge only looks through the papers to see how far you have got in making arrangements. The judge may then ask you to try mediation or talk to a family court welfare officer, who may suggest mediation, or will ask the family court welfare officer to try to help you by seeing if you are nearly in agreement or can reach agreement while you are there. (In some courts such appointments on the day with a family court welfare officer are called 'conciliation appointments'.)

A subsequent court hearing may be fixed if you cannot resolve the dispute. You would not have to attend if you had been able to resolve matters between the first and second court hearing date. If you had not reached agreement and you were invited to attend the court, the judge again would not be wearing robes, but would be in the court waiting to see you. In this case the judge is most likely to talk only to your solicitors (who would be with you). If you had a barrister, the judge would talk to the barrister. If they talk to you, it will not be in a formal way. They will ask you questions. Most family judges will be very understanding and as helpful as possible while they carry out their duty. They will want to find out all about your children, for example.

_____ FAMILY COURT WELFARE OFFICERS _____

What happens if you cannot agree about plans for your children and need a court's help in deciding arrangements?

First of all, try not to feel guilty that you could not manage to resolve matters. It can be very difficult, especially if one or both partners are still feeling very hurt and angry.

The court is a neutral place where judges can use all their experience and skill to decide what is best for a family. Your views will be listened to very carefully and to make the best possible decisions, judges often ask for reports from a Family Court Welfare Officer.

Family Court Welfare Officers are probation officers specially trained in family work who provide the court with detailed information about each parent's plans for their children and also give as clear an idea as possible about what the children think of the situation. Obviously, all children are different and some will be old enough and confident enough to speak freely to the court welfare officer, whereas others may be too young or feel too confused to give clear views.

Because preparing a welfare report is an important and skilled task, Family Court Welfare Officers are usually given about ten weeks to complete it. They will do their best to get to know you and your children in that time. They may wish to see you and your partner together, separately or both. They will visit your home and may talk to other people who have a contribution to make, like schoolteachers and sometimes grandparents.

One of their main tasks will be to meet with the children. They will have to be impartial and not allow themselves to be influenced by one of you more than the other. They have a lot of experience of separation and divorce and are trained to listen to and understand children, using toys sometimes as well as conversation and questions as ways of getting to know them.

The Family Court Welfare Officer will prepare a report for the judge. It is usually available before the court hearing so that you and your solicitors can see it. There is nothing secret about what is written. The task is to try to help resolve matters in the best interests of the children.

Sometimes courts will ask older children to come to court to talk to the judge, but usually it is easier for the Family Court Welfare Officer to see the children in their own environment, so they act rather like judge's helpers.

The Family Court Welfare Officer will also check out whether, even at a late stage, parents can agree and will help them to do so if this is possible.

Family Court Welfare Officers are very busy and delays in preparing reports are not unusual.

COURT DECISIONS

If you cannot reach agreement about financial issues, the court will decide for you. No one can predict exactly what a judge will do, because it is their responsibility to use their own judgement, armed with the evidence before them. Barristers and your solicitor will give you an idea of the parameters within which the judge will decide but the judge is always free to decide. In other countries there are formulae, but not in the UK.

In some cases concerning children or money, justice demands that there is a full hearing. Sometimes this is to settle difficult financial affairs; at other times it happens because of real concerns about the welfare of children. Family judges are appointed (and trained) to have especial understanding. Occasionally they will want to talk to your children, although more usually they use the Family Court Welfare Officer to carry out this sensitive task.

If your case does go to a full hearing, a barrister may become involved and will be 'briefed' by you and your solicitor. Again, there are barristers who specialise in family work and belong to the Family Law Bar Asssociation. They will stay strong and firm in expressing your concerns and will also be working towards the most fair and amicable outcome for you and your children in the short and long term.

Family Assistance Orders

Sometimes the court will consider that a family needs especial help for a few months after they have been to court because, for example, tensions have been great and the court is concerned about the children. The court will then make a Family Assistance Order. This means that the Family Court Welfare Officer will keep in touch for as long as the order stands in order to be of assistance.

Financial Dispute Resolution (FDR)

There is a scheme being piloted in which some family judges will attempt directly to resolve financial issues *between* you. If you are in one of the areas where this is being tried out, you will be required to fill in forms in which you set out all your income, assets and debts and future requirements. These will be used by judges. This differs from the present method, whereby your two solicitors send to the courts 'affidavits' (statements which include financial information and proposals) in which they each set out the proposals you have either agreed upon (via your solicitors) or on which you are disagreed. These new forms closely resemble the forms that mediators use and which you will have seen earlier.

16

DOMESTIC VIOLENCE

THE RIGHT TO SAFETY

The right of a victim of violence to safety at home is now taken seriously by the police, the courts and the law. For many years, police were called out to people's homes, but sometimes believed that this was 'a domestic' and that they had no right to intervene in a private home. This has now changed and the Family Law Act will further strengthen the protection of victims of domestic violence.

The definition of violence

Violence itself is often thought of only as physical harm, whereas it is now interpreted much more widely. It includes verbal and sexual abuse and the persistent devaluing of a woman. Many women describe emotional and verbal abuse as having an undermining and more far-reaching effect on them than physical abuse, yet they may think they can go for help only if they are physically abused. It is clear, however, that the courts are more likely to act when there is *evidence of physical abuse*.

Women as victims of violence

Many women who become victims of their partner's violence find it hard to leave. There is evidence that they will have experienced the violence many times before they actually seek help. The reasons are not hard to understand. A woman may be frightened that her partner will become more violent if she leaves; she may blame herself for the violence (many, many women do); she may have nowhere to go – she may either not know of Women's Aid refuges or be reluctant to go there, having fears about such places and knowing little about them; she may want to maintain her marriage for the sake of her children and feel that she should not deprive them of their father by leaving him. She may also feel ashamed of the violence, feeling responsible for it or contaminated by it. The effect of years of abuse may be to leave the victim feeling powerless and dependent on the abuser.

The Women's Aid Federation offers:

a safe place,
active help and advice from trained staff,
secrecy (no one will be told where you are and your partner will not be
    admitted; there are also other women there to support you),
trained workers who help with children.

There is a Helpline run by the Women's Aid Federation (0345 023468)

Are you afraid of your partner's violence to you?

If your partner is violent to you (hits you or pushes you around) or subjects you to continual harassment (nuisance telephone calls, following you, using crude or violent language to you), you may be able to go to court to get an injunction.

Injunctions

An injunction is a court order designed to protect you. It can order your partner to move out of the home for a period of time and may also order him (and it is usually 'him') not to touch you again. In some circumstances the police can prosecute for assault.

There are two orders under existing legislation:

a non-molestation order or personal protection order, and
an ouster order or exclusion order

Injunctions can be obtained before divorce proceedings start. Legal aid may be available.

In the Magistrates Courts, the orders are called 'protection' and 'exclusion' orders.

In the County Court, they are called 'non-molestation' and 'ouster' orders.

It is possible to get an order without the other partner knowing of the hearing before it takes place. This is called an *'ex parte'* application. It is quite unusual for a court to exclude a partner if there is an *ex parte* application.

In other orders, i.e. not *ex parte*, a violent partner is told of the hearing date beforehand – at the latest, after the first hearing. No order is effective until it is brought to the personal attention of the person to whom it is directed.

Applications to court are made by means of:

an application, in duplicate,
a sworn affidavit, saying why an injunction is wanted and giving
   details of any children, where the person lives and any alternative
   accommodation available to either of them.

If you are the one on whom the injunction is served you can ask a solicitor
to advise you. You may get legal aid if you are financially eligible, if the
solicitor thinks you have grounds to resist the injunction. The statutory
charge may well apply (see page 194).

If you are the one who applies for the injunction and your partner dis-
obeys it, it is normally you who must apply again to the court for the order
to be enforced. This is done by applying for an order that the wrongdoer be
committed to prison. Judges sometimes send people to prison for contempt
of court. Sometimes the order is suspended to give the man (as it usually is)
a second chance.

As the law now stands, if the court is satisfied that there has been actual
bodily harm and there is a likelihood of more such harm, a power of arrest
may in some circumstances be attached to the order. Such a power enables
the police to arrest the injuncted man if he breaks or is likely to break the
order. Powers of arrest will be able to be granted more frequently when the
new law comes into operation. Women's Aid campaigned successfully for
this power to be made more effective (see below).

MEN AS VICTIMS OF VIOLENCE

There is now much more awareness of the difficulty men may have when
their spouse or partner is violent. They may fear ridicule in bringing this to
anyone's attention, but be fearful and helpless to deal with it without retaliation. Many men, as we have learnt, have an inhibition about retaliating –
though many do not, of course.

There is a Helpline for Men (0181 644 9914).

Are you are afraid of your own violence?

Many abusers of their partners do not wish to accept that they are behaving
in this way. They lose control and may feel, in the heat of the moment,
utterly justified in their responses. A feature of the persistent abuser is to
feel so justified. If this is how you see yourself, you must take action. If you
do not feel justified, but feel ashamed, you may not know how to stop your
behaviour and blame your partner for inciting you, when your partner may
be doing no such thing, but is actually afraid of you.

Seeking help for your loss of control is not easy but there are now schemes to help you if you can begin to take responsibility for your behaviour. One such scheme, based in London, acts on any phone calls from frightened women and intervenes, even if the woman later wishes to drop charges, in order to offer a self-control programme. This also keeps the partner involved by requiring them to report on how the abuser is progressing.

Today's society creates many stresses for young men, especially those who are fathers, that erupt in violence. The stresses do not excuse violence, however. They should be grounds for taking action to prevent it.

There are groups for men who have been violent in addition to the Helpline for Men (see above).

CHILDREN AND VIOLENCE

For some years after violence against adult partners gained public acceptance as a crime, it was not realised that children were themselves at risk. Once the definition of violence is widened, as it is in the Family Law Act 1996, it becomes even more obvious that children are at risk. They will witness their parent's abuse, even if they are not themselves physically hit or threatened. Research has shown how damaged they may be by seeing one parent harming the other.

They will be frightened; they may try to intervene; they will recall the violence frequently and have nightmares about it; they will take on responsibility for protecting the abused parent; sometimes they will ally themselves with the abuser and may even become involved in the violence at the inducement of the abuser. Even very young children will remember the violence years afterwards.

DOMESTIC VIOLENCE UNDER THE FAMILY LAW ACT

There are three new orders under the Family Law Act:

1 An Occupation Order. This will have the potential to grant the abused person the right to stay in the home by virtue of the court having the power to decide who shall live in the matrimonial home. (This will be for a limited period only for a cohabitee.)

2 A Non-Molestation Injunction. This will prevent the other partner from molesting, harassing or bothering the abused person and is similar to the previous orders.

3 An Ouster Order. This order will be able to be made in order to protect
children by removing the violent person rather than the children.

Powers of arrest can be attached to any order to take effect if anyone breaks
the conditions of the order.

The new Act will make it possible for more people to apply for such
orders.

There is also a new provision whereby third parties can bring proceedings on behalf of victims of violence.

The Act gives almost as many rights to cohabitees or former cohabitees
as to married persons, but MPs decided in the end that cohabitants might
not always have exactly the same rights as married people. The Act therefore includes a clause saying that the court should take into account that
cohabitants have not given each other the commitment involved in marriage. This might apply when making an occupation order, or when imposing obligations, for example, to repair and maintain the property or to pay
rent or mortgage payments.

Northern Ireland

Northern Ireland may introduce the domestic violence sections of the new
Family Law Act but make less distinction between those who are married
or unmarried in terms of the occupation rights of the woman to the home
after she has become a victim of violence.

17

LIVING IN THE FUTURE

NEW FAMILIES

Separation and divorce lead to new family shapes. There is a bewildering range of possible shapes and you and your children are likely to find yourselves involved in at least one of them.

You could be:

- single again,
- single again, living with your children,
- single again, not with your children, who visit or stay with you,
- living with someone new,
- living with someone new, with your children,
- living with someone new, without your children, who visit or stay,
- living with someone new, with your children and without their children, who visit or stay,
- living with someone new, without your children, who visit or stay, and with their children,
- living with someone new, without your children and without their children, who all visit or stay,
- living with someone new, with your children and with their children.

Your children could be:

- living with you, on your own,
- living with you, and someone else,
- living with you, and someone else, and their children,
- living with you, and someone else, and visiting or staying with their other parent,
- living with you, and someone else, without their children, but who visit or stay,
- living with their other parent, and visiting or staying with you,
- living with their other parent, with their children ,
- living with their other parent, without their children, who visit or stay.

There are even more possibilities if there has been more than one prior parental relationship for any of the four adults. It may seem that on the one extreme there is solitude and on the other, complexity. Furthermore, none of these households may stay as they are for ever. There may be a period of change every so often.

Being separated parents

There are therefore at least three broad ways of being separated parents: having the children almost always with one parent; the other parent seeing the children by arrangement; the children spending an almost equal or flexible time in each home. The age of the children will affect these three broad pictures, their lives taking on their own individual patterns as they grow up.

You will need energy, flexibility and optimism to cope with life after separation and divorce, whether you are in a complex or a small household. Sometimes it will feel like a muddle; at others, so organised that it is difficult to make any spontaneous moves. There may seem to be more consultation between you and your ex-partner than when you were together, although when you were together you may not have noticed how much you checked plans with each other. Or, depending on your style, you may not have needed to talk much about plans before, if it was understood who did what, and now you will have to check more often because of the other's 'need to know'.

Although it is about death, not divorce, the story of one very busy professional medical consultant may be relevant. After his wife died, he opened a file on each child. He had no idea about all the things his children did and used his characteristic way of sorting out matters, to both the despair and amusement of his children.

Whether you are alone, alone with your children or in a complex new household, tiredness may seem more of a problem than before. New living arrangements are usually more tiring than old habits and routines because they have to be thought about and talked about. Tiredness and any lack of health will affect the amount of energy you can bring to the overloads that were mentioned at the very beginning of the book:

- responsibility overload,
- task overload,
- emotional overload.

Words

The experiences of being on your own with your children and on your own without them can be widely and deeply different. The difficulty we have with naming the roles points to the difficulty we have with managing the experience. The Child Support Act coined the terms 'parent with care' and 'absent parent'. These dramatically, and probably unintentionally, capture the negative aspects of both experiences. 'Parent with care' does not sound like the rich experience it can be, but rather has shades of the careworn. 'Absent parent' summons up the gaps in a separated family, but not the thrill of a child or a visiting parent of being together. They are totally negative words.

Other words seem either worse or certainly no better. 'Lone parent' reminds one of the Lone Ranger; 'non-residential parent' implies that you live in a non-residential area; 'visiting parent' sounds as if you have a suitcase. The only thing we have to be thankful for is the banishing of 'custodial' and 'non-custodial' for parents, terms with such criminal overtones. 'Single again parents' may be better, but may be hurtful to those who did not choose to be single. The 'again' also sounds like a backward rather than a forward move. 'On your own with children' is 'not so much a title, more a way of life'.

__ PARENTS ALONE WITH THEIR CHILDREN __

Robert Weiss wrote that 'children grow up a little faster' when they live with parents who are on their own. Some might say that parents grow a little older faster in these circumstances. The numbers of mothers and fathers on their own with children are set out below. They give a glimpse of the hard work life can be on your own with children, whether you are man or woman. (Most of the facts in this part of the book are drawn from factsheets published by the Family Policy Studies Centre, 231, Baker St, London NW1 6XE.)

One-parent Families

About 22 per cent of all families with children have only one resident parent.

90 per cent of parents on their own with children are women.

75 per cent of men living on their own with children have jobs.

50 per cent of women alone with children have jobs, but are less likely to work part-time than married women.

It is the more highly qualified lone mother who works.

The organisation the National Council for One Parent Families publishes many books, some of which are free to lone parents. They also have an information telephone line (see page 219) and can put people in touch with local groups. Gingerbread, Mothers Apart from their Children and Families Need Fathers also offer help of this kind.

___ WOMEN ON THEIR OWN WITH CHILDREN ___

Women's employment

Compared with twenty other countries studied, the UK has the lowest proportion of lone mothers in employment and the lowest proportion working full time.

The following figures are from a study by Jonathon Bradshaw and colleagues at the Social Policy Research Unit at the University of York published in May 1996.

Employment of Lone Mothers (1996 information)

- The proportion of lone mothers in employment has been decreasing.
- Over a period when the employment of married women has been increasing, the proportion of lone mothers in employment has been decreasing.
- There is a sharp increase in housing costs for a lone mother in coming off Income Support. Health and education costs also increase (such as losing free school meals).

Women's earnings

If a lone mother needs to purchase child care, net in-work income is only likely to exceed Income Support if the lone mother's earnings are very high. This is not the case in other countries.

In the UK the net disposable income of a working lone mother (earning half the national average earnings and with one seven-year-old child, for example) are comparatively high, but this does not include the high costs of child care.

Child care costs for women

Out of all the factors studied, the key factor affecting lone mothers' employment in the UK is the very high level of child care costs. The UK has very little subsidised child care.

Schooling does not cover the period of a working day, so mothers have to pay the full market costs of child care outside school hours if they work full time.

In the UK, lone mothers pay an average of £346 per month for a childminder. In other countries this cost is much lower. There is also no statutory leave provision for UK mothers with sick children.

Tax and benefits

The proportion of lone mothers' earnings taken in direct taxation in the UK is in the middle of the range of other countries and there is no difference in the tax they and married mothers pay.

Generally speaking, the plight of women on their own with children has caused concern since the 1970s because of the poverty with which they are so often associated. More recently they have received hostility and criticism from some of the 'pro-family' groups.

____ MEN ON THEIR OWN WITH CHILDREN ____

There is much less known about the 10 per cent of families headed by a lone father. More men than women in this situation work. They tend to be older and to have older children. They seem to be on higher incomes.

Employment of Lone Fathers (1989 figures)

47 per cent of lone fathers *avoid* income support (compared with 15 per cent of mothers)
6 out of 10 lone fathers are in employment.
4 out of 10 work full time.
6 per cent work part-time
8 per cent are self-employed.

They are likely to rely on informal sources of support and to feel, and be seen as, untypical and rather curious. They may be viewed as remarkable for attempting something unusual. The ancestral voices can be heard very strongly in such a household, as men may well be getting more praise and help than women if they are on their own with children.

On the other hand, lone fathers may well feel out of place in the supporting facilities in the community for one-parent families, which are principally used by women. They may feel odd in playgroups and playgrounds, for example.

The income of lone mothers and fathers is compared below. It is clear that they are generally worse off than married couples with children, whether first families or step-families.

Income of Lone Parents (1989)

Average disposable income for lone fathers is £109 per week.
Average disposable income for lone mothers is £88 per week.
Lone fathers' income is lower than that of all men.
Average gross earnings for lone fathers is £162.30, compared with £239.70 for all men's earnings.

SUPPORTIVE FAMILIES

Having gained some insight into the practical difficulties of managing on your own with children, it has probably occurred to you that your main support is likely to be family and friends.

You will manage best if you can acquire:

practical support from friends and family,
enough money,
the co-operation of the other parent and his/her family,
health and energy,
some life for yourself.

If you have none of these, you may struggle. If you have them all, you can do well and so can your children. Research studies indicate that your well-being is a very important factor in how your children fare.

The art of not living with your children

The 'popping-in by her ex' envisaged by Karen in the imaginary family rarely works in practice. Planning is required. Visiting has to respect the new life of both partners. Neither can expect to intrude upon the other parent's new life without warning, nor (usually) upon children's new lives as they increasingly create their own routines. This can feel very excluding until you can 'gather up your differences and throw them in the air', able to put your old life and previous family form behind you. Dealing with the new situation is a priority if you are all to re-establish health and energy. This will also depend crucially upon the level of co-operation maintained with the other parent.

PARENTS NOT LIVING WITH THEIR CHILDREN

Fathers after Divorce

Although it is not only mothers who care for their children full time, there has been more information from research about the ways fathers keep in touch with their children after separation and divorce when they are not living with them. Research was carried out by Newcastle University into a group of 91 fathers no longer living with their children. Some had experienced divorce as long ago as 1985. The researchers (Simpson, McCarthy and Walker) said that even six years afterwards it was not easy for many of these men to talk about their experiences, because it was so painful not to be living with their children any more. The fathers interviewed seemed to fall into the following broad groupings:

no contact – fathers who said they had either lost contact or had contact only rarely,

parallel – fathers who saw their children but had no communication with their ex-spouse,

communicative – fathers whose contact with their children was accompanied by talking to their ex-wives.

In this particular study, 27 per cent had 'no contact', 46 per cent were 'parallel', and 27 per cent were 'communicative'. The researchers pointed out that fathers can move from one group to another. A man may start off with no contact with his children, progress to being a parallel parent and later on become a communicative parent. Of course, the progress can be the other way around. In the past many fathers have lost touch with their children.

One father came into mediation determined to keep in contact with his son because his father had left him when he was a child (at the same age his son was now) and had not kept in touch. He wept in the mediation session whilst explaining to his wife why keeping in touch was so important to him and to his children. He had made contact with his father when he became an adult and regretted the years in which he had longed for but not known his father.

Becoming 'a new kind of father', as one researcher described the transition, depended on the kind of father they had been able to be before separation. Some fathers said that contact caused them to come face to face with their children in an unfamiliar way. The very word 'unfamiliar' evokes the sense of not being within the family any more. Before, perhaps, they had been seen or seen themselves as 'the head of the family' and now did not know how to see themselves. For some it was a 'double whammy', as they were coping not only with the loss of their close partner, but without the familiar help of their ex-partner to manage the experience.

Research has shown that men characteristically describe their partners as the only ones in whom they confide. Some women describe how they had to help their ex-partners to find new ways of relating to their children. Some fathers say they have a closer relationship with their children than ever before, when they were caught up in the busyness of family life.

The fathers with no contact reported more disagreements with their ex-partners than those who had contact. These disagreements were over contact, unsurprisingly, but also about health, religious upbringing and education. The researchers supposed that this reflected how helpless they may have felt about influencing such matters. Communicative fathers reported fewest disagreements.

For most fathers, contact decreased over time. Those who were un-employed lost touch more quickly. The researchers surmised that this may have been a combination of the sheer expense of keeping in touch and a loss of self-esteem. Men were also more likely to keep in touch with sons than with daughters, especially if their families consisted of all girls or all boys. The quotation from the musical *Carousel* was thought by the researchers to have some truth: 'You can have fun with a son but you've got to be a father to a girl.'

Mothers Apart from their Children

Very little is known about the daily lives of mothers whose children do not live with them. Mediators' experience, gained in family mediation, shows that such mothers suffer great personal pain, often of a physical nature. The strained bond of attachment can even result in the loss of menstrual periods.

These mothers also feel that they have little public sympathy, even though they may have given up their children to their ex-spouses because it was the only thing they felt they could do.

One young mother had a very chequered life as a child and later mar-ried her social worker. When her children arrived she experienced great stress in the marriage and believed that her husband could care for her daughters better than she could. He was distraught that she had ended the relationship. He cared for the children willingly and with approbation from everyone for doing so. However, the mother's and her children's distress at their separation from each other went overlooked and unacknowledged. In mediation, the parents negotiated contact. It was arranged regularly and a gap of several months between this mother and her children was painfully and joyfully closed.

───────────── STEPFAMILIES ─────────────

What is a Stepfamily?

According to the National Stepfamily Association, the word 'stepfamily' entered the *New Shorter Oxford English Dictionary* in 1995. The prefix *steop* comes from Old English, meaning 'orphan'. Therefore a step-parent meant one who had become the parent of an orphan. The prefix spread to other words and gradually the meaning has widened. The latest definition, drawn from those who telephone Stepfamily Helpline, is as follows:

A Definition of a Stepfamily

A stepfamily is created when someone who is already a parent forms a relationship with a new partner who then becomes a step-parent to the children. In some stepfamilies both partners have children who then become stepbrothers and sisters. They may not all live in the same household but some with the other birth parent, creating both a full-time and a part-time stepfamily household. All the children who have connections with a parent and step-parent belong to a stepfamily and the structure may include two sets of parents if both parents have formed new partnerships. A stepfamily also exists when the children are adults even if they were adults when the stepfamily was created by a parent's new marriage or partnership. (Batchelor, Dimmock and Smith, 1994)

How many stepfamilies are there?

The General Household Survey (Haskey, 1994) found that just over 1 million dependent children (one in twelve) were living in stepfamilies in 1991. These families contained three times as many stepfathers and stepmothers and were larger than families with only birth parents. The estimates for the future are given below.

Numbers of Children in Stepfamilies

By their sixteenth birthday,

Five children in every 100 can expect to become stepchildren in married couple families.

Seven in every 100 can expect to become stepchildren in cohabiting families.

The numbers of lone parents living alone or cohabiting are given below.

Lone and Cohabiting Parents after Divorce

Women (49 per cent) are more likely than men (11 per cent) to be lone parents.

Divorced men are more likely to be cohabiting (37 per cent) or living alone (42 per cent).

Women are less likely to be cohabiting (25 per cent) or living alone (14 per cent).

How to live in a stepfamily

There are now some very good books describing the nature of stepfamily life and how to cope positively with it. They are listed at the end of this book. The most internationally famous is by two Americans, Emily and John Visher. In 1982, they wrote a book called *How to Win as a Stepfamily*.

UK writers followed, led by Jacqueline Burgoyne, who tragically died before seeing the effects of her pioneering work in changing UK attitudes to stepfamilies from negative to positive.

Jacqueline Burgoyne's research concluded that the happiest stepfamilies were those who did not try to be anything else. They could not be like 'an ordinary family', but they could make a good job of being what they were. Another writer, Donna Smith, writes:

> There is no instant love and loyalty. Rather, for a new step-parent there is unbearable confusion and ambiguity. Every person needs care, nurturing, a sense of belonging and identity. Stepfamilies work when everyone in the family has these needs met.

The Vishers have some very simply expressed perceptions about stepfamily life. A diagram of two overlapping circles with the children in the overlap graphically portrays their experience. They focus on the *different* things: age groups of children in a stepfamily, either concentrated in a narrow age band or spread out over several ages; sexual sensitivities arising from living in close proximity to others of all ages (adult, child and teenager), who are virtual strangers initially; grandparents who 'feel that their family tree is beginning to bear unfamiliar fruit'. They write about grandparents having the capacity to build either bridges or walls. They draw attention sympathetically to the conflict that results when there is more than one adult to each conventional role, i.e. four men and women operating in parental roles where the common expectation is that there should be two.

Adoptions

The greatest number of applications for adoption come from step-parents, yet the majority of step-parents do not want to adopt.

A step-parent can acquire parental responsibility for a child of their spouse by agreement of the birth parents or by an order of the court. This does not remove parental responsibility from the other birth parent. Many families prefer this to adoption.

STAGES OF STEPFAMILY LIFE

Many writers, most of them having had personal experience of stepfamily life, have helped society to recognise the particular characteristics of living in a stepfamily. The National Stepfamily Association and its longest serving chief executive, Erica De'Ath, have helped to put stepfamilies on the

Phase	Emotional process of transition of couple	Second-order changes required in family status to proceed developmentally
New beginnings	Recognition of myths and phantasies about stepfamilies	Recognition of need for co-parenting while resolving emotional divorce Recognition that parent–child bond precedes that of remarriage
Efforts at assimilation	Allowing time and space for stepparent and step-children to develop their own relationships	Recognition of grief, jealousy and loyalty conflicts from loss of original intact family system
Awareness	Reaffirming generational and household boundaries	Recognition of key position and authority of biological parent Recognition of remarriage and place of stepparent
Restructuring	Mobilisation and airing of difficulties	Acceptance by re-formed extended family that changes are necessary for stepfamily to become functional
Action	Beginning to work together	The creation of new rules, rituals and boundaries which are achieved through renegotiations throughout re-formed extended family network
Integrating	Achieving contact and intimacy in stepfamily	The stepparent achieves a unique role which does not compete or usurp roles of biological parents, is accepted throughout the re-formed extended family network and sanctioned by rest of stepfamily, especially the spouse Roles include generational boundaries between stepparent and children
Resolution Becoming a binuclear family	Holding on and letting go	Reliquishing the last hopes of living like a nuclear family Accepting interrupted parenting and family life Ability to negotiate family rituals and changes of access and custody

From *Family transformation through divorce and remarriage*, Margaret Robinson (Routledge, 1991).

political agenda. They regularly raise questions about child support and stepfamilies, for example. They also offer help to people going through the experience via a well-used and well-organised telephone helpline.

There is now much better understanding of the fact that a stepfamily does not instantly work. Like any new family, it goes through stages that help it progressively to cope with all the tasks to be carried out by a modern family. The trouble is that a stepfamily has to go through them rather fast. The problems of overload (responsibility, task and emotional), can seem very stark at times because of the sheer complexity of putting together people with different needs and expectations who are all experiencing change at the same time in different ways.

These stages have been identified and put in chart form by Margaret Robinson, author of *Family transformation through divorce and remarriage* (Routledge, 1991).

Stages of Stepfamily Life
by Margaret Robinson

New beginnings
Efforts at assimilation
Awareness
Restructuring
Action
Integrating
Resolution – becoming a bi-nuclear family

MEDIATION AND STEPFAMILIES

Mediation can help to keep the channels open between households in which one or both have become stepfamilies. In one family, a mother was planning to marry her new partner, whom her daughter greatly liked. This couple applied to adopt the daughter. No one associated this step with the events that then took place. A teacher was approached by the daughter, who accused her mother of hitting her. The school reported the accusation as possible child abuse. It emerged that there had indeed been a series of bitter arguments, leading to blows, that revolved around the daughter staying out late and 'changing her character', as her mother put it. Only gradually did the family realise that the daughter's behaviour was associated with the application for adoption. This had awoken a strong wish in the daughter to reconnect with her birth father, with whom the family had lost contact.

In mediation, contact was negotiated so that the girl could meet her father again on a regular basis. He said he had withdrawn because he thought it best to do so. The adoption move was dropped and, when he had seen his ex-spouse again and discovered what had been happening, the birth father gave his permission for the stepfather to have parental responsibility. The family settled down again.

The relationship of the outside parent to the stepfamily is one that calls for great generosity. It is easier if the parents are able to be co-operative, as the study of visiting fathers shows. The adults hold the key to maintaining peaceful relationships between the two households. If they are not peaceful, it is the children caught in that overlapping circle who hate it so much.

In another family in mediation, two parents had a very bad relationship. They sent notes to each other which the children, especially the older boy, had to deliver. On one occasion he shut himself in the bathroom so that he could not be given another note. During mediation, the parents asked the mediator to consult the children on their behalf to find out what they could do to make life easier. The boy and his sister asked the mediator simply to ask their parents to keep them out of the squabbles and to stop writing notes.

This family revealed another anxiety of some stepchildren: who they look like. In this family, the daughter was very fair, like her father, whereas her mother and stepfather were very dark. On the way out of the mediator's door she said, 'Do you think my hair will grow any darker?'

Whatever family form you and your children live in, it is important to realise that it is not the family form that makes the difference, but how well people's needs within that family are met.

… it is not the family form that makes the difference, but how well people's needs within that family are met.

POSTSCRIPT:
CHILDHOOD INTO THE FUTURE

The researchers Martin Richards and Jane Elliott finished one of their articles by reminding people to look ahead to see how society's concern about separation and divorce should not be limited to the immediate crises:

> In developing policies and institutions to cope with divorce we are pre-occupied with the immediate and the short term. It is the behaviour of children at or around the time of separation which may be used to determine future plans for their care. But there are few indications that the kind and extent of immediate upset have any connection with the longer

term outcomes which we have discussed here. We must raise our eyes to the horizon and consider decisionmaking on divorce from a perspective which stretches into the adulthood of children.

After managing the immediate crises with their experiences in mind, there are two things you can give your children: planning for their futures and loving permission to keep their relationship strong with the other parent. As one mother in mediation said to a researcher:

'We have managed the next best thing to remaining married for the kids' sake.'

PART 3

Reference
Section

18

FINANCIAL CONSIDERATIONS

A husband was in court for deserting his wife. The judge said, 'I award your wife £1,000 a month.' 'That is very generous of your honour,' said the husband. 'I'll try to give her a few quid myself as well.' (A pre-Child Support Agency cracker joke.)

When you start to sort out your financial plans for the future, everything goes into the melting-pot. You will need to weigh up two basic aspects of your lives – your income and your assets (and debts) – in order to work out how they will be divided between you for the benefit of yourselves and your children in the future.

It is a truism that two can live as cheaply as one. Living with children involves much more expense than adding a few extra mouths to feed. Costs grow as the family grows; then separation and divorce create even greater costs. Anyone contemplating separation or divorce must recognise that it is an expensive business. It is the first thing that many divorced parents will tell you. They may refer to legal costs, but they will also talk about the sheer hard work of establishing two households instead of one and funding two life-styles on the same income they had when they were in one household.

Many separated families resort to claiming benefit for the first time in their lives. Poverty may be new to them.

_____ THE COST OF BRINGING UP CHILDREN _____

In a study by the Child Poverty Action Group published in 1994, an attempt was made to draw up a minimum essential budget for children. Groups of parents drew up budgets for children in four age groups, allocating expenses into the 'essential', 'desirable' and 'luxury' categories. They were recommended to refer to Article 27 of the United Nations Convention on the Rights of the Child, to which Britain is a signatory: 'The right of every child to a standard of living adequate for the child's physical, mental, spiritual, moral and social development.'

These costings date from March 1994 and would need to be updated. The most expensive age was between two and five, the totals exceeding the cheapest age (six to ten) by £5 a week and not significantly differing from the older ages (eleven to sixteen). The way the estimates were reached is set out below.

The Cost of Bringing Up Children, 1994

For a child aged 2–5

Food	£9.36 (younger, £6.85 and older, £10.11)
Clothes	
girl	£7.13
boy	£8.65
Equipment	£3.13
Activities	£7.53
Furniture	£0.54
Laundry	£0.86
Toiletries	
girl	£2.18
boy	£2.18
Total	
girl	**£30.73**
boy	**£32.25**

(These costs include pushchairs, car seats, etc.)

(Source: *Poverty: The Facts*, Child Poverty Action Group 1994. Revised 1996.)

These are similar to figures produced a year earlier (1993) by the Family Budget Unit at York University, funded by the Joseph Rowntree Trust. They used two estimates: the costs of an eleven-year-old child in a 'low cost' budget, which was also about £30 a week. However, they also calculated that in a family with 'a modest but adequate budget', the cost of an eleven-year-old was £60 a week.

The Child Poverty Action Group estimates were compared, at the time, with what was granted for children in families who were on benefit. There was a significant shortfall (see below).

Shortfall on Income Support

Children aged 2–5

Income support for boy or girl, plus family premium	£20.68
Shortfall for a girl	£10.05
Shortfall for a boy	£11.57

Not surprisingly, parents not on Income Support spend more on their children than those who are.

In yet another study, average weekly expenditure of all families with two children, was compared with expenditure by families on benefit:

Families on Benefit Compared with Others

The average family spent:

more than 50 per cent more on food,
four times more on alcohol,
five times more on clothing and footwear,
six times more on services and durable goods,
seven times more on transport,

than a family on benefit.

(From *Family Fortunes,* by Jo Roll, Family Policy Studies Centre, 1988.)

These figures give good reasons why the parent living with the children should try to manage without applying for Income Support. Not only will you find it hard to manage, but also you will tend to get stuck in 'the poverty trap'. It is better for both of you to keep earning if possible, even allowing for the fact that this produces another problem: that of child care. Ways of avoiding having recourse to benefit are explored in the section on mediation, where you will see how one couple coped without Income Support.

Working out your own costs for the future

By looking at the expenditure sheets used by NFM mediators (see pages 134–41), you will able to compare your future costs and the costs of your children with the average costs given above.

There are couples who, faced with the mathematics of divorce, have drawn back and carried on their marriage.

Mediation helps you to work out costs together. For parents, the logic of this is that in the short and longer term, the welfare of your children is affected by your income. Their standard of living is something for which you both share responsibility. If you each start thinking that 'she' or 'he' is exploiting you, or that 'he' or 'she' doesn't understand how much it really costs to bring up children, before long, you will stop sharing responsibility and shift it from one to the other.

THE CHILD SUPPORT ACT

Its origins

In the 1980s, magistrates' courts were clogged up with legal actions taken by the Department of Social Security to get fathers to pay the maintenance the court had ordered. It often still went unpaid and not infrequently the father would end up with a prison sentence for not paying it, which benefited the children not at all!

Sometimes the father simply could not pay. Sometimes he argued that he would pay only in exchange for more contact with his children. Good solicitors and magistrates would urge that contact and maintenance should not be so linked, but they often were in the parents' eyes, regardless of the sound argument that contact was for the sake of the child and not a bargaining point for parents in a fight over money. It was a battlefield – which, again, was of no help to the children.

Poverty came almost to be accepted as the fate of separated families, usually women on their own with children.

Then a shift in policy occurred. It became politically acceptable to argue that fathers had a responsibility that continued after separation or divorce. The Children Act shift of thinking (from the rights of parents to the responsibilities of parents) transferred over to financial settlements.

The child support formula

The concept of a statutory formula was gleaned from other countries (Australia and the USA). In January 1990, Mrs Thatcher launched the drive against 'absent parents'.

The formula devised is complex and tries to deal with, for example, the loss of earning power of the parent with whom the children live. New terms were devised: 'absent parent' or 'parent with care'. This antagonised many fathers who did not wish to be 'absent'. Worries were raised in the House of Commons when the Child Support Bill went through its parliamentary stages, but they were not enough to stop its progress, which was assured, it has been said, by an alliance between 'right wing ministers and left-of-centre feminists' (as described in an article by Nick Cohen, in the *Independent* in 1993). The Bill became an Act in 1993.

The Child Support Agency

A new agency was set up to administer the formula, which was to be universally applied – first to those on income support and then, staged over a number of years, to all couples who separated or divorced. The courts would no longer have the power to set levels of maintenance for children.

The intention was that the formula would apply even when settlements had already been made by the courts (by balancing a level of maintenance against a share in the family home). For example, a man might well have been relieved by the courts of realistic maintenance payments for the children if his wife took a larger share of the house instead. This type of arrangement, whereby everything was sorted out once and for all, was called 'a clean break settlement'.

When the CSA got into action, the shock was enormous. Most people will remember the furore and the tragedies reported, when men were faced with bills that they neither understood nor could pay. It is not difficult to understand, in the light of the examples of average costs given above, that many underestimated how much children cost to bring up.

In the past, courts had often been criticised for the wide diversity in amounts awarded, but judges ordering a settlement would have tried to take each individual situation into account. They had often calculated the costs of a child using the rate of foster-parent allowances. In North Yorkshire, the Family Budget Unit found that these rates matched those of the 'modest but adequate' budget. The CSA formula had no such flexibility.

Not only was the formula perceived to be problematic, but its means of collection were also seen to be so. The CSA had a mighty job to perform quickly. As Nick Cohen wrote:

Consultants hired to set up the computer systems at the Child Support Agency's headquarters were among the first to realise that the confused and often bitter experiences of millions of divorced and separated people could not be straightened out by a government imposed equation.

How the formula is worked out

In 1996 efforts were made to adapt the formula to take account, for example, of the costs of second families and of the costs of contact arrangements.

The formula as it applies to you is calculated on a CSA computer by CSA staff. Information is entered from forms completed by both parents (available from all post offices). The formula takes both incomes into account and essential expenditure. Ability to pay is calculated by looking at the income available to both parents after they have met their everyday expenses. The formula is worked out in stages, as set out below.

CSA Formula

Stage 1
The Maintenance Requirement: the basic day-to-day costs of supporting children.

Stage 2
Net Income and Exempt Income

Net income comprises all sources of income available to the parent.

Exempt income represents the income which the parent keeps for their own personal expenses. It will also include allowances for any other children for whom the parent is responsible.

It is calculated as the amount of Income Support personal allowance for a single person aged 25 years of age.

Stage 3
Assessable Income

This is the income available to each parent after allowance is made for net income for day-to-day expenditure. It will be calculated in the same way for both parents, in two stages, i.e. net income received less 'exempt expenditure'. Net income less exempt income equals assessable income.

Stage 4
Additional Element

Where the total assessable income exceeds what is needed to pay the maintenance requirement, the formula provides for an additional amount of maintenance to be calculated and levied.

Stage 5
Protected Level of Income

Protected income provides that an 'absent parent' will retain enough income after paying maintenance to meet their day-to-day needs and that of any second family. An adjustment is made to ensure this when the 'absent parent's' disposable income would otherwise fall below the protected level.

Stage 6
Actual Maintenance

This will be the assessable income (the deduction in Stage 3 and Stage 4 if appropriate) less the protected income.

Minimum Payment

Except where a person is in an exempt (zero-rated) category, every 'absent parent' will be required to pay a minimum amount of maintenance. This will be set at 5 per cent of the amount of the Income Support personal allowance for someone aged 25 or over.

Do you have to pay attention to the CSA?

You may wish to ignore the CSA, especially as it has been widely reported that the CSA makes errors. Up to 1995 these took place in more than 50 per cent of cases. The Agency has since set targets for the degree of accuracy to be achieved. In 1996, 98 per cent of payments were reported to be accurate. They also had managed to deliver payments within ten days, which was a marked improvement.

Unless one of you is on Income Support, when the application of the formula is compulsory, it is still possible to settle matters yourselves co-operatively rather than have the formula applied.

This may not go on for ever, because the intention is eventually to apply the formula in every case. As the CSA has had such difficulty in reaching its targets, the original timetable has been suspended.

However, even if you do not use the CSA formula now, you should work out what it might be in order to assure yourselves that, in any balancing you do as part of any agreement you reach via mediation or via your solicitors, you are properly estimating what the formula would be likely to be if it were applied at any time in the future.

Your solicitor may work this out for you, or you can apply to the CSA to work it out even though they are not to levy it. The Citizens' Advice Bureau would also be able to work it out for you…or you can try to work it out yourselves.

Family mediators and the CSA

Family mediators always advise parents to find out the likely CSA calculation in order to weigh that in the negotiating and balancing act that contributes to a mediated agreement.

Solicitors and the CSA

Solicitors also advise people to work out the CSA figure as a guide – and will often work it out themselves – when they advise or represent parents during a divorce.

Warning

However, no one should assume that their calculation of the CSA figure is correct. The CSA calculation is the only one that can be viewed as official. A 'ball-park' figure is all that anyone else can arrive at.

Cohabitation, stepfamilies and the CSA

Under the changes introduced into the CSA in 1995, if you are living with a new partner whose children therefore live with you, an allowance can be made for their housing costs.

Spousal maintenance

This used to be called 'alimony'. Nowadays, you cannot be sure that any court would impose spousal maintenance, as the assumption is usually that a separated person can earn and not need 'a meal ticket for life'. The courts adopt what is called a 'needs and resources' approach, which means that they look at each situation on its merits. In relation to tax, there are no longer ways of getting around tax by maintenance arrangements as there once were.

However, you may arrange in your own agreement that it is fair for one of you to continue to support the other – at least over a period of time – if that parent stays at home to care for the children, depending on their ages and your circumstances. In marriages that have lasted a long time, it may be very unfair to expect an older woman to begin work if she never has, or not for many years; in this case maintenance might well be expected and perceived to be fair.

The CSA originally said that it would take over the collection and enforcement of forms of maintenance other than child support (such as spousal maintenance) if child support maintenance is in payment. However, the timetable for this measure has also slipped.

Maintenance for a spouse does have an effect upon means-tested welfare benefits. For example, each pound of maintenance for an adult partner means that Income Support goes down by a pound. Maintenance for a spouse does not affect benefits that are not means-tested, like Child Benefit, for example.

Cohabitation and remarriage

You might ask, can the means of a cohabitee be weighed in the balance when a married couple divorce? There is no obligation for a cohabitee to disclose their income. The court can order a cohabitee to attend court as a witness, but has no obligation to do so.

The law imposes no obligation upon a cohabitee to support their partner's children. However, the law does take into account the extent to which a cohabitee's income reduces their partner's living expenses and thus increases disposable income for maintenance to a former spouse.

PENSIONS

A pension is an asset. It is often worth as much as any house you own. It should not be disregarded and courts now view pensions and associated lump-sum payments as capital and income available for redistribution by agreement or by order of a court.

However, until the whole of the Family Law Act is implemented, the court cannot split a pension. Formerly, the pension holder believed that the pension was due to him or her (usually him) alone for having worked. Nowadays, however, pensions are viewed as joint assets, as the benefit was accrued in the marriage even though only one partner may have been working outside the home. The other is viewed as having given up their right to a pension by working at home.

State pensions

State pensions will have no direct effect on any negotiations to settle financial matters. There is no capital value and so there is nothing to redistribute and no loss by either partner. However, the wife can rely on her husband's contribution record during the marriage to entitle her to a pension in her own right. Once the marriage is over, she is responsible for her own pension contributions. If she is approaching 60, there can be advantages in deferring the divorce until after her sixtieth birthday.

Occupational and private pensions

Common benefits of a pensions scheme are:

a capital sum payable on retirement,
a pension paid to the pensioner after retirement,
a widow's pension payable on death or retirement (the non-pensioned partner is usually a widow rather than a widower),
a lump sum to be paid on death prior to retirement,
a pension for the widow (usually) on retirement.

The above are usual benefits of a pension scheme, showing what a non-pensioned partner stands to lose. Many women, particularly if experiencing divorce later in life, find themselves with no pensions and no prospect of any widow's pension other than from the State. Many older women bitterly begrudge their ex-husband living comfortably off a pension earned during the marriage, to which they, as an ex-spouse, are no longer entitled.

Parliament has recently made two major attempts to correct this injustice. It is principally women who have striven to get this injustice tackled by the Government and this was a major issue in the passage of the Family Law Bill. The groups that campaigned included the Philippa Fawcett Society, Fairshares and the Law Society. As a result of such campaigns there are now three ways of dealing with pensions where, before 1996, there was only the one – the first in the following list.

Three ways of dealing with pensions

There are three ways of dealing with pensions. Only two of them are available at the time of writing.

1 Using other assets to compensate the one with no pension or a smaller pension

You will need to ask the pension company to give the pension holder an estimate of the tranfer value of the pension. This should be given annually as of right, but you can apply for the information at other times, in which case you have to pay for this to be calculated.

You then weigh that asset in the balance when you divorce (this is what the imaginary couple, Karen and Pip, proposed).

2 Earmarking

This possibility came into being in July 1996. It means that you can choose whether to act as in (1), above, or wait until the pension is due and then divide it, having agreed, at the time of the divorce, on the percentage that the non-pensioned partner should have, i.e. having earmarked a portion of the pension either as a lump sum or as a regular, periodical payment. The calculation base is the current transfer value of the pension, i.e. what you would have to take out at the time if you wished to begin another pension scheme, for example. (This is similar to what Tricia and Mike proposed.)

The advantages of this course of action are that you then know what the pension is worth after all the life chances have passed by (any unemployment, job changes, illnesses, etc).

The disadvantage is that there is no 'clean break'. You go on being dependent on each other throughout your adult working lives, waiting for the final settlement.

3 Pension-splitting

The Family Law Act 1996 includes a provision to split pensions at the time of divorce. The non-pensioned partner would take their share of the current transfer value in order to put it into their own pension scheme or start a pension scheme.

There are many advantages to this provision, but it is complicated to work out and the Government has to adjust other legislation to a considerable extent before implementing this section of the Act. It will therefore take some time before this is available. A White Paper was published on 26 February 1997.

Occasionally pensions schemes are able to assign some rights to a person other than the pension-scheme member – perhaps a lump sum on retirement – but this is very rare and is not, for example, possible in the case of servicemen's pensions.

Questions to Ask about Pensions

1 When did the pension-holder join the scheme?

2 What do the rules say? (You would have to bring the rules of a pension scheme and any explanatory booklet to a mediation session.)

3 What are the latest benefits? (A copy of the latest benefits statement is sent you annually but you may have to ask for an extra copy at any other time.)

4 What is the current transfer value? The pension fund will send you a statement of this.

5 Is there enough capital available to fund lost benefit for the other spouse?
   If there were enough capital then the money could be invested in the spouse's own scheme or invested to produce a future income in lieu of the pension or used to buy an annuity.

The questions you need to ask if you are working out a compensatory package are set out above. In mediation, this is always done. The information is shared between you so that you can choose together how to deal with any pensions fairly. If your solicitor is acting for you in these matters, they will want to know the answers to the questions, whether it is your pension or your partner's pension. The answers will help you decide what to propose to your partner so that your solicitor can then negotiate with your partner's solicitor to find a solution. If there is no agreement, a court will have to impose a solution.

In some areas a new form of Financial Dispute Resolution is being tried out by the courts on the basis of forms which you would have to fill in. These are similar to the forms NFM uses. If you use mediation and do not reach agreement, the work you have done is taken to the next stage. It is not wasted.

THE FAMILY HOME

Your house may well be your major asset. You may have invested time and money in it. However, the courts will see it primarily as a home, especially if you have children.

Rented property

The question is, who will live in it? This may be easy to decide. However, you need to consider the following:

- If you are to transfer the tenancy from both of you to one spouse or from one spouse to the other, you may need a court order. This is not likely to be necessary if the house is a council or housing association house. It may be necessary if it is a private tenancy.
- If it is a council house, there may be a right to buy at a significant discount. This then becomes an asset and needs careful consideration as you think through how to balance and divide your assets.

Houses on a long lease

This is more common in some parts of the country than others. A lease may have a capital value with a right to buy the freehold. You will need legal advice in these circumstances.

Houses owned by one or both of you

Your House

Options:

- sell the house and divide the proceeds,
- transfer the house outright to one of you (usually to the one caring for the children)
- transfer the house to one of you on condition that the recipient buys out the interest of the other,
- transfer the house with a 'charge back' to the other; this can release money for the partner giving up the house to use at a later stage,
- a combination of the above two options,
- keeping the house in joint names but deferring the sale and division of the proceeds until later (this is often called a Meshev Order in the courts or a Martin Order if the occupier has a right to occupy during his/her lifetime until remarriage).

It is clearly wise to consider all these options carefully – *together,* if you can – as they affect your future lives and the security of your children, both in the home where they will mainly live and the home where they will spend time with the other parent. Mediation will help you to work out your decision together. Your solicitor will also advise you about these options, either alongside mediation or, if they are representing you, by negotiating your proposals with your partner's solicitor.

The value of the house

In deciding what to do about any house you own, you will have to know what the equity is in the house, i.e. what is yours rather than what still belongs to the mortgage company. You will have to arrange for a value to be put on the house that you can both accept as fair. Often two valuations are needed to be sure; take into account how any other similar houses in the road are selling.

Mortgages

Most mortgages are either repayment or endowment mortgages. There is sometimes more than one mortgage. The person whose name is coming off the title deeds will also want their name to come off the mortgage so that they can get another mortgage elsewhere in the future. The lender is likely to agree if the track record is good and there are no arrears and the income of the remaining spouse is sufficient. However the lender may not agree if any of these conditions are not present. These things will have to be checked before you get too far down the line with this option. There are also costs associated with these changes and you will need to sort out who should pay them.

If the mortgage is an endowment mortgage, there will be life policies assigned to the lender. They will have a current surrender value and a projected maturity value if all the premiums are paid over the years. These must also be taken into account as you value and divide your assets.

Homelessness

It is important to understand that if a spouse agrees to the house being sold and hopes to be housed by the local authority, they could find themselves treated as 'intentionally homeless' with no obligation, therefore, on the part of the council to do anything about it.

Warning about Homelessness

There have been instances in which a couple have agreed to sell the house and split the proceeds. This has sometimes left the spouse with the income in the comfortable position of having a deposit for another home and the income to arrange for a new mortgage. But the other spouse may be left with the children and no income, a lump sum of, say £10,000 and no home. She (if it is a woman) will lose her entitlement to Income Support because the capital sum is over the limit that the Department of Social Security disregard. She would also be considered

'intentionally homeless'. This is a disastrous outcome and you should be
very wary of slipping into it. Similarly, if you agree to defer the sale,
you must be sure that each person will have the means to pay for alternative accommodation when the house is sold.

These aspects are considered in mediation, but the mediator is also
likely to advise you to seek legal advice to be sure that you are not
taking any personal risks and slipping into homelessness.

Tax considerations

Legal advice should be sought on whether from the tax point of view it is
better to keep the house in joint names as 'tenants in common' and divide
the assets when it is sold or transfer the house to one of you with a charge-
back which secures the interest of the spouse in the same way as would be
agreed when it was sold.

Receiving a charge-back may make you subject to Capital Gains Tax if
fairly large sums are involved. Capital Gains Tax does not operate if the
house is sold and to the proceeds are divided within three years of your
leaving it, providing that the house was where you lived while you owned it.

If the house is in only one name

There are particular concerns if your house is in only one name. If the
house is not in your name, you may have to protect your interest quickly,
particularly if you are at serious odds with your spouse and do not trust
him or her. You may, as explained earlier, need to register your interest on
a public register, depending on whether or not your home is registered at
the Land Registry. You can ask your bank or building society about this. If
your house is registered, your district Land Registry will advise you how to
register your right of occupation and give you the appropriate forms to
complete and return. HM Land Registry in London (HM Registry, 32 Lin-
coln's Inn Fields, London WC2A 3PH, telephone 0171 405 3488) will tell you
where to go locally. If your house is unregistered, you will have to register
at the Land Charges Department.The fee is £1 per person and the form is
called K2. You can ask a solicitor about this. Lawyers call this 'registering
a class F' because it is registering a class F land charge. This is a strangely
unknown procedure that usually comes to light only at the time of a separation or divorce.

Clean breaks

Courts are under an obligation to consider whether there should be a 'clean
break' as soon after the grant of the decree as the court considers just and

reasonable. You will want to discuss this in mediation and with your solicitor. The seriousness of a clean break is that it is irreversible.

Clean breaks were routine before the CSA because it was learnt, from
experience, that the main alternative (keeping the house and selling it later)
might result in the parent living with the children in the house not being
able to afford to buy alternative housing when the time came. The idea of
keeping the house for the children and selling it later may become more
acceptable again in the light of the CSA. You will want to consider this as
an option.

COHABITATION AND HOUSING

If you are unmarried, the divorce law is not available to you to protect your
property rights. You can only use the ordinary law of property. This is very
limited. The court can only order a sale of the property or sometimes establish a trust. The court has no statutory discretion to deal justly between the
parties. In other words, it does not have to be fair.

There are two ways of jointly owning property:

- As joint tenants – each owner owns all the property in question. If one
  dies, the survivor automatically inherits the property. This is what usually happens to married couples.
- As tenants in common – each owner has a definite share, e.g. 60:40. Each
  owner is free to leave their share by will or under intestacy (i.e. not having
  made a will). This is more flexible but also more complicated and each
  partner should make a will.

If the title deeds state the shares in which an unmarried couple own the
property, this is usually conclusive for the court. If the house is in one
person's sole name, then the situation is difficult for the other, who will have
only a very limited right of occupation unless they can establish an interest
under a trust. It is very important to remember that there is no such thing
in law as a 'common-law' husband or wife. Cohabitees do not acquire rights
by living together.

Cohabitation, domestic violence and rights of occupation

The new Family Law Act will give limited rights of occupation to an
unmarried woman if she has been the victim of domestic violence, but her
rights, though greater than under previous laws, are not as assured as those
of a married woman who has become a victim and needs to stay in the
house to the exclusion of her violent husband.

THE NEED FOR LEGAL ADVICE

You are well advised to weigh up all the factors covered here before making your final arrangements concerning property and lump sums. You must think of the future, even though you will never know precisely what may happen to you or your partner. It is wise to seek legal advice before making any permanent arrangements. It is better to be safe than sorry. Court orders on capital and property are final.

Even though in All Issues Mediation you will look at all these factors, mediators cannot advise you individually. They will therefore expect and advise you to check the implications of the proposals you reach for your own situation, in the present and in the future.

Other assets

When you prepare your information for All Issues Mediation or for your solicitors, you will need to collect the complete range of information about your other assets. Some of the assets under consideration are mentioned below. Everything goes into the melting-pot.

Bank accounts

There are many different kinds of bank account. You will have to identify each type of account. You will have to produce statements for each account, with the account number.

Life insurance

Details of the surrender value can be obtained by writing to the insurance company. They will provide annual details of any bonuses added to a with-profits policy. There is usually a cash surrender value after two to three years.

Share options

A share option is the right the company gives to employees to purchase shares at a fixed or reduced price. Thus, if the price of the share goes up the employee may be able to buy it at the earlier price. If either of you has share options you will have to produce the documents describing the plan.

Profit-sharing schemes

Some companies give a direct share in the company profits as bonuses. This information is also needed in calculating what you have to consider in your financial package.

Debts

It is important to establish the extent of what you owe and work out who will be responsible for each debt. Most bank and finance houses are paid by direct debit or standing order or there may be a payment book with slips that you post each month. The counterfoils will show the outstanding balance. Both of you will have to understand these debts.

If you have worrying debt problems, it is worth contacting the Citizens' Advice Bureau, who provide debt-counselling. Debt can often become a new problem, or a worse problem at the time of separation. Neither partner may know what the other is doing, perhaps for the first time, and so routines slip. Each thinks the other is doing what they usually do, whereas both may change their habits or get out of sequence because of the muddle and trauma. It is always better to seek help than to let matters drift on. A person driven by anger may go on a spending spree out of vengeance or defiance. Unfortunately there is only one melting-pot for the future and such sprees deplete it for everyone concerned, including the children.

Inheritances

If you or your spouse inherit something during your marriage, it is part of the marriage and not yours alone; it will have to go into the melting-pot, as will inheritances that are foreseeable. In practice this only applies where a spouse is almost certain to inherit from an old or gravely ill relative. This can come as a shock if you are not already aware of it. One husband's father died while he and his wife were in mediation and the inheritance went into the pot. He became depressed for a while when he realised that his father's gift to him was not his alone at the very point when his marriage was ending – but that is the law.

Inheritance tax is on the way out, according to what the Chancellor of the Exchequer said in the 1996 Budget, when the value of the inheritance tax threshold was raised to £215,000.

WELFARE BENEFITS

When you are separating or divorcing, it may be an option for one of you to apply for Income Support (this is usually the one with children). There are advantages in this in that you can apply for other benefits, like getting your rent or mortgage paid, free school meals and a right to apply to the social fund for a loan for some special items. There are disadvantages, however, in that the level of Income Support is very low.

You will have to take care that if you get a lump sum (as set out above), you may lose entitlement to Income Support. If your partner falls into arrears in paying maintenance and you get extra Income Support to make up for the shortfall, you may have to pay back the benefit you received in lieu if your partner pays it off later.

There are other benefits that may well leave you better off if you can each manage to work.

Family Credit

On Family Credit you can be better off. You can apply for it if you work for more than sixteen hours a week (1996). If you are in receipt of Family Credit, Housing Benefit, Council Tax Benefit and the first £15 of any maintenance you receive will not be taken into account.

This will of course depend on the age of your children and the work you can do. We saw earlier what Pip and Karen managed to do when Karen increased her working hours to sixteen. To get the maximum effect of Family Credit, you must earn less than £73 a week (1996).

Mortgage and Income Support

If you are paying a mortgage, it will be considered how much of the interest can be paid by Income Support. Income Support will not pay capital repayments or endowment policy premiums.

One-parent Benefit

One-parent Benefit was frozen at £6.30 in the 1996 budget and it was announced that it would not be payable from April 1998 onwards. Until then, it is payable after you have been apart for thirteen weeks, or immediately after you have legally divorced unless you are living with someone else. Existing claimants will continue to receive it but it will begin to disappear after April 1998. The National Council for One Parent Families reckoned that it would leave lone parents £10.75 worse off because of the knock-on effect it would have on other benefits. It would also make it harder for lone parents to work.

Housing Benefit and Council Tax Benefit

You can apply for these if you are on low income and have capital of less than £3,000 (1996). If you have more than this in savings, it will be counted as income (at the rate of £1 per £250), but you can still be eligible for Housing Benefit if you have up to £16,000 in savings.

A chart listing the latest current welfare benefit rates is readily available from the Department of Social Security.

The Melting-pot

All of these financial considerations will go into the melting-pot when you divorce. In the section on All Issues Mediation in Part 2 you will see the forms that NFM Services use to help couples in mediation to collect and share all this information. If you are using a solicitor to negotiate for you, they will need the same information. They will pass it to your partner's solicitor, who will pass your partner's back to you via their solicitor. The courts oversee the extent of the disclosure and the evidence for the facts cited before granting a divorce. There are measures that can be taken against those who conceal financial information.

One advantage of mediation is that you put all the information together and check it there and then with the help of a mediator. You can both see how it all adds up and begin to work out what is fair to each of you and to your children.

19

LEGAL AID

Either of you may be eligible for legal aid, although it is still more usual for women to be eligible (70 per cent of women initially and 11 per cent of men). This is because legal aid is worked out according to your separate incomes. If you are eligible, the Legal Aid Board currently will pay your solicitor an amount for costs and expenses following scrutiny of the solicitor's bill by the Court and the Legal Aid Board. In the future, your costs in mediation will also be paid by the Legal Aid Board, if you are eligible for legal aid.

A loan, not a gift

Legal Aid is not a gift; it is a loan which you will have to pay back by instalments.

THE STATUTORY CHARGE

The Legal Aid Board will also be able to reclaim legal costs from any assets you 'recover or preserve', at the end of the proceedings, particularly from the sale of the house from which you have benefited. This is called 'the statutory charge', i.e. the State's charge on what you have borrowed.

If you have kept or recovered property worth more than £2,500 you will have to repay to the Board, from the excess, the sum they paid to your solicitor. If the retained or recovered property is to be used as a home for you or your dependants, you may be able to postpone repayment to the Board, but interest will be added to the outstanding debt. Until the money is repaid the Board has the benefit of the statutory charge over the property. This works therefore rather like a mortgage. You will be given credit for the money you paid as a contribution and any costs paid by your ex-spouse or ex-partner under a court order.

Cohabitation and the statutory charge

If either person is in receipt of legal aid and the property is sold, the statutory charge applies as for married partners if either person benefits from the sale and can be seen to be able to repay the Legal Aid Board from the proceeds of the sale. But with unmarried couples there is no exemption for up to £2,500 (1996), as is allowed to married partners.

THE GREEN FORM SCHEME

There are two main types of legal aid: the Green Form Scheme (because the form on which you apply is green) and the full Legal Aid Certificate.

The Green Form Scheme is for initial advice and assistance from a solicitor. The scheme entitles you to a certain amount of free legal advice – up to three hours if you start the proceedings and up to two hours if your partner does.

Eligibility for Green Form advice

Eligibility for Green Form assistance is, however, limited. You will be eligible if you are on benefit (Income Support, Family Credit or Disability Allowance) of if you earn a more or less equivalent amount (in 1996, £72 a week). Your capital will also be taken into account – there is a limit as to how much you can have and still be eligible for Green Form advice. This amount is about £1,000, more if you have dependants. The value of your home is *not* counted.

For details about what a solicitor can advise you upon under the Green Form, see pp. 146–7

You are normally entitled to only one Green Form, but you can get an extension if there is good reason, for a mediator to help you make arrangements for the children, for example.

These arrangements will change under the Family Law Act in that solicitors and mediators are likely to have block grants so that they may not have to apply to the Legal Aid Board for every case.

FULL LEGAL AID CERTIFICATE

A full legal aid certificate can only be granted if there is a 'public interest' in resolving issues in your case. This means that there are issues to be resolved that concern, for example, a house that could be sold or children who will be affected. This is called 'the merits test', as getting such an issue sorted out merits public funding. The Legal Aid Board decides and there is usually a wait after your solicitor has sent off your application form.

Eligibility for a full legal aid certificate

If you want your solicitor to *represent* you, i.e. to negotiate on your behalf, and you think you are eligible for legal aid, you will have to apply for civil legal aid. Your solicitor will give you a form to fill in and you have to make a statement of your financial circumstances. This goes to the Legal Aid Board, who decide whether you are eligible.

Means testing

In calculating your disposable income in order to see whether you are eligible for legal aid, the following are deducted:

> employment expenses,
> mortgage or rent,
> council tax,
> any insurance commitments,
> any maintenace you pay to your spouse,
> allowances for dependants (children: £1,384 per adult and between
> £833 and £1,921 per child).

If, after these deductions, your disposable income is less than £2,425, you should be eligible. If it is more than £2,425 but less than £7,187 you will be asked to contribute 1/36th of the excess until the work is finished. If you have more than £7,187, then you will not be eligible.

Your capital and legal aid

In calculating your disposable capital, the following are not counted:

> the value of the house you are living in,
> any other property that either of you is seeking from the other,
> cars, furniture, etc.

If your disposable capital is between £3,000 and £6,750, you will have to contribute the difference over and above £3,000 and the statutory charge will be applied. Allowances may be made for some debts.

There is a duty upon all solicitors (and mediators once they are franchised) to tell you about legal aid and about likely costs.

Legal aid in Northern Ireland

Because it is very difficult for people to conduct their own divorces in Northern Ireland, legal aid is more available and people do not have to go through the merits test – only the means test. Because it is less expensive in Northern Ireland, there has been less concern about the rising cost of divorce there. Mediation is not yet legally aided.

Legal aid in Scotland

Legal aid in Scotland is available for mediation for a trial period.

20

CURRENT LAW

THE LAW IN ENGLAND AND WALES AT PRESENT

According to the existing law, in England and Wales, there is one ground for divorce: the irretrievable breakdown of the marriage. However, people applying for a divorce ('petitioners') have to establish this by proving one of five facts. These are set out below.

Divorce Reform Law 1969

The divorce law that remains in force until 1999, the Divorce Reform Act 1969, is based on the concept of irretrievable breakdown of the marriage to be proved by one of five facts:

adultery – and the petitioner finds it intolerable to live with the respondent,

unreasonable behaviour – the respondent has behaved in such a way that the petitioner cannot reasonably be expected to live with the respondent,

two years' desertion – for a continuous period of at least two years,

two years' separation – for a continuous period preceding the petition with consent of the respondent,

five years' separation – for a continuous period preceding the petition.

How the current law works in practice

Three-quarters of all petitions are based on the first two facts, which are called 'the fault facts', and divorce is granted in most cases within six months. The current 'adversarial' character of divorce is linked to the fact that most petitions, because they are based on the fault facts, have to establish fault in the other party to the satisfaction of a judge, even though it is in only a tiny percentage of cases that a judge actually has to decide who is at fault. This is something judges can scarcely be expected to do, in any case.

Since the early 1980s, it has also been possible to handle your own divorce. You can collect the papers from your nearest county court, fill them in and return them yourselves. Concern about the 'quickie divorce' stems from the introduction of this legislation, which, linked to the fault clauses, is blamed for the speed with which many people have divorced.

THE COURT PROCEDURE
FOR GETTING A DIVORCE

Nine steps

1 The petitioner

Whoever begins the proceedings sends to the court:

1 A petition (Form D8); three copies.
2 A Statement of Arrangements for Children (Form M4); two copies.
3 Marriage certificate.
4 Fee £150 (£20 on Income Support).

Note: If you have lost your marriage certificate, write to:
OPCS General Register Office,
PAS Smedley Hydro,
Trafalgar Road,
Southport PR8 2HH.

2 The respondent

The other spouse receives from the court:

1 A copy of the Petition (Form D8).
2 The Statement of Arrangements for Children for signature and approval.
3 A Notice of Proceedings.
4 An Acknowledgement of Service.

3 Court sends to petitioner:

a Notice of Issue of the petition.

4 Respondent sends to the court:

an Acknowledgement of Service with consent to divorce

5　When the Acknowledgement of Service is returned, the petitioner sends to the court:

　　1　An application for Directions for Trial (Form D84). (This is optional in many district registries.)
　　2　Affidavit of Evidence (Form 7(a–e)).

6　District judge:

　　considers arrangements for children and divorce papers,
　　issues certificate of entitlement to a decree if satisfied, and decides whether the court needs to exercise its powers under the Children Act 1989.

7　The court pronounces Decree Nisi.

8　Petitioner sends to the court, after six weeks:

　　application for Decree Nisi to be made absolute (Form D36).
　　Fee £20.

9　The court sends the Decree Absolute.

Note:　The total court fees (1996) are £170.

Slow down, consider mediation and take legal advice

Mediators will usually recommend that people take at least initial legal advice, to be sure that nothing is overlooked, and suggest that you slow down the process so that you both have a chance to come to terms with what is happening in order to take *equal* control of it. In the past there were many women whose divorce was rushed through without their realising, for example, that they had lost out on pension rights. Women who have joined Fairshares (see page 218) tell powerful stories of how they were disadvantaged for their rest of their lives by swift actions on the part of their partners which they were unable, at the time, to challenge because they did not know that they could. There are also many couples who never discussed the end of their marriage together, with the result that one, perhaps both, subsequently felt that a chapter of their lives ended abruptly, giving them no opportunity to make sense of it together.

THE CHILDREN ACT 1989

(in force since 1991 in England and Wales)

Any divorce law must dovetail into the Children Act, 1989. The ideas behind the Children Act fit well with the new divorce law. They guide the courts and all the professionals you will meet. The Children Act is a good backcloth for mediation even though mediation is not specifically mentioned in the Act.

Family Law in this country and in other European countries has moved in the direction of expecting parents to make their own decisions in a responsible way rather than asking the law and the courts to decide matters for them. Parents are encouraged to exercise their 'parental responsibility' by making their own agreed, practical arrangements for their children. The court therefore makes no court orders for children unless it thinks these are in the children's best interests. The court retains a responsibility to oversee the fairness of parents' decisions and their impact on the welfare of children. This is not easy for the court to do and there is concern about how much the court can or should do, if the parents are agreed. The Family Court Welfare Officer is there to advise the court on the best interests of the child when asked to do so. In some circumstances a Guardian *ad litem* is appointed to represent the child in court.

The judge also has to make sure that there are no undue delays. This does not mean imposing restrictions that deny parents a sensible amount of time to make their own decisions; rather, it prevents courts taking too long to get to hear cases.

The basic approach is that everyone must consider the needs of the child as the paramount factor. 'Parental responsibilities' therefore replace 'parental rights' and parental responsibility continues for each parent after divorce.

Parental responsibility is automatic for parents who were married at the time of the birth of a child. It continues for each parent after divorce.

Unmarried parents

If parents were not married at the time of the birth of a child, parental responsibility is automatic for the mother, but the father can apply to the court to be granted parental responsibility or to be given parental responsibility by the mother. (Forms can be collected from the County Court Office and need to be returned with the signature of the mother and witnessed. This provision has been very little publicised.)

Court orders

If the court considers that it is in the best interests of children to make an
order it can make any of the following orders, called Section 8 orders. These
are:

- Residence orders: 'settling the arrangements to be made as to the person
  with whom the child will live'.
- Contact orders: 'requiring the person with whom the child lives or is to
  live to allow the child to visit or stay with the person named in the order
  or for that person and the child otherwise to have contact with each other'
  (for example, by letter).
- A prohibited steps order: requiring that certain steps cannot be taken by
  a person without the consent of the court.
- A specific issue order: determining a specific question that has arisen
  (e.g. which school a child should attend).

Other people acquiring parental responsibility

A person who is not a parent does not acquire parental responsibility
simply by assuming the physical care of the child. However, if the child is
in anyone's care, this person may do what is reasonable to safeguard or protect the welfare of the child. This would apply, for example, to any new
partner of a child's parent.

Other people will acquire parental responsibility if they have a residence order granted by the court so long as the residence order is in force.
For example, a step-parent can apply for a contact or residence order which
then results in their acquiring parental responsibility.

Grandparents

Grandparents may acquire parental responsibility by way of a residence
order if, for example, a child has lived with them for at least three years or
with permission of the court at any time if it is in the best interests of the
child.

Children

Children can participate in decision-making, but cannot have the final say.
They are persons 'to whom duties are owed rather than objects of welfare
or possessions over whom power is wielded' (an excerpt from *The Mediator's Guide to the Children Act*, written by Marian Roberts, (NFM)).

The court is required to 'ascertain the wishes and feelings of children' in
the light of their age and understanding and to give them 'due considera-

tion' when it makes decisions concerning them. There is a checklist of factors that courts have to consider when making decisions and this is the first
in the list.

Children have a right to approach the court themselves, but must be
given permission to do so. No orders can be made after they reach sixteen
years of age unless there are exceptional circumstances. Older children (six-
teen- and seventeen-year olds) can be treated more as adults.

How children are given a voice in their parents' separation and divorce
is still a matter that the courts are working out and these issues were raised
prominently during the passage of the Family Law Bill. It is possible that,
at some time in the future, there will be a special service of information and
assistance to children in their own right.

Abduction

Where there are no court orders, parents can take a child out of the country
without special consent. If there is a residence order to one parent then the
other cannot do so. If you are worried that your ex-spouse may take the
child away for longer, you can apply for a specific issue order to prevent
this. The court could require the child's passport to be kept by the court.

If you are worried that your child may be removed before you can get to a
court, your solicitor can apply for an emergency order. Your solicitor can also
contact the police, as abduction is a criminal offence under the Child Abduction Act. Your child may already be abroad. About 26 countries have agreed
to work together to notify each other in order to protect children under the
Hague Convention. Reunite (see page 219) or your solicitor will have a list of
which these are; they also include most of the states of Canada and the USA.

Northern Ireland

Divorce law in Northern Ireland is spread over various orders: the Matrimonial Causes Order (NI) 1984, Family Law Miscellaneous Provisions (NI)
Order 1984 and Matrimonial and Family Proceedings Order (NI) 1989.
Unlike England and Wales, all but a very few divorces in Northern Ireland
are handled by solicitors. The 'do-it-yourself quickie divorce' was never
made possible in Northern Ireland, where solicitors have generally recommended the two-year period of separation with consent. Because of this,
Northern Ireland may not be so committed to introducing the divorce sections of the new Family Law Act. The Department of Law Reform in
Northern Ireland has commissioned some research to help it decide whether
or not to do so.

The Children Act came into force in Northern Ireland in 1996, seven
years after it was passed in England and Wales.

Scotland

The Divorce Scotland Act 1976 is based on the same principles as the Divorce Reform Act 1969 in England. Divorce is granted when irretrievable breakdown of marriage is proved by the same five facts. More than 50 per cent of divorces in Scotland where children are involved are sought under the first two fault facts.

The Children (Scotland) Act 1995 established the relationship between parents and children in terms of parental responsibilities. It defines parental responsibilities as the duty of a parent:

- to safeguard and promote the child's health, development and well-being,
- to provide direction and guidance for the child,
- if not living with the child, to maintain direct contact and personal relations with the child,
- to act as the child's legal representative.

This Act presumes that parents will consult the child and each other before making decisions in relation to this child and this duty is not affected by marital breakdown. Children over twelve in Scotland will be asked when their parents apply for a residence or contact order by the court if they wish to express a view.

The orders available to the court are the same as those in the English legislation. Unlike the English law, however, the Act places a *duty* on parents and on courts to have regard to the children's views in making major decisions affecting them.

United Nations Convention on the Rights of the Child

Mediation, which will be at the centre of the new Family Law Act when it comes into force, will be one of the ways best able to help parents to give their children's views due consideration. This brings the UK into line with the United Nations Convention on the Rights of the Child. (The words of this Convention are set out on pp. 109–10.)

European Convention on the Rights of the Child

The European Convention goes further than the United Nations Convention in terms of mediation by referring to it as one way of assisting the fulfilment of the rights of the child during separation and divorce.

21

THE FAMILY LAW ACT 1996

This new law should come into effect by the year 2000. The principles of the the Family Law Act 1996, have already begun to influence the practice of most professionals you are likely to meet.

The new law seeks to establish the irretrievable breakdown of a marriage *by a passage of time*. It makes the assumption that, once one of you has taken the first legal step to divorce, if either or both still want to divorce at the end of a set period of time, you will have had an opportunity to be sure. For those with no children the time is twelve months; if you have children it is eighteen months. There will be a possibility of either lengthening the period (if you have no children) or shortening the period (if you have children) if the court considers this to be justified.

There is a focus on saving your marriage, if you can, and, if you cannot, reducing the bitterness and considering the needs of your children. The principles of the new law are set out in the Introduction (see page 6). The diagram opposite shows how the Act will work.

THE PROCESS OF THE NEW LAW

1 Information

The first formal step is an Information Meeting. The shape of these meetings is not yet determined, but the person initiating the proceedings will be required to attend to learn about how the Act will work and about the services available to them. You will not be required to go with your partner. It may be possible, however, for you to go together if you both wish that. The person who is not initiating the proceedings may have to attend if they are to initiate any legal action themselves.

It is not yet clear who will be giving this information. The best ways of giving information will be tried out in a Government pilot scheme.

Note: People seeking divorce may no longer be called 'petitioner' and 'respondent'. The Law Commission, who originally proposed the changes, thought that the language should be simpler.

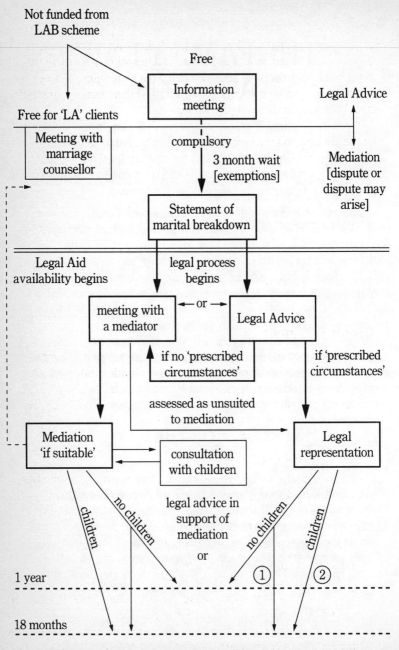

Not funded from
LAB scheme

Free

Information
meeting

Legal Advice

Free for 'LA' clients

Meeting with
marriage
counsellor

compulsory

3 month wait
[exemptions]

Mediation
[dispute or
dispute may
arise]

Statement of
marital breakdown

Legal Aid
availability begins

legal process
begins

meeting with
a mediator   ← or →   Legal Advice

if no 'prescribed
circumstances'

if 'prescribed
circumstances'

assessed as unsuited
to mediation

Mediation
'if suitable'

consultation
with children

Legal
representation

children   no children

legal advice in
support of
mediation

or

no children   children

1 year   ① ②

18 months

1 One year respondent can ask for 6 more months.
2 Can shorten 1 year if injunction for domestic violence or 'significantly
   detrimental' to children.

2 Three months' wait

After receiving information, which will include a pack of information about what is available locally, you will have to wait three months before you take any more legal steps. The intention is that you should reconsider your decision and seek marriage counselling if there is a chance of saving your marriage. A meeting with a marriage counsellor should be free for those eligible for legal aid.

During this time, legal aid will be available for urgent actions. You will be able to go for mediation of issues about arrangements for children under the Children Act or to a solicitor for legal advice; it is to be hoped that legal aid will be available for you to do this even though you cannot yet take any further legal steps to divorce.

3 Statement of marital breakdown

After three months you can make a statement that you believe your marriage has broken down irretrievably. This will have to be sworn and could be made at court. Your partner is then formally informed that you have done this.

4 Choose your route

This is the point at which you choose your route. You or your partner can apply for legal aid for whatever route you decide to take – mediation of all issues; mediation of children only or financial issues only; solicitor representation for all issues or for financial issues only or for children issues only.

5 An intake meeting for mediation

If you go to a solicitor and there is no obvious reason why you should not consider mediation, the solicitor will send you to meet a mediator for an intake meeting to discuss whether mediation is suitable for you both, taking into account all the circumstances.

There will be several routes into mediation:

direct access (before you do anything else),
access after the information meeting,
access from a mediation intake meeting after the statement of marital breakdown, if mediation is suitable,
access from a mediation intake meeting referred by a solicitor,
access from a court referral for an intake meeting, if the court at some point thinks you should consider mediation and you have not yet previously attempted it.

6 *Work during the period of reflection and consideration*

Although the details of what you will have to do during this period have
yet to be worked out, you will be expected to make your arrangements
before the end of the year, or 18 months if you have children. The judge
will probably hold hearings in which they ask for information about
your progress. If you are not resolving matters, they may order an
appointment to consider mediation, refer to a court welfare officer for a
report about the children, or hold a hearing at which they would make
decisions (and perhaps a financial dispute resolution appointment if
they are found to be effective).

7 *Applying for your divorce*

Towards the end of the period you would have to submit, with your
application for a divorce:

> your Memorandum of Understanding (if you have used mediation),
> drafted as a legally binding document, or
> proposals drafted by your solicitors,which would include financial
> proposals and proposals for the children.

If you have not reached agreement, the judge would make a decision,
but they are likely to have learned that you were not agreed via hearings
held during the period. The judge might, on application, consider a
change in the length of the period. They might decide not to grant the
divorce if either applied for the order not to be granted on the grounds
that it would result in substantial hardship for either party or the children and the judge thought this had been established.

8 *Divorce granted*

USEFUL ADDRESSES

THE PROFESSIONALS YOU MAY MEET

A multi-cultural society

We live in a multi-cultural and multi-racial society. Marriage means different things to different people and divorce and separation carry very different meanings and implications for different cultural groups and communities. When choosing a professional to assist you – a mediator, solicitor, barrister or counsellor – you may want to look for someone who is knowledgeable about, and sensitive to, your cultural values. Such resources may still be scarce in some parts of the country.

1 FAMILY MEDIATORS

How will you know that the mediator works to a high standard?

UK College of Family Mediators
PO Box 3067
London WC1H 9SP

The UK College of Family Mediators sets standards for all family mediators, however they operate, whether they work from a specialised Service base (as in NFM and FMSco) or in some other way.

You can find out whether your mediator is a member of the UK College by looking them up in the *UK College Directory of Family Mediators*.

'The UK College of Family Mediators has been established to provide the foundation for mediation services throughout the country. It will set and maintain standards, protect the public and speak with a strong voice for all its members.' (Dame Margaret Booth DBE, Chair of the UK College of Family Mediators, founded 1 January 1996)

National Family Mediation (NFM)
9 Tavistock Place, London WC1H 9SN
Tel 0171 383 5993 Fax 0171 383 5994

National Family Mediation is the longest standing body of family mediators in the UK. It has about 70 local Family Mediation Services in England, Wales and Northern Ireland which specialise in family mediation in separation and divorce. Each local Service is independently and locally managed as a charity; selection, training and accreditation are carried out nationally by NFM. Services work to NFM quality standards, mediators are supervised by trained supervisors and work to the College Code of Practice. Mediators are drawn from a range of relevant disciplines. Many Services work with all issues; all focus upon children's issues and are committed to equal opportunity. There is a full list of Services on page 211.

Family Mediation Scotland (FMSco)

127 Rose Street, South Lane
Edinburgh EH2 4BB
Tel 0131 220 1610 Fax 0131 220 6895

Family Mediation Scotland is very similar to NFM in its organisation and commitments and has twelve Services affiliated to it. FMSco selects, trains and accredits mediators. FMSco also has an educational and a contact centre department. It is a founder member of the UK College. See page 216.

The Family Mediators Association (FMA)

PO Box 2028, Hove
East Sussex BN3 3HU
Tel/Fax 01273 747750

The Family Mediators Association selects, trains and accredits mediators, who usually (but not always) work in pairs made up of a lawyer mediator and a mediator from another professional background. They do not work from a Service base, but are organised in regions. FMA is a founder member of the UK College and adheres to its standards, codes and equal opportunities policies.

The Solicitors Family Law Association (SFLA)

PO Box 302, Orpington, Kent
Tel 01689 850227 Fax 01689 855833

The SFLA is an association of family solicitors who work to achieve fair and amicable divorces. They work to a Code of Practice.

The SFLA now train some of their members to mediate and are developing standards in conjunction with the Law Society and the UK College. A lawyer mediator cannot mediate in a situation where they, or their firm, are advising one of the parties.

The British Association of Lawyer Mediators (BALM)

The Shooting Lodge, Guildford Road
Sutton Green, Guildford
Surrey GU4 7PZ
Tel 01483 235000 Fax 01483 237004

BALM is an association of lawyers who also mediate. They may also mediate in fields other than family law.

Comprehensive Accredited Lawyer Mediators (CALM)

42 Carden Place, Aberdeen AB1 1UP
Tel 01224 621 622 Fax 01224 621 623

CALM is the Scottish equivalent to BALM. They have been established for longer and specialise in family mediation.

Alone in London

3rd Floor, 188 King's Cross Road
London WC1X 9DE
Tel 0171 278 4486 Fax 0171 837 7943

Offers mediation for the homeless young to re-establish family contact.

Post Adoption Centre

5 Torriano Mews, Torriano Avenue
London NW5 2RZ
Tel 0171 284 0555

Offers mediation on contact and other matters in open adoptions.

Mediation UK
82a Gloucester Road, Bishopston
Bristol BS7 8BN
Tel 0171 924 1234

An umbrella body for community
mediation schemes which deal with
community and neighbour disputes.

Irish Family Mediation Service
Irish Life Centre, Lower Abbey Street
Dublin
Tel 00 353 1 872 8277

Offer family mediation.

Mediators Institute Ireland
c/o 13 Royal Terrace West
Dun Laoghaire, Dublin, Ireland
Tel 00 353 1 284 5277
Fax 00 353 1 280 0259

This is the umbrella body for mediators
working in different fields in Ireland.

**National Association of Family
Court Welfare Officers**
Court Welfare Office, East House
9 East Street, Swindon
Wiltshire SN1 5BU

Family Court Welfare Officers are court
officers and work within the framework
of the Children Act specifically to focus
on the interests of the child. They are
professionally trained social workers.
They devise and work to Home Office
standards. Many Probation
Departments assist NFM Services.

Their main activities are to resolve
disputes at court, write welfare reports,
supervise Family Assistance Orders and
talk to children at the request of the
judge. In places they provide Contact
Centres (see Community Help, pp
218–224).

Local addresses will be found from
County Probation Services.

_____ 2 NATIONAL FAMILY MEDIATION _____

Affiliated Services (under regions)

* Asterisked entries offer All Issues Mediation (children, finance and property
issues)

FMS = Family Mediation Service   FCS = Family Conciliation Service

SOUTH EAST (LONDON)

**Barnet, Haringey & Hertsmere,
Family Mediation Service**
267 Ballards Lane, Finchley
London N12 8NR
Tel 0181 343 9899

**Central Middlesex Family
Mediation**
Civic Centre Complex, Station Road
Harrow, Middlesex HA1 2XH
Tel 0181 427 2076

**Divorce Mediation & Counselling
Service**
38 Ebury Street, London SW1W 0LU
Tel 0171 730 2422

Eye to Eye Mediation
231 Camberwell New Road
London SE5 0TH
Tel 0171 701 1114/703 2532

***The Family Mediation Service –
Institute of Family Therapy (IFT)**
24–32 Stephenson Way
London NW1 2HX
Tel 0171 391 9150

*Mediation for Families (East London & City)
74 Great Eastern Street
London EC2A 3JL
Tel 0171 613 1666

*Mediation in Divorce
13 Rosslyn Road East, Twickenham
Middlesex TW1 2AR
Tel 0181 891 6860

Merton Family Links
Mediation Service closed.
Contact Centre open
Tel 0181 543 9691

South-East London FMB
5 Upper Park Road, Bromley
Kent BR1 3HN
Tel 0181 460 4606

Provisionally affiliated

African Caribbean FMS
Suite 85, Eurolink Business Centre
49 Effra Road, Brixton
London SW2 1BZ
Tel 0171 737 2366

SOUTH EAST (HOME COUNTIES)

Berkshire FMS
3rd Floor, 160–163 Friar Street
Reading, Berkshire RG1 1HE
Tel 01734 571 159

Chiltern FMS (Amersham & Watford)
1 King George V Road, Amersham
Bucks HP6 5TT
Tel 01494 732 782 (24-hr answerphone)

*Chilston Mediation & Family Service
The Lodge (Ravensdale)
Pembury Road, Tunbridge Wells
Kent TN2 3QJ
Tel 01892 511 468

Hampshire FMS
Hilsea House, Hilsea Lodge
Gatcombe Drive, Hilsea
Portsmouth PO2 0TX
Tel 01705 660 919

Kent FMS
8 Park Road, Sittingbourne
Kent ME10 1DR
Tel 01795 476 949/01795 429 689

Milton Keynes Family Mediation
City Counselling Centre
320 Saxon Gate West
Central Milton Keynes
Bucks MK9 2ES
Tel 01908 231 293 (24 hr)

*Sussex FMS
Garton House, 22 Stanford Avenue
Brighton, East Sussex BN1 6DD
Tel 01273 550 563

*Surrey FMS
316 High Street, Dorking
Surrey RH4 1QX
Tel 01306 741 777

*Thames Valley FMS
Windsor Magistrates Court
Juvenile Court Entrance, Alma Road
Windsor, Berkshire SL4 3ER
Tel 01753 830 770

EAST

*Cambridge & District FMS
The Family & Divorce Centre
1 Brooklands Avenue
Cambridge CB2 2BB
Tel 01223 576 308

Essex South FMS
29 Harcourt Avenue, Southend on Sea
Essex SS2 6HT
Tel 01702 436 466

Essex West FMS
Sewell House, 349 The Hides, Harlow
Essex CM20 3QY
Tel 01279 426 749

Norfolk FCS
Charing Cross Centre
17–19 St John Maddermarket
Norwich, Norfolk NR2 1DL
Tel 01603 620 588

*Peterborough & District FMS
71 London Road
Peterborough PE2 9BB
Tel 01733 347 353

Suffolk FMS
43 Elm Street, Ipswich
Suffolk IP1 2AP
Tel 01473 225 845
Bury Office: 01284 755142
Lowestoft Office: 01502 501935

MIDLANDS

*Birmingham & District FMS
3 Kingston Row, Birmingham
West Midlands B1 2NU
Tel 0121 233 1999

*Coventry & Warwickshire FMS
Palmer House, Palmer Lane, Coventry
West Midlands CV1 1FN
Tel 01203 258 915; 01203-228814 (24 hr)

Dudley FMS
200 Wolverhampton Street
Dudley DY1 1DZ
Tel 01384 255 440

Herefordshire FMS
Community House, 25 Castle Street
Hereford HR1 2NW
Tel 01432 264087

Northamptonshire FMS
49 York Road, 1st Floor
Northampton NN1 5QJ
Tel 01604 36651

*Oxfordshire FMS
1st Floor, 123 London Road,
Headington, Oxford OX3 9HZ
Tel 01865 741 781 (24 hr)

Stafford Mediation
SDVS Centre, North Walls, Stafford
Staffordshire ST16 3AD
Tel 01785 214 933
(Information line: 01785 56617)

Staffordshire South FMS
33 Park Road, Cannock
Staffordshire WS11 1JN
Tel 01543 572 600

Shropshire Family Mediation
PO Box 571, Telford
Shropshire TF3 2WD
Tel 01952 502 447

Worcestershire FMS
3 Shaw Street, Worcester WR1 3QQ
Tel 01905 610925 (24 hr)

*Provisionally affiliated
(Midlands)*

**North Staffordshire Family
Advisory and Mediation Service**
The Art Centre, Pitfield House
Brampton, Newcastle-under-Lyme
Staffs ST5 0QP
Tel 01782 717 411

Nottinghamshire Children and Families Mediation Service (FAME)
Warren House, Pelham Court
Pelham Road, Nottingham NG5 1AP
Tel 0115 985 8855

NORTH

Bradford and Keighley FMS
The Law Courts, Exchange Square
Drake Street, Bradford BD1 1JA
Tel 01274 732 768

Cheshire Mediation Service
Goss Chambers, Goss Street
Chester CH1 2BG
Tel 01244 400 658

*Cleveland FMS
St. Mary's Centre
82–90 Corporation Road
Middlesbrough, Cleveland TS1 2RW
Tel 01642 222 967

Cumbria FMS
Stricklandgate House
92 Stricklandgate, Kendal LA9 4PU
Tel 01539 733 705

Durham County FMS
Alington House, 4 North Bailey
Durham DH1 3ET
Tel 0191 386 5418

The Family Mediation Service (Greater Manchester)
21 Knowsley Street, Bury
Lancashire BL9 0ST
Tel 0161 797 9910

Family Mediation Service (North-West Yorkshire)
13 Dragon Parade, Harrogate
North Yorks HG1 5BZ
Tel 01423 525 156

Lancashire FMS
15 Victoria Road. Fulwood, Preston
Lancashire PR2 8PS
Tel 01772 787557

Merseyside FMS
5a Swiss Road, Liverpool L6 3AT
Tel 0151 260 9155 (24 hr)

North Derbyshire FMS
NCH Action for Children
32a Newbold Road, Chesterfield
N. Derbyshire S41 7PH
Tel 01246 277 422

*Northumberland and Tyneside FMS
4th Floor, MEA House
Ellison Place, Newcastle-upon-Tyne
Tyne & Wear NE1 8XS
Tel 0191 261 9212

South Yorkshire FMS
14–18 West Bar Green, Sheffield
South Yorks S1 2DA
Tel 0114 275 2227

Sunderland and South Tyneside FMS
4 Toward Road, Sunderland
Tyne & Wear SR1 8DG
Tel 0191 510 9525

West Yorks Family Mediation Council
Oxford Chambers, Oxford Place, Leeds
West Yorks LS1 3AX
(Offices at: Leeds, Wakefied, Kirklees & Calderdale)
Tel 0345 419 403

*York FMS
82 Bootham, York
North Yorkshire YO3 7DF
Tel 01904 646 068

WEST

*Bristol FMS
25 Hobbs Lane, Bristol, Avon BS1 5ED
Tel 0117 929 2002

Dorset FMS
43 Oxford Road, Bournemouth
Dorset BH8 8EY
Tel 01202 314 600 (24 hr)

Exeter and District FMS
49 Polsloe Road, Exeter EX1 2DT
Tel 01392 410 529 (24 hr answerphone)

North Devon FMS
6 Bridge Chambers, Barnstaple
Devon EX31 1HB
Tel 01271 321888

*Salisbury and District FMS
24b St Edmund's Church Street
Salisbury, Wilts SP1 1EF
Tel 01722 332 936 (24 hr)

*Swindon FMS
37a Regent Street, Swindon
Wiltshire SN1 1JL
Tel 01793 527 285

Provisionally affiliated (West)

Plymouth Mediation
St Peter's Centre, 18 Hastings Street
Plymouth PL1 5BA
Tel 01752 671 078

Somerset FMS
The Myrtle Tree, 34 Bridge Street
Taunton, Somerset TA1 1UD
Tel 01823 352013

South Devon FMS
4 East Street, Torquay, Devon TQ2 5SO
Tel 01803 214 242
(Temporarily closed 1996)

WALES

Cardiff FMS
4th Floor, St David's House
West Entrance, Wood Street
Cardiff CF1 1ES
Tel 01222 229 692

Provisionally affiliated (Wales)

Gwent Mediation Service
Ty Asha, 30 Stow Park Avenue
Newport NP9 4FN
Tel 01633 263 065

North Wales Mediation Service
8 Riviere's Avenue, Colwyn Bay
Clwyd LL29 7DP
Tel 01492 533919

NORTHERN IRELAND

Northern Ireland Family Mediation Service
76 Dublin Road, Belfast
Northern Ireland BT2 7HP
Tel 01232 322 914

IRELAND

Family Mediation Ireland
Block 1, Floor 5, Irish Life Centre
Lower Abbey Street, Dublin 1, Eire
Tel 00 353 1 872 8277

Provisionally affiliated but not operational

Thomas Coram Foundation for Children
The Meeting Place
40 Brunswick Square
London WC1N 1AZ

Scarborough and District FMS
Allatt House, West Parade Road
Scarborough
Tel

Mid-Essex FMS
47 Broomfield Road, Chelmsford
Essex CM1 1SY
Tel 01245 258 680

SCOTLAND

Family Mediation Borders
PO Box 13753, Peebles EH45 8ZY
Tel 01721 724170

Family Mediation Central
16 Melville Terrace, Stirling FK8 2NE
Tel 01786 472984

**Dumfries & Galloway Family
Mediation Service**
The Family Centre, 4 Creswell Gardens
Dumfries
Tel 01387 263185

Family Mediation Fife
30 North Street, Glenrothes KY7 5NA
Tel 01592 751095

Family Mediation Grampian
27 Huntly Street, Aberdeen AB1 1TJ
Tel 01224 630050

Family Mediation Highland
62 Academy Street, Inverness IV1 1LP
Tel 01463 712100

Family Mediation Lothian
37 George Street, Edinburgh EH2 2HN
Tel 0131 226 4507

Family Mediation Orkney
43 Junction Road, Kirkwall, Orkney
KW15 1AR
Tel 01856 870571

Family Mediation Tayside
132a Nethergate, Dundee DD1 4ED
Tel 01382 201343

Family Mediation West
1 Melrose Street, Glasgow
Tel 0141 332 2731

Family Mediation Service
63 Titchfield Street, Kilmarnock
Tel 01563 572429

Family Mediation Western Isles
The Bridge Community Centre
Bayhead, Stornoway, Isle of Lewis
Tel 01851 706868

3 LEGAL SERVICES

ENGLAND

The Citizens' Advice Bureaux
keep a list of local family solicitors
and family mediators and of local
services. They also provide advice
(particularly on welfare benefits) and
debt-counselling.

Divorce and Family Courts
Most divorces are handled by district

judges. Applications can be to any
county court or to:

Principal Registry of the Family
Division, Somerset House, The Strand
London WC2R 1LP

The Family Law Bar Association
Secretary, Queen Elizabeth Building
Temple, London EC4Y 9BS
Tel 0171 797 7837

The Law Society
113 Chancery Lane, London WC2
Tel 0171 242 1222

The Law Society governs the
professional standards of solicitors.
They have a complaints bureau for the
public.

The Legal Aid Board
85 Gray's Inn Road, London WC1X 8AA
Tel 0171 813 1000
The Legal Aid Board franchises family
solicitors to provide publicly funded
legal advice and representation.

The Legal Aid Board grants £25.35
for a 'report' by a mediator to a solicitor
on what has or has not been agreed
about children if clients are on the
Green Form Scheme.

When the Family Law Act comes in
there will be legal aid for mediation.

SFLA (see above for address) will
supply lists of solicitor members in
your area.

NORTHERN IRELAND

Belfast Law Centre
Tel 01232 321307

**Probation Headquarters
(Northern Ireland)**
Tel 01232 242935

SCOTLAND

The Citizens' Advice Bureaux
keep a list of local family solicitors and
family mediators and of local services.
They also provide advice (particularly
on welfare benefits) and debt
counselling.

Divorce and Family Courts
Most divorces are handled by the
Sheriff Court. An initial writ should be
lodged in the Sheriff Court which is
nearest to the partner starting the
action.

The Family Law Association
Fordyce & Co, 1 Glenview Place,
Main Street, Alexandria
Tel 01389 759811
This organisation can supply a list of
solicitors who specialise in family law.

The Law Society of Scotland
26 Drumsheugh Gardens
Edinburgh EH8 7YR
Tel 0131 226 7411 Fax 0131 225 2934

The Law Society of Scotland governs
professional standards for solicitors in
Scotland. It can provide a list of
solicitors in any area of Scotland and
information about solicitors' fees.

Scottish Child Law Centre
Cranston House, 108 Argyle Street
Glasgow G2 8BH
Business Line 0141 226 3434
Fax 0141 226 3043
Advice Line (for adults) 0141 226 3737
Freephone (*for under 18s only*)
0800 317 500

Gives free confidential information and
advice on law and policy affecting
children and young people. Free
confidential helpline for under 18s.

The Scottish Legal Aid Board
44 Drumsheugh Gardens
Edinburgh EH8 7SW
Tel 0131 226 7061

The Scottish Legal Aid Board
franchises family solicitors to provide
publicly funded legal advice and
representation.

4 COMMUNITY HELP

There is a wide range of agencies that can help you with family changes in the community. Imaginative schemes have grown as more and more people become aware of the pressures and overload on families. There are groups providing help in marital matters, parenting, direct services to families and to children. Sometimes these are professional services; at others, helplines staffed by trained volunteers, or clubs and courses and information providers.

Special concern for separation and divorce

CONTACT

Network of Access and Child Contact Centres (NACCC)
St Andrew's with Castle Gate United Reform Church, Goldsmith Street
Nottingham NG1 5JT
Tel/Fax 0115 948 4557

Scottish Access and Contact Centre
Development Officer
Family Mediation Scotland
Details as on p. 210.

There are 200 centres which provide places for children to meet parents, usually on Saturdays and Sundays. They have staff on hand, toys and games and resources for preparing food and drink. These can be invaluable for parents who do not live with their children and do not have accommodation that can easily adapt to the needs of children. NACCC publishes a directory of centres and is open to provide information on Mondays, Tuesdays and Wednesdays from 10 am to 3 pm.

Thomas Coram Foundation
40 Brunswick Square
London WC1N 1AZ

This long-established children's charity provides a contact centre (and a mediation service) in Central London.

SUPPORT AND ACTION

Fairshares
14 Park Road, Rugby
Warwickshire CV21 2QH
Tel 01788 570585

A campaigning group concerned with pensions on divorce.

Families need Fathers
Postal address:
BM Families, London WC1N 3XX
Office:
134 Curtain Road, London EC2A 3AR
Tel 0171 613 5060
Tel 0181 886 0970 (Helpline)
Northern Ireland:
Tel 01232 814662

Advice, support and representation for parents (particularly non-resident parents) following separation and divorce. They produce a magazine called *Access*.

Gingerbread
16–17 Clerkenwell Close
London EC1R OAA
Tel 0171 336 8184

A support organisation for lone parents and their families, with over 275 groups in England and Wales. Also publishes advice and information leaflets.

Gingerbread (Scotland)
19 Chester Street, Edinburgh EH3 7RF
Tel 0131 220 1585

Gingerbread (Northern Ireland)
169 University Street, Belfast BT7 1HR
Tel 01232 231417

Harmony
41 Morehampton Road, Donnybrook
Dublin 4 Tel 00 353 1 660 5233
Fax 00 353 1 668 2320

Give support to ethnic minority groups,
and people involved in intercultural
marriages in Ireland. Pressure
government to introduce anti-racist
legislation.

**MATCH (Mothers Apart from
their Children)**
c/o BM Problems, London WC1N 3XX

MATCH, Northern Ireland
Tel 01247 464174

Links together mothers who are living
apart from their children.

**National Council for the Divorced
and Separated**
PO Box 519, Leicester LE2 3ZE
Tel/Fax 0116 2700595

Northern Ireland
Tel 01232 794476 (Billy)

A national network of social clubs for
separated and divorced people.

**National Council for One Parent
Families**
255 Kentish Town Road
London NW5 2LX
Tel 0171 267 1361

This long-established body runs an
information line, produces valuable
literature and publicly represents the
concerns of lone parenthood.

NI Council for Ethnic Minorities
c/o Chinese Welfare Association
17 Eblana Street, Belfast BT7 1LD
Tel 01232 238220

Umbrella organisation representative
of ethnic minority groups and their
support organisations.

One Parent Families Scotland
13 Gayfield Square
Edinburgh EH1 8NX
Tel 0131 556 3899

Reunite
PO Box 4, London WC1X 3DX
Tel 0171 404 8356

Self-help for parents whose children
have been abducted.

Rights of Women
52–54 Featherstone Street
London EC4Y 8RT
Tel 0171 251 6577

Provides free legal advice to women.

**Stepfamily (National Stepfamily
Association)**
Chapel House, 18 Hatton Place
London EC1N 8RU
Tel 0171 209 2460
Tel 0990 168 388 (Helpline)

Stepfamily Scotland
5 Coates Place, Edinburgh EH3 7AA
Tel 0131 225 8005

Stepfamily is a membership body
which provides a range of services,
books and newsletters for adults and
children. Its helpline is very well used.

Counselling services for married and unmarried couples

Accord
Cana House, 56 Lisburn Road,
Belfast BT9 6AF
Tel 01232 233002

CMAC aims to help people initiate, sustain and enrich their marriage and family relationships through its services – marriage counselling, fertility counselling, sexual therapy, marriage preparation courses and educational service.

Asian Family Counselling Service
74 The Avenue, London WC13 8LB
Tel 0181 997 5749

Beginning Experience
Regional Office, c/o St Clements Retreat and Conference Centre
722 Antrim Road, Belfast
Tel 01232 776500

A support group for the separated, divorced and widowed of all denominations.

British Association of Counselling (BAC)
1 Regent Place, Rugby,
Warwickshire CV21 2PJ
Tel 01788 578328

Keep a register of approved counsellors.

Cara Friend
Tel 01504 263120
Tel 01232 322023

Gay and lesbian counselling.

FLAME (Family Life and Marriage Education)
All Saints Vicarage
20 Burcot Lane, Bromsgrove
Worcestershire B60 1AE

Jewish Marriage Council
23 Ravenhurst Avenue
London NW4 4EE
Tel 0181 203 6314 (Advisory service)
Tel 0181 203 6211 (Helpline)
Tel 0345 581999 (Crisis helpline)

London Marriage Guidance Council
76a New Cavendish Street
London W1M 7LB
Tel 0171 580 1087

Marriage Care (formerly Catholic Marriage Guidance)
Clitheroe House 1 Blythe House
Blythe Road London W14 0NW
Tel 0171 371 1341

Marriage Counselling Scotland
105 Hanover Street, Edinburgh EH2 1DJ
Tel 0131 225 5006 Fax 0131 220 0639

Marriage Enrichment
Enquiries to: Churches Together for Families, 27 Tavistock Square
London WC1H 9HH

Money and Relationship Counselling (MARC)
Northern Ireland
Tel 01232 240649

Northern Ireland Mixed Marriage Association
28 Bedford Street, Belfast BT2 7FE
Tel 01232 325835

NIMMA exists for the mutual help and support of people involved in, or about to be in, a mixed marriage. It provides advice and information through a telephone rota system.

Relate
Herbert Gray College
Little Church Street, Rugby CV21 3AP
Tel 01788 573 241 Fax 01788 535 007

Relate (Northern Ireland)
76 Dublin Road, Belfast BT2 7HP
Tel 01232 323454

Samaritans
National helpline: 0345 909090

Samaritans are volunteers who provide their services to those who call who are feeling depressed or suicidal. They offer service of listening to people who are going through a time of crisis. Anything said is in complete confidence between caller and volunteer.

Scottish Catholic Marriage Care
113 Whitehouse Loan
Edinburgh EH9 1BB
Tel 0131 440 2650

Tavistock Institute of Marital Studies
The Tavistock Centre, 120 Belsize Lane
London NW3 6BA

Provides couple and marriage therapy.

Direct services for children involved in separation and divorce

CHILDREN'S COUNSELLING

Family Mediation Scotland
127 Rose Street South Lane
Edinburgh EH2 4BB
Tel 0131 220 1610
Fax 0131 220 6895

Three family mediation services provide counselling and support for children whose parents separate or divorce.

National Family Mediation
9, Tavistock Place, London WC1H 9SN
Tel 0171 383 5993 Fax 0171 383 5994

Some NFM Services provide a counselling or listening service for children who have experienced separation and divorce. Some also work in groups in schools.

Relateen in Northern Ireland
Relate, 76 Dublin Road
Belfast BT2 7HP
Tel 01232 320709

A counselling service for teenagers whose parents separate or divorce. Referrals can come from parents, teenagers or professionals. The range of provision includes one-to-one counselling for teenagers, family counselling with families with younger children and group work for teenagers.

SERVICES FOR CHILDREN

Barnardo's
Tanners Lane, Barkingside, Ilford
Essex IG6 1QG
Tel 0181 550 8822

235 Corstorphine Road
Edinburgh EH12 7AR
Tel 0131 334 9893 Fax 0131 316 4008

Barnardo's is a large nationwide charity with no special focus on separation and divorce, although its focus on all children in need includes a large number of children whose parents are separated or divorced. They provide one mediation project (Chilston).

Children First (RSSPCC)
41 Polwarth Terrace
Edinburgh EH11 1NU
Tel 0131 337 8539

The Children's Society
Edward Rudolf House, Margery Street
London WC1X 0JL
Tel 0171 837 4299

The Children's Society identifies the same areas of work as Barnardo's, although it also becomes involved in moral debates because of its link with the Church. It builds school links re education for parenthood.

NCH Action for Children
85 Highbury Park, London N5 1UD
Tel 0171 226 2033

NCH Scotland
17 Newton Place, Glasgow G3 7PY
Tel 0141 332 4041

NCH Action for Children is very actively concerned about children in separation and divorce. They manage several Family Mediation Services within the NFM and Family Mediation Scotland framework in England, Wales and Scotland. Their Family Mediation Services are very likely also to manage counselling services for children.

NSPCC
67 Saffron Hill, London EC1N 8RS
Tel 0171 825 2500

The NSPCC is also a large organisation and has a preventative and protection focus. It has no specific focus on separation or divorce but provides family centres and advocacy for children, work with survivors of abuse and perpetrators of abuse, helplines, training for listening to children and preparation for parenthood.

Young Minds
102–108 Clerkenwell Road
London EC1M 5SA
Tel 0171 336 8445
Tel 0345 626376 (Helpline)

A telephone service offering advice and information for parents concerned about children or young people.

CHILDREN'S RIGHTS

Groups concerned with the rights of children include:

The Association of Lawyers for Children
c/o Ronald Prior & Co
163–165 Hoe Street, Walthamstow
London E17 3AL
Tel 0181 520 5632

The Children's Rights Development Unit
235 Shaftesbury Avenue
London WC2H 8EL
Tel 0171 240 4449

Children's Legal Centre
University of Essex, Wivenhoe Park
Colchester, Essex CO4 3SQ
Tel 01206 873820 (Helpline)

Gives advice on law and policy affecting children and young people.

IRCHIN (Independent Representation for Children in Need)
1 Downham Road South, Heswall
Wirral, Merseyside L60 5RG
Tel 0151 3427852

Many fifteen- and sixteen-year-olds contact IRCHIN for help on a helpline. IRCHIN works towards a comprehensive information, advice and representation service for children.

The National Children's Bureau
8 Wakley Street, London EC1V 7QE
Tel 0171 843 6000

These groups are concerned that English law should not be in breach of the UN Convention, Article 12, ratified by the UK, or of the European Convention (Strasbourg).

Help for Families and Parents

The following list of organisations that offer help to families is mainly drawn from a report by the Family Policy Studies Centre of work sponsored by the Department of Health. Entitled 'The Parenting Initiative', this project began at the end of the International Year of the Family. They are set out alphabetically here.

Black Fathers
Moyenda Project
National Parenting Development Centre
Exploring Parenthood
4 Ivory Place, 20a Treadgold Street
London W11 4PB
Tel 0171 221 4471

The Moyenda project, run by Exploring Parenthood, runs groups that focus on black fathers and their particular cultural experience.

Child Poverty Action Group
Citizens' Rights Office
4th Floor, 1–5 Bath Street
London EC1V 9PY
Tel 0171 253 3406

They produce valuable information about benefits and poverty in families.

Christian Link Association for Single Parents
6A Millstream Court, Lame BT40 3ER
Tel 01574 272647

Seek to administer to those who feel isolated and damaged by broken relationships and widowhood and who have the responsibility of bringing up their children alone.

Family Helpline
Tel 01574 260206

If you have a problem or need someone to talk to, then telephone the above. Also acts as a contact point and source of information and makes referrals to other organisations.

Family Resource Centre (NHSSB)
2 Westland Road
Cookstown BT80 8BX
Tel 01648 766668

Offers both individual programmes of work and/or group work services which aim to improve the quality of family life.

Family Rights Group
The Print House
18 Ashwin Street
London E8 3DL
Tel 0171 923 2628

They are especially concerned about the rights of children within the family and provide a high quality of information and direct initiatives to help children in care.

Family Service Unit
207 Old Marylebone Road
London NW1 5QP
Tel 0171 402 5175

They operate in some urban areas, offering direct help to families.

Family Welfare Association
501–505 Kingsland Road
London E8 4AU
Tel 0171 254 6251

They publish useful information and offer direct social work help to families. They focus on poverty issues.

Grandparents Federation
Room 3, Moot House, The Stow
Harlow, Essex
Tel 01279 444964 (12 noon–3 pm)

This organisation links grandparents
and provides volunteers to help
children out of care.

Home-start UK
2 Salisbury Road, Leicester LE1 7QR
Tel 0116 233 9955

Home-start UK offers local direct help
to families in their own homes with
managing the overloads of family life.

Home-start Northern Ireland
Tel 01232 668725
Tel 01232 459429

Newpin
Sutherland House, Sutherland Square
Walworth, London SE17 3EE
Tel 0171 703 6326

Offers seminars and groups for fathers.

One Plus One
12 New Burlington Street
London W1X 1FF
Tel 0171 734 2020

They produce research information and
literature to help couples identify early
signs of difficulty.

Parentline
Westbury House, 57 Hart Road
Thundersly, Essex SS7 3PD
Tel 01268 757077 (Parents' helpline)

Provides voluntary help for parents.

Parent Link Scotland
15 Saxe Coburg Street
Edinburgh EH3 5BR
Tel 0131 332 0893

DOMESTIC VIOLENCE

Helpline for Men
0181 644 9914

**Men Against Domestic Violence,
Northern Ireland**
Tel 01232 262400

Northern Ireland Women's Aid
129 University Street, Belfast BT7 1HP
Tel 01232 249041
Tel 01232 666049

Scottish Women's Aid
13/19 North Bank Street, The Mound
Edinburgh EH1 2LP
Tel 0131 2210401

Southall Black Sisters
52 Norwood Road, Southall
London UB2 4DW
Tel 0181 571 9595

Counselling and advice for Asian and
black women experiencing domestic
violence. Their advice also covers
immigration, housing and matrimonial
questions.

Welsh Women's Aid
38–48 Cruwys Road
Cardiff CF2 4NN

Women's Aid Federation
PO Box 391, Bristol BS99 7WS
Tel 0345 023468 (Helpline)

Support and advice for any woman
worried about violence, whether
physical or mental. Provides temporary
secret refuge for women and children.
There is a helpline and access to legal
advice. In the refuges there are workers
with a special focus on children.

RECOMMENDED READING

———— HELPFUL BOOKS FOR ADULTS ————

Couples in Crisis Chris Belshaw and Mike Stutt (Cassell, 1996)

Dad's Place – A Practical Guide for Divorced Fathers, Jill Burrett (1996).

Divorced Parenting – How to Make it Work, Dr Sol Goldstein (Mandarin, 1987).

The Divorce Handbook, F. Shackleton and O. Timbs (Farrer, 1992).

Helping Children Cope With Divorce, Rosemary Wells (Sheldon Press, 1989/93).

How to Cope with Separation and Divorce, Green (1995)

How to Win as a Stepfamily (Advice on challenges in early stages of remarriage), Visher (Available from Stepfamily).

If Divorce is the Only Way, John Bieber (Alma House, 1995).

Learning to step together, building and strengthening stepfamilies (Stepfamily 1996)

Life After Divorce – How to Grieve and Let Go, Wegscheider-Cruse.

Loving Other People's Children, Fowler (Available from Stepfamily).

Marriage – Fact and Fantasy (to help couples develop better understanding of themselves), Marsh.

The origin of everyday moods. Managing energy, tension and stress Robert E Thayer (O.U.P. 1997)

Other People's Children (advice for step-parents and children), Hayman (Available from Stepfamily).

Parenting Threads – Caring for children when couples part, Stepfamily (1992).

The Separation Survival Handbook, Helen Garlick, (Penguin, 1989).

Splitting Up, National Council for One Parent Families.

Straightforward Guide to Divorce and the Law, Lowton (1994).

Surviving Divorce (Women's resources after separation), Mavis Maclean (Macmillan, 1991).

To and Fro Children – A Guide to Successful Parenting After Divorce, Jill Burrett (Thorsons, 1991).

The Which? Guide to Divorce 1996, Helen Garlick.

NCOPF Publications for lone parents

The National Council for One Parent Families publishes a wide range of useful guides concerning lone parents and tax, maintenance, children's rights, pregnancy, returning to work, etc. They are available for sale, but are free to lone parents. (Please send an s.a.e. for further details – address on page 219).

Booklets for parents

Child Support Maintenance for Parents who Live Apart, Child Support Agency.
Divorce – What About the Children? (Available from Relate).
What Can we Say? – for parents who are separating, Swindon Family Mediation Service.
When Parents Split Up, Scottish Television.

BOOKS FOR CHILDREN

Children Don't Divorce, R. Stones and N. Spooner (Dinosaur Publications, 1991; available from Relate). Ages 7+.
Dinosaurs Divorce – a guide for changing families, L. Krasny Brown and M. Brown (Little, Brown & Co., 1986; available from Relate). Ages 5–8.
The Divorce Express, Paula Danziger (Pan Piper, 1987; available from Relate). Ages 10–13.
The Growing Pains of Adrian Mole, Sue Townsend.
It's My Life, Robert Leeson (Lion Tracks, 1981/92). Teenage.
It's not the End of the World, Judy Blume (Pan Piper, 1994; available from Relate). Ages 10–13.
It's Not Your Fault, Rosemary Stones (Piccadilly).
Kidnap, Ian Strachan (Methuen).
Let's Talk About Divorce, Angela Grunsell (Watts, 1989; available from Relate). Ages 7+.
Madame Doubtfire, Anne Fine (Penguin, 1987; available from Relate). Ages 9+.
Mike's Lonely Summer, Carolyn Nystrom (Lion Books, 1986; available from Relate). Ages 8+.
My Family and Other Natural Disasters, Josephine Feeney (Viking).
Sam Sticks and Delilah, Diana Hendry (Walker, 1993). Ages 7–10.
The Suitcase Kid, Jacqueline Wilson (Yearling, 1993). Ages 9–12.
We Don't All Live with Mum and Dad, National Council for One Parent Families (Available from Relate).
We Have Two Homes (Talk Over Series, 1989). Photo picture book, no words. Ages 5–12.
What's Happening? Splitting Up, Karen Bryant Mole (Wayland, 1992; available from Relate). Ages 8–12.
Where Has Daddy Gone?, Trudy Osman (Heinemann; available from Relate). For under-sevens.

Children's books about Remarriage and new partners

Goggle Eyes, Anne Fine (Penguin, 1989; available from Relate). Ages 10+.
It's an Aardvark-Eat-Turtle World, Paula Danziger (Pan Piper, 1988; available from Relate). Ages 10–13.
Let's Talk About Stepfamilies, Angela Grunsell (Watts, 1990).
Step by Wicked Step, Anne Fine (Hamish Hamilton, 1995; available from Relate). Ages 8–12.
Stepfamilies Talking, Elizabeth Hodder (Macdonald Optima). *Out of print.*
Step Trouble, William L. Coleman (Comp Care Publishers, 1993; available from Relate). Teenage.

BIBLIOGRAPHY

Being There: Fathers after Divorce, Bob Simpson, Peter McCarthy, Janet Walker, Relate Centre for Family Studies, Newcastle University, 1995.

The Best of Friends, Joanna Trollope, Bloomsbury, 1996.

Children in the Middle: living through divorce, Ann Mitchell, London, Tavistock Publications, 1985.

The Exeter Study, Monica Cockett and Dr John Tripp, University of Exeter, 1995.

Factsheets, Family Policy Studies Centre.

Family Transformation through Divorce and Remarriage: a systemic approach, Margaret Robinson, Tavistock/Routledge, London and New York 1991.

How To Do Your Own Divorce: a step-by-step guide, Jeremy Rosenblatt, Vermilion, London, 1993.

How to Win as a Stepfamily, John and Emily Visher, Brunner/Mazel, New York, 1982.

Long Walk to Freedom, Nelson Mandela, Abacus 1994.

Marital Separation: Coping with the End of a Marriage, Robert Weiss, NY Basic Books, 1975.

Mediation: the Making and Re-Making of Co-operative Relationships. An Evaluation of the effectiveness of comprehensive mediation, Janet Walker, Pete McCarthy, Noel Timms, Relate Centre for Family Studies, Newcastle University, 1994.

National Stepfamily Newsletter, April 1996.

Factsheets, One Plus One

'Parental Divorce and the Life Chances of Children', Jane Elliott and Martin Richards, University of Cambridge, *Family Law*, Volume 21, p. 449–500.

Surviving the Breakup: How Parents and children Cope with Divorce, Judith Wallerstein and Joan Kelly, London, Grant McIntyre, 1980.

The Which Guide To Divorce, Helen Garlick, Consumers Association/Penguin Books, 1996.

INDEX

Page numbers in *italics* indicate diagrams and forms,
bold indicate major references.

abductions 203
'absent parent' 161, 178, 180
accusations *see* blame game
adoptions 168, 170
affairs 37–41
    case studies 27–8, 29–31,
        35–5
    and children
    case studies 74–5
    keeping secret from 25
    gay and lesbian
        relationships 41–2
    statistics 37
alimony *see* spousal
        maintenance
All Issues Mediation 88,
        116–44, 147–8
    benefits of 142–3
    case study 125–41
    clients' comments 143
    failure of 149–50
    information sheets
        117–19
'Alternative Dispute
        Resolution' (ADR) 82
attachment 43–6
    children 62
    untying the knots 46–8

bank accounts 190
benefits *see* welfare benefits
bitterness 45–6
    avoiding and reducing 48–9
blame game 34–5
bonding *see* attachment

Child Abduction Act 203
Child Benefit 147
Child Support Act 161, **178**
Child Support Agency (CSA)
        146, 178–9
    calculation of formula
        178–81

and cohabitation 182
and family home 189
and mediation 181
and remarriage 182
and solicitors 181
and stepfamilies 182
children
    abductions 203
    adoptions 168, 170
    and affairs 74–5
    age-related factors 57–8,
        113
    All Issues Mediation 116
    arrangements for **104–15**,
        159, 201
    case studies 110–12, 129
    future focus 171–2
    communication with
        breaking the news 59,
            65–9
    counselling 91
    parents after divorce 7,
        107–8, 113–15
    'views, wishes and
        feelings' 109–12, 202–3
    conflict 56, 58, 60
        domestic violence 59, 64,
            69, **157**
        as focus of 56, 87, 107–8
    cost of bringing up 175–8
    court orders 202
    emotional reactions 53–4,
        55–6, 62–4
        separation anxiety 113,
            114–15
        understanding and
            helping 54–5, 61–2
    family court welfare
        officers 152
    friends 62, 78
    gay or lesbian parents 41
    gender-related factors 58
    in 'Grand National' 62

health problems 60
laws relating to *see*
        Children Act; Family
        Law Act
loyalty to both parents 24
and mediation 66, 67,
        105–12, 147, 201, 204
needs of **50–64**, 82, 105
in new families
    multiple reordered 40, 58
    stepfamilies 167
research studies 51–60
    cohorts 55–6, 59–60
rights of 109–10, 175,
        202–3, 204
schools 55–6, 77, 162
self-esteem 48, 56, 60, 61–2
siblings 62
staying together for 24–7
Children Act 73–4, 87, 146,
        201–4
as base for mediation 6
language of 104
Northern Ireland 203
parental responsibility 178
principles of 7
Scotland 204
Citizen's Advice Bureau 92,
        181, 191
cohabitation
    and Child Support Agency
        (CSA) 182
    and housing 189–90
    new partner's income and
        child support 182
    parents after divorce 167
    rights of cohabitees 157,
        158
    and statutory charge 195
cohort studies *see* children,
        research studies
common law husband or wife
        see cohabitation

confidentiality
  exceptions to 87
  judges 87
  mediation 84, 86–7, 150
conflict
  see also children, conflict
  families, case studies 71–2
  friends, case studies 74–5
  stepfamilies 168
consent orders 8, 142
contact centres 108
contact orders 202
council tax benefit 122,
    192–3
counselling
  children's 91
  divorce 49, 91
  marriage and couple 14, 15,
    91, 207
    agencies 17
    aims of 18
court orders
  consent orders 8, 142
  contact orders 202
  family assistance orders 153
  on finance 144
  if homelessness threatened
    187
  injunctions 155–6, 157–8
  Martin Order 186
  prohibited steps orders 202
  property 186, 194
  residence orders 202
  Section 8 orders 104, 202
  specific issues orders 202,
    203
courts 144, **151–3**
  divorce procedure 199–200
  fees 200
  non-intervention by 7
cultural influences
  case studies 32–3
  cross-cultural divorce 76–7
  dependency 15
  family and friends 70–8
  loyalty of marriage 16
'custody' 104, 161

debts 191
detachment 13, 34, 38
Disability Allowance 195
disillusionment 13, 24, 37–8
divorce
  applying for 207
  bereavement analogy 43,
    45–6
    graph of recovery *48*

do-it-yourself guides 145
experience courses 41
fair and amicable 81–2
family and friends after 76
law reforms 5, 198
process 205, *206*, 207–8
'quickie' 199, 203
risk factors 19
seven levels of 12
statistics 14, 18–19
domestic violence 154–8,
    189–90
  see also children, conflict

erosion 13, 16, 34, 38
exclusion orders *see*
    injunctions
Fairshares 184, 200
families, new 159–61
  See also stepfamilies
family assistance orders 153
family court welfare officers
    201
  and the blame game 35
  children 152
  conciliatory appointments
    151
  Family Assistance Orders
    153
Family Credit 122, 124, 195,
    192
Family Law Act
  aims of 18, 34, 48
  and children 7, 107–8, 109,
    203
  divorce process under 205,
    206, 207–8
  domestic violence under
    157–8
  Green Form Scheme
    changes 195
  information meetings 8, 92,
    205
  language of 205
  mediation 144, 204
  Northern Ireland 158, 203
  pensions 183, 184
  principles of 6
  Scotland 204
  solicitors obligations under
    149
  time management 14, 151
Family Law Bar Association
    153
family mediation *see* All
    Issues Mediation;
    mediation

Family Mediators'
    Association 92, 144
Family Mediation Service
    89–90, 91
family relationships 45, 70,
    72–4, 164
fathers *see* men, fathers
'fault facts' 198–9
finance 175–93
  All Issues Mediation 116,
    190, 193
  case studies 122–3, 124–5,
    129–30
  Child Support Agency
    (CSA) 146
  court decisions 153
  court fee 200
  failure to reach agreement
    149–50
  income sheets *132–41*
  information sheet *121*
  solicitors 145, 147, 148–9
Financial Disputes
    Resolution (FDR) 153,
    185
flexibility 87, 105–7
friends 45, 74–6, 164
future focus 1–2, 84, 171–2

gay relationships 41–2
gender differences 23–5, 58
  see also men; women
'Grand National' analogy
    25–7, 62
grandparents 73–4, 168, 202
Green Form Scheme 146, 195
grieving 38, 43, 45, 48
  see also divorce,
    bereavement analogy
  children 62
  mourning the marriage 13,
    39

health 44, 45, 162
  children 60
homelessness 187–8
homosexuality *see* gay
    relationships; lesbian
    relationships
housing
  see also property, family
    home
  benefit 122, 191–2
  cohabitation 189–90

impartiality 86
income sheets *132–41*

Income Support 162, 195, 191–2
  imaginary case study 122
  'intentional homelessness' 188
  and mortgages 192
  shortfall on 176
  spousal maintenance 182
information, full exchange of 83
information meetings 8, 92, 205
information sheets
  Agreement to Mediate *120*
  All Issues Mediation *117–19*
  case study 126
  financial *121*
inheritances 191
injunctions 155–6, 157–8
integrating the trauma 13, 40–1

joint decisions, mediation 84
judges 8, 35, 87, 142, 151

kin *see* families
kith *see* friends

leavers 20–2, 46
legal advice 91
  financial assets 190–1
  home ownership 188
  in mediation 144, 200
legal aid 194–7, 207
  capital 196
  certificate 148, 195–6
  eligibility for 146, 147, 148, 194, 196
  Green Form Scheme 146, 147
  injunctions 155, 156
  means testing 196, 197
  for mediation 144, 194
  Northern Ireland 197
  Scotland 197
  solicitors' franchise 145–6
  statutory charge 194–5
Legal Aid Board 194, 196
lesbian relationships 41–2
life insurance 190

maintenance *see* child support; spousal maintenance
marital breakdown
  reasons for 11–12, 22

seven stages of 12–13
  statement of 207
marriage enrichment courses 16–17
Marriage Guidance Council *see* Relate
marriages, saving 16–18, 24–7
mediation 81–7
  benefits of 4–5
  and Child Support Agency (CSA) 181
  and children 66, 67, 105–12, 147, 201, 204
  clients' comments 90
  confidentiality 84, 86–7, 150
  cost of 143–4
  and courts 8
  definition of 4
  and different cultures 77
  and divorce law reform 5
  future focus 3–4
  grandparents in 73
  legal advice in 143, 200
  legal aid for 144, 194
  may not be suitable 84
  Northern Ireland 197
  preparing for 88–95
  principles of 83–4, 85
    in practice 85–7
  process 96–103
    first contact 89–90, 92–3
    from argument to negotiation 94–5
    how it works 82–3
    imaginary case study 97–103, 116, 122–4
  reducing bitterness 49
  routes into 207
  safe environment and fair process 83
  safeguards in 87
  Scotland 197
  and solicitors 143, 147–8, 149, 207
  and stepfamilies 170–1
  training of mediators 73, 85
  'unfolding' characteristic of 144
Memorandum of Understanding 123–4, 128–30
men
  see also gay relationships; gender differences

bitterness 46, 49
  and domestic violence 156–7
  expression of feelings 45
  fathers 163, 164–6
  reasons for dissatisfaction in marriage 21–2
  who are left 22
mortgages 187, 192
mothers *see* women, mothers

National Family Mediation (NFM), Code of Practice 85
National Insurance contributions 147
negotiation
  by solicitors 81–2, 88
  disputes 108–9
  in mediation 94–5
new families 159–61
  see also stepfamilies
new relationships 37–42
non-molestation injunctions 155, 157
Northern Ireland
  Children Act 203
  Family Law Act (1996) 203
  legal aid 197
  mediation 197

one-parent benefit 192
one-parent families
  see also parents, lone
  lone fathers 163
  organisations 161
ouster orders 155, 158
overload 11, 37, 160

'parent with care' 161, 178
parental responsibility 7, 201
  financial settlements 178
  others aquiring 202
parenting plans 105, *106*, 107
parents
  lone 11, 161–4, 163, 167
  not living with children 164–6
  returning to, after divorce 43–4
  separated 160
  taking on each other's roles 47
  unmarried, at time of birth of child 201

pensions 183–5, 200
  case study 130
  occupational and private
    183
  questions to ask about 185
  state 183
  ways of dealing with 184
profit-sharing schemes 190
prohibited steps orders 202
property
  All Issues Mediation 116
  failure to reach agreement
    over 149–50
  family home 185–9
    imaginary case study 124
  home ownership 186, 188
  and legal aid 194
  long lease 186
  mortgages 187
  rented 186
  tax 188
  value of 187
protection orders *see*
    injunctions

'quickie' divorce 199, 203

Relate 17, 49, 91
residence orders 202
rights *see* children, rights of

schools 55–6, 77, 162
Scotland 197, 204
second adolescence 13, 39–40
Section 8 orders 104, 202
self-esteem 45
  children 48, 56, 60, 61–2
separation
  case studies 28–3, 35–6, 45,
    66, 93–4
  parenthood in 160

physical 13, 38–9
process of 28–36
temporary 28–9
separation anxiety, children
    113, 114–15
share options 190
siblings, children 62
solicitors
  and the blame game 34–5
  and Child Support Agency
    (CSA) 181
  choosing 145–6
  different approaches 149
  fees 148–9
  financial matters 147
  Green Form Scheme 146–7,
    195
  legal advice from 91
  and legal aid 147, 149
  and mediation 143, 144,
    147–8, 149, 207
  negotiations through 8,
    81–2, 88, 90
  obligations under Family
    Law Act 149
  tasks in representation 148,
    151
Solicitors Family Law
    Association 91, 149
  Code of Practice 145
specific issue orders 202, 203
spousal maintenance 182
statutory charge 194–5
stepfamilies 166–71
  and Child Support Agency
    (CSA) 182
  definition of 166–7
  and mediation 170–1
  the 'outside' parent and 171
  stages in life of *169*, 170
  statistics 167

tax 163, 188
tiredness *see* overloads

unmarried couples *see*
    cohabitation; parents,
    unmarried
unmarried women 189–90

violence *see* domestic
    violence
visiting 164
voluntariness 85

welfare benefits 92, **191–3**,
    195
  see also individually named
    benefits
  families on 177
  imaginary case study 122
  lone mothers 162
welfare officers *see* family
    court welfare officers
women
  see also gender differences;
    lesbian relationships
  bitterness 49
  and domestic violence
    154–5
  legal aid 194
  mothers
    child care costs for 162
    employment 162
    unmarried at birth of child
      201
  who leave their children 46,
    166
  pensions 183–4, 200
  unmarried, rights of
    189–90, 201
  who are left 22–3
  who initiate divorce 20–1

Acknowledgements

Thanks are due to the many dedicated people in National Family Mediation in local Family Mediation Services who have contributed to the development of family mediation over the last nineteen years in order to help parents find solutions for their children in the midst of family breakdown. Those who have particularly contributed to this book include:

National Family Mediation:
Clare Alcock, Sheena Adam and Marian Roberts (NFM); Kay Begg and Paul Foster (Bristol FMS); Kate Gardner (Swindon FMS); Diane Elliott and Jean Craggs (Sussex FMS); Linda Kerr (Northern Ireland FMS); Denise Shepherd, Janet Ward, Alison Norton and Mike Gascoigne (Coventry FMS); Arnold Gordon (African Caribbean FMS).

UK College of Family Mediators:
Dame Margaret Booth DBE.

Other Organisations:
Maureen Lynch, Family Mediation Scotland; Ruth Hindley, the Family Mediators Association; The Solicitors Family Law Association; Margaret Robinson, Donna Smith and Erica De'Ath (Stepfamily); Jan Laithwaite (Relate); Penny Mansfield, One Plus One; Karen Pappenheim, National Council for One Parent Families; The Women's Aid Federation; The Family Policy Studies Centre; Judge Dick Greenslade; Julie Hamlett.